S0-CID-173

SPORTS FANS 2.0

How Fans Are Using Social Media to Get Closer to the Game

David M. Sutera

THE SCARECROW PRESS, INC.
Lanham • Toronto • Plymouth, UK
2013

Published by Scarecrow Press, Inc.
A wholly owned subsidiary of The Rowman & Littlefield Publishing Group, Inc.
4501 Forbes Boulevard, Suite 200, Lanham, Maryland 20706
http://www.scarecrowpress.com

Estover Road, Plymouth PL6 7PY, United Kingdom

British Library Cataloguing in Publication Information Available

Library of Congress Cataloging-in-Publication Data

Sutera, David M., 1967-
Sports fans 2.0 : how fans are using social media to get closer to the game / David M. Sutera. pages cm
Includes bibliographical references and index.
ISBN 978-0-8108-9076-3 (cloth : alk. paper) -- ISBN 978-0-8108-9077-0 (ebook) 1. Sports spectators. 2. Sports--Computer network resources. 3. Social media. I. Title.
GV715.S97 2013
306.4'83--dc23
2013000111

The paper used in this publication meets the minimum requirements of American National Standard for Information Sciences Permanence of Paper for Printed Library Materials, ANSI/NISO Z39.48-1992.

Printed in the United States of America

In memory of Professor Dale Warren Elrod from the University of Utah. Thank you for being my introduction to the world of film and media studies.

CONTENTS

ACKNOWLEDGMENTS

I would like to thank Brenda Sieczkowski for her assistance with editing during the writing of this book. Thanks to Richard Benak for his help with visual design and for sharing his experience on *Mike and Mike in the Morning*. Thanks to Patrick Terry for producing the cover photo and offering excellent feedback on several chapters. Thanks to Zach Ingle for helping me work through rough spots in the manuscript and for telling me to get back to work when I wanted to talk about the Nebraska game. Thanks to Ron Wilson, Chris Lippard, Catherine Preston, Zach Saltz, Matt Jacobson, Isley Unruh, and Chuck Berg for offering encouragement in seeing this project to the finish line. Thanks to Max Utsler and Scott Reinardy, who allowed me to play on their Men's Senior Baseball League team, the Kansas City Cubs, and to Scott, in particular, for reminding me about Morganna the Kissing Bandit, the Rainbow Hair Guy, and the Boom Goes the Dynamite incident. Thanks to John Rinnert at the University of Kansas and the entire staff at Media Productions Studio for their patience and assistance with visual design. Thanks to Josh Wille for pointing out several new social media applications available to sports fans and for some great insights on the future of sports video gaming. Thanks to Jack Blankenship, Candice Sortino, and K. T. King for their help in researching the topic and for providing the photos that appear in the book. Finally, I'd like to extend special thanks to my editor, Christen Karniski, for giving me the opportunity to share my thoughts and ideas on the world of sports, and for her patience and guidance throughout the entire process.

INTRODUCTION

MONDAY NIGHT FOOTBALL, DECEMBER 26, 2011

It was December 26, 2011, and the Atlanta Falcons were facing off against their conference rival, the New Orleans Saints, in the Superdome for a late-season matchup with playoff implications. The winner was set to take the NFC (National Football Conference) South Division title and earn a possible first-round bye into the playoffs. Adding to the drama of the game, Saints' quarterback Drew Brees was only nine yards away from breaking Dan Marino's long-standing single-season passing record of 5,084 yards.

Third and goal from the 13-yard line, the Saints had the ball with two minutes and fifty-one seconds remaining in the game. Drew Brees took the snap from the shotgun and narrowly escaped a blitz by the Falcons' defense. Brees scrambled out of the reach of a charging linebacker and stepped up in the pocket to scan down the field for an open receiver. He proceeded to deliver a strike to Saints' running back Darren Sproles for a nine-yard touchdown, thus breaking the record. The Superdome erupted in cheers and applause.

I immediately rushed to my computer and opened my Facebook page, eager to post the following about Brees' historic touchdown pass: "Drew Brees just scored his fourth touchdown for the night, breaking Dan Marino's single-season passing record. Oh, and by the way, his fourth touchdown puts my team, the Mount Etna Vulcans, in the MIFL [Middle American/International Football League] championship game next week. Suck on that, Rick Benak!" My Fantasy Football opponent that week, Rick Benak, immediately responded to my comment by posting, "You lucky bastard! Enjoy your little moment of glory. I still have more championships than you ever will!" My teenage niece, Emily, quickly followed up with the following derisive comment on my conversation with my friend, which drew 17 "likes" from my Facebook friends in a matter of minutes: "You Fantasy Football guys are nerds! Get a life!"

While I admit to being a bit obsessive when it comes to Fantasy Football, the previously mentioned reaction to "my team's" win and the desire to share "my victory" with as many people as possible and as quickly as possible through social media is not exceptional. These types of interactions are becoming more and more common among sports fans worldwide due to the increased availability in such social media outlets as Facebook and Twitter. These and other social media applications provide sports fans with an unprecedented ability to communicate their opinions and thoughts about sports to a nearly limitless audience on the Internet. Recognizing the impact of social media on contemporary popular culture, high-profile sports mass media outlets like ESPN are devising programming that incorporates applications like Twitter and Facebook as major features, not only to attract more viewers, but also to encourage sports fans to take a more active role and directly participate in the world of sports media.

Sports Fans 2.0: How Fans Are Using Social Media to Get Closer to the Game explores the increasingly participatory nature of contemporary sports fandom brought on by the expansion of new digital media technologies and the proliferation of social media. It illuminates the roots of the desire for many sports fans, mostly American men, who crave more direct involvement in professional and college sports and fulfill this desire by utilizing smart devices to take advantage of new avenues of expression in mass and social media. This book examines the ways in which these forms of digital media create and facilitate new channels for sports fan engagement and how these manifestations of expression shape and enhance a fan's perception of participating in contemporary popular sports culture.

In researching *Sports Fans 2.0*, I took on the role of participant–observer ethnographer. I collected data through direct observations and interactions with sports fans groups and analyzed prevailing fan sentiments evident in mass media sports broadcasts and such social media documents as Twitter feeds, Facebook posts, and Internet blogs. I write from the multiple perspectives of media scholar, frustrated athlete, and avid sports fan. In this way, I consider myself part of a burgeoning field of hybrid scholars in the area of fan studies, what Henry Jenkins alludes to in his official blog as *acafans*.[1] This approach allows me to simultaneously write about sports fandom as an academic, drawing on aspects of sociology, psychology, and media studies, and as a fan with an intimate knowledge of the customs, vernacular, and traditions of many sports fan communities. My research and insights straddle the line between popular culture and sports media scholarship, which, I believe, permit me to generate a unique melding of theory and practice in analyzing emerging patterns in digitally mediated sports fandom. I am aware of the potential dangers and criticisms of this method of study (losing my objectivity, "going native"); however, the ever-changing structure of the mediated world and the mercurial activities of contemporary sports fans in relation to social media lends itself well to this approach. And, since I already have an intimate knowledge of the sport fan community and am an active sports fan participant (Fantasy Football, among many others), going native is unlikely simply because, for the most part, I already am one of the "natives."

I carry out ethnographic fieldwork concentrating on sports fans' use of social media through direct observation and participation in various rituals and practices surrounding such live sporting events and televised sports programs as on-site stadium promotions, as well as monitor and engage in Twitter comments generated during a variety of sports event broadcasts as sites of study. When examining sports fan engagement with social media entities between games, I use the Internet accessed through personal computers, tablet computers, and mobile viewing devices (iPhones/Android Smartphones) as main sites of analysis. In addition, I provide content analysis of sports fan participation trends in live sporting event game broadcasts and sports talk show programs on ESPN. Furthermore, I comment on how mass media outlets incorporate social media through the Internet and mobile viewing devices as effective ways to reach an ever-increasing number of sports fans and enhance their sense of participation in mediated sports. Moreover, I highlight examples of high-profile athletes' use of social media to engage their fan base, for example, Chad Johnson, former NFL star and Twitter aficionado, who have experienced both the positive and negative effects of using social media as a form of personal promotion.

While I explore the activities of sports fans around the world, I focus mainly on American male sports fans 18 to 49 years of age as the main group of study in my analysis. I make this distinction because, along with belonging to this cohort myself, this demographic comprises a significant majority of active sports fans in the United States with access to and the wherewithal to use both mass and social media as part of their engagement with sports. In addition, this group represents considerable buying power as potential consumers, which, in turn, makes them one of the most highly sought after and analyzed demographics in sports media programming and marketing schemes. Consequently, a sizable body of research and data surrounding the consumption and viewing habits of this group exists in relation to sports spectatorship, which I draw upon when exploring and describing various case studies of sports fans and athletes using social media.[2]

I avoid further breaking down this group on the basis of other demographic profiles, including race or gender. While these are important distinctions and characteristics worthy of in-depth study, these dimensions go beyond the scope of my analysis and lie outside my area of expertise. As such, I defer to more qualified scholars in the areas of cultural anthropology and gender studies specializing in racial or gender bias in sports spectatorship to conduct those types of studies.

The main intention of this project is to show that developments in social media are the primary mechanisms through which contemporary fans are becoming more actively involved in mediated popular sports culture. *Sports Fans 2.0* explores this concept by first identifying the pivotal role sports plays in popular culture and what it means to be a sports fan in the United States and other parts of the world. Then it examines some of the motivations behind the desire of sports fans to be more directly involved in popular sports culture. Next, it identifies the specific mass media and social media outlets that make increased fan interaction possible and provides specific case studies of the practical application of social media by sports fans in enhancing their sense of participation and interaction with mediated sports. *Sports Fans 2.0* also shows how high-profile athletes are using social media to increase their fan base and promote their own celebrity status, both of which were once primarily determined by how much mass media provided coverage of their activities to the general public. Finally, the book speculates on future developments in technologies and social media applications that will allow for even greater fan interaction in mediated sports.

My motivation in writing *Sports Fans 2.0* is to explore the important role sports plays in popular culture and shed light on the emerging trends in sports spectatorship in relation to the widespread utilization of social media. Throughout this book, it is my intention to write in plain language, avoiding technical jargon whenever possible, while still operating from a sound methodological approach in substantiating my claims. In addition, by writing from the standpoint of both a sports fan and media scholar (acafan), I hope to bridge the gap between popular culture and academia in sports media studies and, more importantly, offer a perspective that simultaneously appeals to both mainstream and scholastic audiences.

NOTES

1. Henry Jenkins, "Acafandom and Beyond: Concluding Thoughts," *Confessions of an Acafan: The Official Weblog of Henry Jenkins*, 22 October 2011, http://henryjenkins.org/2011/10/acafandom_and_beyond_concludin.html (28 June 2012).

2. "Sports Fans Continue the Conversation Online: Brands Seek Opportunities Outside the Commercial Breaks," *eMarkerter.com*, 6 July 2012, www.emarketer.com/PressRelease.aspx?R=1009174 (7 August 2012).

1

SPORTS IN AMERICAN SOCIETY

SPORTS AND THE AMERICAN DREAM

In late September 2005, after turning in a videotaped audition for Spike TV's new reality television program *Pros vs. Joes*, I received the following email message:

> ROUND 2
> Congratulations! You have been selected to go on to the next round of casting for *Pros vs. Joes*. What this means is that we are *very interested* in what we have seen so far of you and would like to get to know you even better. Please answer all the following questions (it's a pretty long application, please accept our apologies but we just need to cover as many bases as possible). When you've finished, please fax your completed and signed application to us at 310-566-6136 and then mail the original signed application to us at:
>
> *PROS VS. JOES* ROUND 2 CASTING
> 1831 STANFORD STREET
> SANTA MONICA, CA 90404
> 310-566-6136
>
> WE NEED TO HAVE AT LEAST THE FAXED COPY OF THIS IN OUR OFFICE BY OCTOBER 10 AT 3PM FOR YOU TO REMAIN IN THE GAME! Thank you again for your effort in this process and we look forward to getting to know you better and possibly seeing you take on the PROS!

I have to admit, the prospect of being cast as one of the contestants for the inaugural season of the sports-oriented reality series *Pros vs. Joes*, where I would have had the chance to display my athletic talents against such famous retired professional athletes as Dennis Rodman (Detroit Pistons and Chicago Bulls), Jerry Rice (San Francisco 49ers), and Bo Jackson (Kansas City Royals and Los Angeles Raiders),[1] seemed to be the answer to living out my dreams of athletic glory—and on national television no less. Unfortunately, I failed to make it past the final round of auditions. Making matters worse, after watching one of the Joes who beat me out—a late thirty-something amateur athlete with whom I share many physical attributes—fail miserably during the first segment of the series, "Could You Cover Jerry Rice?,"[2] as Jerry Rice effortlessly dodged his inept coverage on the way to three straight touchdowns, I indulged in the fantasy that I would have performed much better against this former All-Pro NFL wide receiver. As I watched subsequent episodes that season, I grew more frustrated, actually believing I was a better athlete than the other Joes on the show, and that I would have had a realistic chance at winning the grand prize of $20,000 if only the producers had chosen me as one of the contestants.

One manifestation of the American Dream, especially for many men, is to become a professional athlete. A series of articles published in the *North American Journal of Psychology* in 2007 asserts that,

> stories about athletes who went from rags-to-riches are so common and so widely circulated that they have created an American myth, namely that any poor boy [or girl] who is willing to devote some time and energy to sports can become a wealthy professional athlete. Both the myth and the prevalence of the myth are well documented.[3]

The mainstream media fuels this myth by generating an onslaught of movies and television programs aimed at a wide range of audiences that glorify athletic achievement as one way to achieve the American Dream. Hollywood sports films like *The Natural* (1984), *Rudy* (1994), *Invincible* (2006), and the entire Rocky series (1976–2006) bolster this perception, as evidenced by their box-office success and the iconic status in American culture of the real-life and fictional sports characters in these films. In addition, nonfictional "feel-good" stories on ESPN of athletes enduring extreme personal hardships in making it to the big leagues (e.g., New York Mets knuckleball pitcher Robert Allen "R. A."

Dickey), along with other representations in the media of self-made success through athletics, attract attention from mainstream audiences as a popular narrative trope.

Successful athletes are often afforded unquestioned celebrity status in the United States. For instance, a popular American sports figure like New England Patriot's Pro Bowl quarterback Tom Brady from the National Football League (NFL) is not only idolized by avid male sports fans for his on-field success, with three Super Bowl rings and two NFL MVP Awards, but also because he is married to the Brazilian model Gisele Bündchen. Female fans, even those who do not regularly follow football but view Tom Brady as a sexy heartthrob, follow his exploits both on and off the field, attention that manifested itself most prominently by the interest his long hair garnered during the 2011 season. In fact, the topic of Tom Brady's long hair was a popular trend on Twitter and the Internet, even after he cut his hair later in the 2011 NFL season, and it led to the creation of a comical Twitter feed known as Tom Brady's Hair @BradyHair. [4] Social media sites devoted to athletes in general, especially those that focus on such peripheral aspects of an athlete's life as Tom Brady's hair, are a testament to the power athletes have in attracting attention in popular culture. Moreover, social media applications like Twitter and Facebook allow for an even greater propagation of this myth to an expanding fan base that primarily engages with popular culture through the Internet.

In some instances, athletes are compared to comic-book superheroes.[5] This appears in various forms in popular culture and mass media. For example, All-Star center Dwight Howard, as a member of the National Basketball Association's (NBA) Orlando Magic, donned a Superman cape while performing in the slam-dunk competition of the 2008 NBA All-Star Game, a move that was met with great fanfare through extensive media coverage as he dominated and won the highly publicized event. Continuing with the NBA, because of his speed and quickness on the basketball court, Dwayne Wade of the Miami Heat has earned the nickname "Flash,"[6] drawing a comparison between Wade and the iconic, long-standing DC character the Flash, who possesses the ability to run at superhuman speeds—for those uninitiated in the world of comics. In 2011, Marvel Comics, in conjunction with the NBA, published an entire series of comic-book mash-ups that featured such prominent figures LeBron James, Kobe Bryant, and Kevin Durant as replacements for superhero characters like Iron Man, Wolverine, and the Human Torch in popular comic series including *The Avengers*, *X-Men*, and *The Fantastic Four*.[7]

The NFL has its own superhero comparisons, for example, Calvin Johnson of the Detroit Lions who earned the nickname "Megatron," while Houston Texans' wide receiver Andre Johnson was dubbed "Optimus Prime," both in reference to the main villain and hero from the series *The Transformers*, respectively. And, of course, Captain America's professional athlete counterpart is none other than the already highly regarded Tom Brady of the New England Patriots.[8] The Nickelodeon television network produced an animated cartoon called *NFL Rush Zone: Rise of the Guardians* to air on its Nicktoons channel in 2012. This superhero/action cartoon features a group of preteen crime fighters who don superpowered armor and team up with animated versions of current NFL players the likes of Tom Brady, Calvin Johnson, and Demarcus Ware, all of whom provide the voices for their characters, to fight the forces of evil led by the villain known as "Wild Card."[9] These examples reinforce the mythic status already assigned to athletes in popular culture. More importantly, corporate mass media outlets bolster this perception by comparing athletes and superheroes as previously described, most likely as an appeal to crossover audiences among sports fans and comic-book fans in generating new revenue streams from consumers.

Along with this heavy emphasis on the success of professional athletes in American society as a form of spectacle entertainment, individual athletic accomplishment on the playing field often serves as a metaphor for success in enterprises outside the world of sports. The concept of self-made success, as epitomized through athletic achievement, pervades almost all aspects of American culture, most especially through the use of sports-oriented language in everyday conversation. For instance, in the business world, people often articulate such sports clichés as "keep your eye on the ball" or "hit a home run" when referring to closing an important deal. In addition, famous sports quotes like Vince Lombardi's "winning isn't everything, it is the only thing," along with Will Ferrell's line in *Talladega Nights: The Ballad of Ricky Bobby* (2006), "if you ain't first, you're last," both speak to the importance of success in American culture regarding all aspects of an individual's existence.

Similarly, the concept of teamwork, another important aspect of the sports culture, invades the lexicon of other components of American society. Such sports euphemisms as "taking one for the team" or "scoring one for our side," which overzealous inspirational speakers utter ad nauseam to the chagrin of most attendees at team-building conferences and seminars across the United States, epitomize the symbolic importance of teamwork in areas outside of athletics. In many instances, sports talk is considered the unofficial small talk of American business; in fact, individual credibility in the business world often depends on one's conversational competence in appropriate sports jargon to impress potential clients.[10] Demonstrating the ability to speak effectively in sports parlance in American business culture gives those men and women a definite advantage over their competitors.

The importance of success and widespread acclaim associated with winning are persistent in many aspects of American society, especially in sports. Sports mass media outlets contribute to this perception by focusing primarily on the winners in sports competitions and marginalizing teams and players who finish second. For example, ESPN's flagship program *SportsCenter* features a rapid-fire montage of all the current league champions of major professional and college sports teams celebrating their victories, often drawing emphasis to the team's most prominent player hoisting the championship trophy surrounded by cheering fans, as a lead-in to every episode. With representations like this, among countless others in the media, it is no wonder that the intense societal pressure to be "number one" or "finish first" in the United States can dominate and even cloud an individual's thinking and actions when engaging in almost any professional endeavor or leisure activity.

It is important to point out that although a person might fail to finish first in a particular activity, sports or otherwise, he or she will often perform quite well by engaging in said competition; often infinitesimal details separate the victors from the losers. For instance, in the men's 100-meter butterfly in the 2012 London Summer Olympics, U.S. Olympic swimming star Michael Phelps beat Chad le Clos of South Africa and Evgeny Korotyshkin of the Russian Federation for the gold medal by only 23 hundredths of a second (0.23 sec).[11] Consequently, even though both silver medalists tied for second and almost beat Michael Phelps in this event, they are unlikely to receive as much international media attention as Phelps will as the gold medalist.

Unfortunately, in competitive American society, finishing second rarely comes with any long-lasting recognition or accolades, especially in the world of sports. For instance, while many sports fans can easily rattle off all of the winners of the NFL's Super Bowl in chronological order, many of these same individuals would be hard-pressed to identify all the teams that lost the Super Bowl. Even though actually making it to the Super Bowl is an astounding accomplishment for any team, given the intense competition of the NFL and the numerous injuries to key players during the regular season, if that team fails to win the game, they will be either lost in memory or fall into notoriety and, ultimately, be classified as losers, most notably, the Minnesota Vikings and Buffalo Bills, who both lost the Super Bowl four times. Often missing from this analysis, however, is that the New England Patriots, considered one of the most successful sports franchises of all time and frequently associated as exemplars of winning in the spirit of American Exceptionalism, also lost in the Super Bowl four times. It seems obvious that since the Patriots won the Super Bowl three times, many sports media analysts and fans tend to forget New England's Super Bowl losses, which supports the sports cliché that most transgressions committed by athletes—O. J. Simpson notwithstanding—and sports teams will be forgiven and forgotten if they win a championship.

Sadly, this perception bleeds through into many other aspects of American society. The unrealistic objective of always winning downplays the genuine quality of one's so-called unsuccessful efforts in pursuit of a particular goal—even though a person likely reached a high level of achievement in the process—a pursuit that is often damaging to an individual's self-esteem when the goal is unmet. Regardless, this emphasis on winning is endemic to the American zeitgeist and appears to be a permanent fixture in American culture. Furthermore, it seems evident that athletic achievement will continue to serve as a metaphor for achieving the American Dream, and that mass media will bolster this perception by creating programs and covering live sporting events with winning as the ultimate climax to the vast majority of the featured sports narratives.

WHY CAN'T I BE A PROFESSIONAL ATHLETE? IT LOOKS SO SIMPLE ON TV

I bought into the myth of becoming a sports hero and all the misconceptions associated with how easily it could be attained hook, line, and sinker. Growing up in Omaha, Nebraska, in the 1970s and 1980s, I believed I had only a few socially respectable career options available to me as a young man. My father was a dentist, and my two brothers were lawyers. This meant that the medical and legal professions were both acceptable potential career paths—as my mother drilled into me on a regular basis. With these familial encouragements and the fact that I had an aptitude for science, I started out as a premed student at Creighton University in Omaha, Nebraska. That was, until I learned I was squeamish when it came to blood and other bodily fluids, to say nothing of my aversion to the thought of having to cut other people open for a living. The military was another looming option, especially since my father and brothers were army officers, my sisters were married to air force pilots, and we lived near Offutt Air Force Base during the latter stages of the Cold War, the home of the Strategic Air Command (SAC)—a common reference in Stanley Kubrick's classic *Dr. Strangelove or: How I Learned to Stop Worrying and Love the Bomb* (1964). Before I ultimately decided against the military as a career, I made it through ROTC (Reserve Officer Training Corps) basic training as a cadet pilot with several athletic and physical fitness awards and a full scholarship to pay for my last two years of college.

However, the third and most appealing option for me was to become a professional athlete. This aspiration was inevitable because I spent a good portion of my youth idolizing Nebraska football in its heyday, first with Heisman Trophy winner Johnnie "the Jet" Rogers and the 1971 and 1972 National Championship teams, and later with legendary coach Tom Osborne and such standout players as Turner Gill, Mike Rozier, and Irving Fryar in the 1980s. In addition, I regularly attended the National Collegiate Athletic Association's (NCAA's) Division I College World Series (CWS) at Rosenblatt Stadium in Omaha, Nebraska—the highlight of my summers as a child. During the years at the CWS, I had the privilege of watching future major-league stars Dave Winfield[12] (University of Minnesota), Roger Clemens (University of Texas), and even Barry Bonds (Arizona State University) play on the hallowed grounds of Rosenblatt Stadium. Watching the adulation these and other athletes received, both in person and on television, was intoxicating to me as an impressionable youth. From an early age, even at the harsh discouragement of my mother, becoming a professional athlete was my number one career goal.

What made this a remote possibility for me was that I possessed some natural athletic talents. I may have been small in stature, but the ability to run faster than most of my contemporaries allowed me to excel in certain sports, especially football and baseball. I even caught the attention of a few college and professional baseball scouts early in my high school career after they witnessed me run the fastest 40-yard dash time (4.4 seconds—electronic-timed *not* hand-timed) at a baseball tryout camp with more than 500 other hopeful young athletes. Having the "God-given ability to run fast"—as the scouts indicated in their official assessment of my athletic talents—was all the encouragement I needed to believe I might have a chance at making it as a college and professional athlete. Sadly, my dreams of athletic glory faded soon after high school. Even though I had baseball scholarship offers from a few small colleges, the untimely death of my father during my senior year in high school and an ACL (anterior cruciate ligament) injury to my right knee soon thereafter made me realize that considering other career options outside athletics was prudent.

My personal story of athletic disappointment is all too universal. The harsh reality for the vast majority of aspiring athletes is that they will never reach the professional level. To put this into a numerical perspective, let's look at the current statistical odds of a single individual becoming a professional athlete as their main source of income in the United States. According to the U.S. Department of Labor's *Occupational Outlook Handbook, 2010–11 Edition*, there are approximately 17,000 professional full-time athletes in the United States, and that number is likely to remain constant for the foreseeable future.[13] The U.S. Census Bureau lists the current U.S. population at 312,564,274.[14] Therefore, simply dividing the number of total athletes at 17,000 by the total current U.S. population, the odds of making it as a professional athlete are 0.0000544. Adding to these desperate statistical odds, other determining factors like natural talent and body size, which cannot be enhanced significantly enough through hard work or practice, even with performance-enhancing drugs, make it nearly impossible for most human beings who lack these native, natural skills and physical attributes to make athletics their sole profession. In addition, professional athletics is one of the most competitive career fields because "an athlete can lose his or her job because of an injury, or can be replaced by a 'better' player at any time."[15] As such, professional athletics offers little job security even to those who possess the natural physical talents and the proper training and development needed to compete at the highest levels of athletic competition.

Being a professional athlete is also a strenuous and often dangerous occupation. While many spectators may assume that athletes have an easy life of merely playing a sport for a living, the physical demands on athletes are, in fact, quite staggering. Admittedly, some sports, for example, golf and tennis, are easier on the body than other more strenuous contact sports like football and hockey; however, the breadth of a professional athlete's career in any sport is often brief. For instance, even though such famous NFL all-star quarterbacks as Peyton Manning of the Denver Broncos and Tom Brady of the New England Patriots might have seemingly interminable careers, because of intense competition and frequent injuries, the average career for most NFL players is 3.5 years.[16]

Ickey Woods, a fullback for the Cincinnati Bengals from 1988 to 1991, best known for his popular touchdown celebration dance, the Ickey Shuffle, is a prime example of how quickly an athlete can fall from the spotlight to relative obscurity due to injury. During his rookie season in 1988, Woods rushed for 1,066 yards, scored 15 touchdowns, and achieved a NFL-best 5.3 yards per carry on the way to a Super Bowl XXIII appearance and selection to the NFL's All-Pro Team.[17] Along with his impressive rookie stats, Woods earned great popularity through his Ickey Shuffle, which "sparked a nationwide craze, with Ickey songs, Ickey shirts, Ickey commercials, and even an Ickey milk shake."[18] Unfortunately, Woods tore his left ACL during a preseason game in 1989, keeping him out of action for the entire season, and he injured his other knee early in the 1991 season, which ultimately led to the Bengals cutting him from the roster, ending his four-year career in unspectacular fashion.

Even though many athletes seem invulnerable to pain as they perform at such high levels during competitions, the sheer physical demands an athlete places on their body often go unnoticed during the regular course of a game. Yes, it is true that live game broadcasts and recap programs like *SportsCenter* will play back devastating injuries—usually in the form of cringeworthy slow motion replays of severe joint injuries like blown-out knees or badly twisted ankles—as a spectacle; however, sports media outlets rarely elaborate on the daily physical suffering of almost all professional athletes in preparing for and enduring competition during the course of a sports season. The saying in many sports clubhouses that "there is a difference between pain and injury" serves as an axiom in preparing athletes for games through extended seasons that can last as long as seven months and entail more than 162 games, as in Major League Baseball.

Not surprisingly, to simply make a living or earn bonuses for playing in a certain number of games, as per their contracts, most athletes play in great pain throughout the majority of the season and their careers. This frequently requires them to endure extended rehabilitation regimens. When these attempts at therapy proceed too slowly, many athletes are pressured by coaches and management to subject themselves to powerful painkilling medication in the form of such synthetic opiates as Oxycontin, Percocet, and Darvocet to deaden their injured body parts. These powerful drugs are often administered by medical professionals minutes before each game time so that athletes can simply compete at a nominal level.[19] A vivid illustration of this practice is evident in the sports film *North Dallas Forty* (1979), which is based on the autobiographical novel of the same name written by former Dallas Cowboys wide receiver Peter Gent. In a poignant scene leading up to an important game with playoff implications, the main character, Phil Elliot (Nick Nolte), who has a terribly injured knee and can barely walk, receives an injection of an intense painkiller pregame in the locker room. The medication deadens his knee and allows him to play in the game with no pain. While this is a fictional cinematic account of what happens in most NFL locker rooms, many NFL players attest to the accuracy of this depiction and view the long-standing practice of prolonged and widespread drug use in helping athletes get through the season illustrated in the film as routine and simply an occupational necessity in functioning as a professional athlete.

Furthermore, while those NFL players lucky enough to enjoy extended careers may become famous for their longevity, they subject themselves to long-term, irreversible, and sometimes life-threatening physical damage. One early example of the long-term physical damage that can result from a professional career in sports is the famous center Jim Otto of the Oakland Raiders. Otto's career spanned 15 years, from 1960 to 1974, first in the American Football League (AFL) and later the NFL, which earned him a first ballot spot in the Professional Football Hall of Fame in 1980 and the ranking of 78 on the *Sporting News'* list of the Greatest Football Players of all time in 1999. However, as a result of such a lengthy career, Otto endured 40 surgeries, including 28 knee operations alone, and he even had his right leg amputated on August 1, 2007; he now deals with multiple debilitating conditions, including chronic arthritis and back and neck pain.[20]

Greater awareness of head trauma injuries has recently come to light in mass media, especially concerning NFL players and those in other contact sports. Past NFL superstars like the outspoken and flamboyant Jim McMahon, quarterback of the 1985 Super Bowl champions the Chicago Bears, now suffers from short-term memory loss, claiming in an interview with Yahoo! Sports that, "My memory's pretty much gone. There are a lot of times when I walk into a room and forget why I walked in there."[21] In addition, the tragic suicides of NFL veterans Junior Seau of the San Diego Chargers and New England Patriots and Dave Duerson of the Chicago Bears have been partly attributed to the head trauma both suffered during their playing careers. In fact, Duerson, who fatally shot himself in the chest to leave his brain fully intact, left a suicide note requesting that his brain go to researchers for study on head trauma on football players.[22] Many former NFL athletes with brain injuries are bringing new awareness to the dangers the sport poses to the human brain. Current and former players and coaches alike hope to reduce similar brain injuries for the next generation of football players by advocating that proper tackling techniques, for instance, avoiding helmet-to-helmet contact, are taught to young players as early as possible.

This practice is not limited to players in the NFL. For example, during the 2012 NBA Finals, All-Star point guard for the Miami Heat, Dwayne Wade, regularly had his injured left knee drained of fluids and endured numerous cortisone shots before numerous games with the Oklahoma City Thunder just to allow him to function on the court on par with his performance earlier in the season before his injury. Even though this practice caused him to eventually miss playing as a member of the U.S. men's Olympic basketball team in the 2012 Summer Olympics in London due to a subsequent surgery to repair any long-term damage to the knee, Wade received accolades for "toughing it out" and sacrificing his body on a nightly basis to help bring home another NBA championship to the Miami Heat.

These examples clearly show that participation in sports is both highly competitive and extremely dangerous. While many professional athletes are afforded celebrity status during their playing careers, many veterans of all sports must deal with the adverse physical and mental repercussions of their athletic exploits later in life. Sadly, even though more advanced surgeries and rehabilitation techniques are widely available, along with greater emphasis on preventative care for athletes at all levels of play, this trend is likely to continue as new generations of professional athletes endure many of the same rigors and traumas as their predecessors during the course of their playing careers to meet the increasing demand of delivering high-quality sports entertainment to the general public.

OKAY, SO I CAN'T BE A PROFESSIONAL ATHLETE. HOW ELSE CAN I PARTICIPATE IN SPORTS?

Given the astronomical odds against becoming a professional athlete, along with the inherent dangers and physical demands associated with the profession, it is highly unlikely and ill-advised for the average person to actually engage in the playing action of professional sport. Regardless, many athletes who never make it past the high school or college levels still want to participate in sports as they get older. These individuals, mostly men, are known colloquially as "frustrated athletes." Since I could find no nomenclature to qualify a frustrated athlete, and for the sake of clarity, I offer the following definition:

> *frustrated athlete* /frəs trātid aTHlēt/ noun: 1. A person, usually male, who lacks the natural or acquired traits, such as strength, agility, and endurance, necessary for success in physical exercise or sports, but adheres to the deluded belief that either lack of opportunity, injury, or some other external circumstance thwarted his poten-

tial success in athletics. 2. Someone having feelings of dissatisfaction or lack of fulfillment in failing to gain recognition for their athletic accomplishments. Synonym: *Jock*.

Anyone who has ever attended their high school reunion can easily identify former classmates who match this description, especially if he or she had the misfortune of enduring a boring and pitiful conversation with one of these guys gloating about his days as captain of the football team or some anecdote about how he won the big game.[23]

Along with recounting their past athletic exploits to friends at parties and sports bars, another common behavior of frustrated athletes is that they attempt to relive their days of athletic glory or fulfill unrealized moments of athletic achievement by participating in adult recreational sports leagues.[24] These organizations, in both large cities and small towns across the United States, provide those unable to participate in professional sports with ongoing athletic venues ranging from traditional sports like flag football, basketball, and softball to the more esoteric, for example, Ultimate Frisbee, kickball, and even an actual variation of the game Quidditch from the *Harry Potter* series.[25] Plunkett Research, Inc. indicates that consumer activity in adult recreational sports leagues is one of the few industries unaffected by the 2011–2012 economic recession, and that "amateur participation in team sports such as lacrosse, volleyball, and rugby is extremely high as of 2011"; furthermore, they claim that "health clubs in the United States [many of which sponsor recreational adult sports leagues of all varieties] enjoyed revenues of $21.4 billion in 2011."[26] With all the time and money devoted to amateur sports in the United States, adult recreational sports leagues comprise a sizable, profitable, and stable industry that, according to Plunkett Research, is likely to grow in the foreseeable future.

THE MEN'S SENIOR BASEBALL LEAGUE (MSBL)

While I abandoned my dreams of becoming a professional athlete long ago, I still play baseball (not softball) two times a week during the summers on a team in a national sports recreational league known as the Men's Senior Baseball League (MSBL) in Kansas City, Missouri. The MSBL is a national organization that appeals to aging baseball players who still want to be active in the sport at a more competitive level than what exists in most recreational softball leagues. This sentiment is epitomized by the league's official motto of "Don't Go Soft, *Play Hardball!*," and MSBL players will take offense if you incorrectly refer to it as softball in casual conversation. The MSBL has been in existence since 1988, and the league currently has "325 local affiliates, 3,200 teams, and 45,000 members who play organized baseball in local leagues, 30 regional tournaments, and six national tournaments."[27] Teams are required to wear full, matching baseball uniforms, and all participants must use wooden bats on par with the specification for those in professional baseball. These last two distinctions are important because—in sharp contrast with recreational softball—they help make the playing experience in the MSBL more ceremonial and authentic in recreating a heightened competitive atmosphere or "live game" feeling for participants.

Further enhancing the level of competition in the MSBL is that, along with the accomplished high school and college baseball players who comprise the majority of participants, there are also many former Major League Baseball and Minor League Baseball players who play in the league. For instance, "Sacramento is home to almost a dozen former major leaguers who play on MSBL teams, including former San Francisco Giant pitcher Jim Barr, who was said to have held his own against the likes of future Hall of Famers Henry Aaron, Roberto Clemente, and Johnny Bench."[28] In addition, such former major league players as Bert Campaneris, Orlando Cepeda, Ron LeFlore, Bill Lee, Jose Cardenal, Tito Landrum, Jim Willoughby, Luis Tiant, and Bob Oliver all played on MSBL teams in the United States.[29] Former Kansas City Royals players from the 1985 World Series champion team, including Willie Wilson, Greg Pryor, and Danny Jackson, all played on past incarnations of my current team, the Kansas City Cubs, and they sometimes play on our team when we compete in national tournaments in Phoenix, Arizona, Orlando, Florida, and Las Vegas, Nevada. While these former professional baseball players are obviously past their prime, their active involvement as players in the MSBL elevates the league's status and level of competition beyond that of most recreational softball leagues. Consequently, by either playing against or with some of these former major leaguers, participation in the MSBL is as close as nonprofessional athletes can get to competing as professional athletes, which can be accomplished simply by possessing modest athletic talent, the proper equipment, and the ability to pay a $500 (sometimes much larger) entry fee.

Playing in the MSBL gives many "has-been" or "never will be" baseball players the opportunity to live out small fragments of athletic achievement with and against former professional baseball players on a reasonably competitive and safe playing field. While my physical skills have noticeably deteriorated with age, in one of my latest games, I went 3–4 at the plate with two stolen bases, two RBIs, and two runs scored, along with having made a diving catch in the outfield that, in my biased estimation, would have made *SportsCenter's* "Top 10 Plays of the Day." Even though I need to wear so many orthotic neoprene protective compression sleeves that I sound like a rain stick with every step, at 45 years of age, I will likely play in the MSBL for as long as I am physically able.

What I find encouraging about my prospective, long-term involvement in the MSBL is that many of the players, including some of my teammates, can still compete at amazingly high levels in their late 60s. For example, Bill Harmon, a 66-year-old tire shop owner dealing with chronic heart disease and one of the founding members of the Kansas City MSBL, has the league's highest lifetime batting average (.375). Our starting pitcher, Dave Welsh, a 62-year-old stockbroker who has developed an ulcer due to prolonged use of anti-inflammatory drugs during the course of his 24-year career in the MSBL, needs multiple cortisone shots just to make it through each season. Even so, Dave frequently pitches complete games and has a respectable ERA (earned run average) with a winning record.[30]

Despite all the positive qualities of the MSBL's composition and relative competitiveness, since the league gets little media attention, it, for the most part, goes unrecognized by the general public. Not to belittle the league, but, without widespread recognition in a public forum, participation in the MSBL will seem about as insignificant or trivial in the eyes of the casual observer as any other recreational sports league. In fact, recognition and acclaim in sports are important factors that motivate many potential professional athletes in choosing a particular sport over another. Olympic historian David Wallechinsky elaborates on this concept when describing why the United States does poorly in certain Olympic events:

> The United States used to be very strong in weightlifting . . . and then just fell by the wayside due to lack of role models. For example, if you were a big, heavy, strong guy from, say, Russia or Ukraine or Iran or Bulgaria or Turkey, then you knew—you know—that if you won a gold medal in weightlifting, you could become a national hero. But, if you won a gold medal in weightlifting for the United States, nobody's going to hear about you the day after the closing ceremony. So somebody—that same person who's a great athlete, strong, a big person—is instead going to go into football instead of becoming a weightlifter.[31]

A lesser-known fact about Robert Griffin III, Heisman Trophy-winning quarterback from Baylor University and first-round draft pick for the NFL's Washington Redskins, is that he is also a world-class hurdler. Griffin's former track coaches say that he had a good chance of competing in the 2012 London Games as a hurdler for the U.S. team if he hadn't decided to devote himself full-time to football.[32] Griffin himself was quoted as saying, "My dad was talking to me about it and he was saying that a lot of my peers, the guys that I beat growing up, are running at the trials. And . . . it does suck. I mean, that's the only way to say it. It sucks."[33] While Robert Griffin claims that "it sucks" to watch the Olympics, knowing that he could have competed as a hurdler in the games, his life is anything but "sucky," especially since he already has multiple sponsorships, including Subway, Gatorade, and Adidas, among many others, along with appearing on NBC's *The Tonight Show with Jay Leno* and other popular programs. It is safe to assume that Griffin would not even come close to gaining the current level of fame if he was a world-class hurdler, even if he won multiple gold medals in the Olympics, that he enjoys with the Washington Redskins as their quarterback of the future, and all without having taken one snap from center at the time he gained these high-profile corporate sponsorships.[34]

Historically, many U.S. Olympic medal-winning sprinters have gone on to NFL football careers, starting with Bob Hayes, 100-meters gold medalist from the 1964 Tokyo Olympics who played 10 years for the Dallas Cowboys, to the most recent U.S. sprinter, Jeff Demps, part of the U.S. silver medal-winning 4x100 relay team who signed a contract with the New England Patriots soon after the 2012 London Olympic Games.[35] What these examples suggest is that athletes who excel in multiple sports are more likely to choose a sport over another based on the one that receives more mass media coverage to spotlight his or her talents on a much broader and more visible stage and that often delivers greater monetary rewards as a result of this recognition.

In the same way, even though the MSBL has gained some national media attention in recent years, it is often limited to small-scale outlets that rarely reach audiences beyond those who are directly involved in the league itself.[36] I can personally attest that at most of my MSBL games the few spectators present are usually devoted spouses and restless children of teammates and opponents. Furthermore, when I interviewed those in attendance, most claimed that the baseball action is boring and openly admitted that they would not be there if it wasn't so important to their spouses for them to attend. All of my past girlfriends who braved watching me play in the MSBL quickly lost interest in the game after only a few innings, wishing they would have brought a book or something else to help pass the time. Even one of my best friends and fellow sports media scholar, Zach Ingle, an avid baseball fan and quite possibly the most diplomatic person I know, after attending only one game, described the MSBL in the following painfully accurate terms, "It is like little league for 50-year olds."

I use the MSBL as a primary example because of my direct participation in the league for over eight years with different teams at various locations across the United States, including the Omaha Indians, the Burbank Yankees, the Salt Lake City Astros, and, my current team, the Kansas City Cubs. As such, my long-term involvement gives me a wide frame of reference and an intimate knowledge of the MSBL's inner workings. More importantly, it makes me keenly aware of how most MSBL spectators view the games as boring or uninteresting, which I have found to be the consensus among attendees at all the locations where I have played and conducted audience research. In many ways, the clichéd philosophical question regarding observation and knowledge of reality "if a tree falls in the forest and no one is around to hear it, does it make a sound?" metaphorically applies to participation in the MSBL, although I should modify the question to fit my experience: "if an MSBL player makes a great play and no one is there to see it, does it matter if it occurred?" While this is meant somewhat jokingly, there is a bitter reality to the answer of this question. For example, even though I know I might have made a spectacular diving catch or hit a home run, if the only people who saw it were those at the ballpark who happened to be paying attention at that particular moment and no pictorial or video evidence exists to verify it, the catch, in essence, ceases to exist. Sadly, this is the reality for almost everyone who participates in recreational sports. Indeed, if no one actually witnesses you perform that amazing athletic feat, no matter how much you recount the details of the event to friends over beers, it goes unnoticed and ignored and ultimately fails to gain the recognition you feel it so rightly deserves.

With this bleak assessment in mind, how, then, can those who are unable to participate in sports due to physical limitations or other obstacles be a part of the American sports narrative? One of the surest and most reliable ways for the average citizen to have any hope of being recognized in the world of sports is as a sports fan. While sports fans have always played an important role in American culture, recent advancements in digital technologies, especially in the areas of personal computing and social media, allow for an unprecedented level of fan control over the flow of sports information that will likely increase exponentially in the near future and allow sports fans to make a name for themselves in the world of sports for their remarkable sports fan exploits.

NOTES

1. "Full Cast and Crew," *Pros vs. Joes* (2006), www.imdb.com/title/tt0497304/fullcredits#cast (11 August 2012).

2. "Could You Cover Jerry Rice?" *Pros vs. Joes*, Season 1, Episode 1, Spike TV, original air date 6 March 2006.

3. Jay Coakley and Richard Lapchick, "Psychology and the Road to Professional Baseball." *North American Journal of Psychology*, Special Issue (2007), p. 3.

4. Tom Brady's Hair @BradyHair, https://twitter.com/bradyhair (7 August 2012).

5. Comparing contemporary athletes to superheroes is no longer a far-fetched idea, given the proliferation of performance-enhancing drugs in sports, along with the fact that most professional athletes already possess exceptional natural physical abilities compared to average humans, including super strength, incredible speed, and remarkably fast reflexes.

6. According to Brian Windhorst of ESPN.com, Dwayne Wade no longer likes the nickname "Flash" because of his strained relationship with former teammate Shaquille "Shaq" O'Neal, the person who gave him that name, and his desire to distance himself from the past team and more directly associate with his new teammates, LeBron James and Chris Bosh. It is also significant to note that, early in his career, Shaq also adopted the persona of Superman and even appeared in the film *Steel* (1997) as the film's main character, DC's superhero Steel. See http://espn.go.com/blog/truehoop/miamiheat/post/_/id/360/dwyane-wade-dont-call-me-flash-anymore (13 July 2012).

7. Brandon Mendelson, " Every Team Makes Theirs Marvel in *ESPN Magazine* , " *Comics Alliance* , 25 October 2010, www.comicsalliance.com/2010/10/25/espn-magazine-nba-marvel-covers-gallery/ (24 July 2012).

8. Eli Marger, "Which Athletes Are Most Like These Superheroes?" *Los Angeles Times*, 13 October 2011, http://bleacherreport.com/articles/891052-which-athletes-are-most-like-these
-superheroes (3 December 2012).

9. "Behind the Scenes: *NFL Rush Zone Season of the Guardians*," *Nick.com*, http://nicktoons.nick.com/videos/clip/rush-zone-bts.html (5 December 2012).

10. B. O. Murphy and T. Zorn, "Gendered Interaction in Professional Relationships." In *Gendered Relationships: A Reader*, ed. T. J. Wood (Mountain View, CA: Mayfield, 1996), 218.

11. "Men's 100m Butterfly: Day 8 Review, Phelps Ends Career in Golden Fashion," *London2012.com*, 2 August 2012, www.london2012.com/swimming/event=swimming-men-100m-butterfly/ (7 August 2012).

12. While best known for his Hall of Fame major-league career as an outfielder with 3,110 hits, 465 home runs, 223 stolen bases, and a career batting average of .283, as a college All-Star, Dave Winfield is most noted for his pitching, especially in the championship game of the 1973 CWS. See "CWS Memories: Dave Winfield's Final Pitch," *The Quad: The New York Times College Sports Blog*, 28 June 2010, http://thequad.blogs.nytimes.com/2010/06/28/c-w-s-memories-dave-winfields-final-pitch/ (18 July 2012).

13. This number excludes athletes abroad; however, the number of American professional athletes in other countries is small by comparison to other occupations. See athletes, coaches, umpires, and related workers in U.S. Bureau of Labor Statistics, *Occupational Outlook Handbook, 2010–11 Edition* (Lanham, MD: Bernan Associates, 2010).

14. U.S. Census Bureau, www.census.gov/ (6 November 2011).

15. U.S. Bureau of Labor Statistics, "Professional Athlete," 19 March 2010, www.bls.gov/k12/sports02.htm (6 November 2011).

16. According to current NFL commissioner Roger Goodell, 3.5 years is misleadingly low because this number does not include those who earn a roster spot as a scout team player. While many of these players will never see live action in a regular-season NFL game, they earn a regular salary exclusively as an athlete. Regardless, even with figures adjusted for scout team players, most NFL careers are brief. Moreover, Goddell's claim reflects his vested interest as NFL commissioner in portraying the league as being sympathetic to the players, especially in light of the NFL labor dispute leading into the 2011 season. See "What Is the Average NFL Player's Career Length? Longer Than You Might Think, Commissioner Goodell Says," *NFL Communications*, 18 April 2011, http://nflcommunications.com/2011/04/18/what-is-average-nfl-player%E2%80%99s-career-length-longer-than-you-might-think-commissioner-goodell-says/ (21 July 2012).

17. "Ickey Woods," *Pro-Football-Reference.com*, 2012, www.pro-football-reference.com/players/W/WoodIc00.htm (7 August 2012).

18. Paul Gutierrez, " Catching Up With Bengals Running Back Ickey Woods, " CNNSI.com, 9 December 1997, http://sportsillustrated.cnn.com/features/1997/weekly/catchingup/1215/ (7 August 2012).

19. "Sports and Painkillers," *The Sporting Body Themes and Issues: Investigations into the Organisation of the Body in Sports*, http://sportingbody.edublogs.org/painkillers-and-sport/ (7 August 2012).

20. "Raiders Legend Otto Undergoes Right Leg Amputation," *ESPN.com*, 1 August 2007, http://sports.espn.go.com/nfl/news/story?id=2957868 (21 July 2012).

21. Doug Farrar, "Jim McMahon: 'My Memory's Pretty Much Gone,'" *Shutdown Corner, Yahoo! Sports Blog*, 10 November 2011, http://sports.yahoo.com/nfl/blog/shutdown_corner/post/Jim-McMahon-My-memory-s-pretty-much-gone-?urn=nfl-284214 (21 July 2012).

22. Mark Walker, "Oceanside: Football Great Junior Seau, 43, Dead in Apparent Suicide," *North County Times*, 2 May 2012, www.nctimes.com/article_bccb943a-ba7e-56f3-8756-13d9c81a8258.html (21 July 2012).

23. Based on my own definition, I qualify as a frustrated athlete. Even though I make it a point to spare my friends the details of my past athletic accomplishments at get-togethers when the liquor flows, I meet the basic criteria because I honestly believed at one point in my life that the main reason why I failed to make it as a professional baseball player was because I tore my ACL.

24. Clearly, not everyone who participates in recreational sports is as a frustrated athlete. The majority of people who engage in amateur or recreational sports do so because they enjoy the activity as part of a healthier lifestyle or use it as a positive outlet in relieving stress from their daily lives.

25. Most of the Quidditch players are *Harry Potter* fans more so than sports fans. Regardless, the league's existence speaks to the importance of recognition for performing in athletic competition, which is often one of the main reasons people engage in any type of sport in the first place. See International Quidditch Association, www.internationalquidditch.org/ (31 July 2012).

26. "Introduction to the Sports Industry," Plunkett Research, Inc., 2012, www.plunkettresearch.com/sports-recreation-leisure-market-research/industry-and-business-data (27 July 2012).

27. Men's Senior Baseball League, www.msblnational.com/About-Us.html (7 July 2012).

28. Marc Wortman, "Over 30s Play Ball: Once a Game Only for the Boys of Summer, Amateur Baseball Leagues Are Now Filled With Thousands of Men Over 30," *Cigar Afficionado*, September/October 1998, www.cigaraficionado.com/webfeatures/show/id/Over-30s-Play-Bal_7391 (27 July 2012), 1.

29. Wortman, "Over 30s Play Ball," 3.

30. Even though we only play seven innings in the MSBL as opposed to the standard nine, this should not diminish the accomplishments of my teammates, given the stamina and coordination required to operate effectively for this many innings as a pitcher at any level of baseball competition.

31. Audie Cornish, "Don't Count on a U.S. Medal in Badminton, Canoeing: Audie Cornish Talks to David Wallechinsky about the United States' Olympic Weak Spots. What Are the Sports and Events Americans Rarely—If Ever—Win Medals For? And What Countries Excel in Those Areas?" *All Things Considered*, NPR, 23 July 2012, www.npr.org/2012/07/23/157248905/dont-count-on-a-u-s-medal-in-badminton-canoeing (24 July 2012).

32. Jeffery Eisenband, "Robert Griffin III Could've Been an Olympic Hurdler," *ThePostGame*, *Yahoo! Sports*, 9 August 2012, www.thepostgame.com/blog/london-calling-2012/201208/robert-griffin-iii-olympics-hurdles-baylor-track-heisman (16 August 2012).

33. Michael David Smith, "Robert Griffin III: 'It Sucks' Watching Olympic Track Trials," *NBC Sports*, 29 June 2012, http://profootballtalk.nbcsports.com/2012/06/29/robert-griffin-iii-it-sucks-watching-olympic-track-trials/ (4 August 2012).

34. Dan Steinberg and Sarah Kogod, "DC Sports Bog: RGIII on Two Catalog Covers," *Washington Post*, 25 July 2012, www.washingtonpost.com/blogs/dc-sports-bog/post/rgiii-on-two-catalog-covers/2012/07/25/gJQADkpt8W_blog.html (5 August 2012).

35. James Walker, "Patriots Pull Shocker with Jeff Demps," *ESPN NFL, AFC East Blog*, http://espn.go.com/blog/afceast/post/_/id/46315/patriots-pull-shocker-with-jeff-demps (17 August 2012).

36. According to the official website, the MSBL/MABL has been featured in more than 600 local radio, television, and newspaper accounts and has reached national prominence, with major articles in *Sports Illustrated*, *Sport*, *Baseball America*, *USA Today*, *Sporting News*, and *U.S. News and World Report*. In addition, MSBL/MABL has been in the spotlight on broadcasts of the *Today Show* and *Good Morning America*. One of the foremost articles featuring MSBL appeared in *Cigar Afficionado*. Regardless, most of these stories are marginal and do not offer ongoing coverage of the league, which, for the most part, leaves prospective involvement in the league unnoticed by the general public. See Men's Senior Baseball League, www.msblnational.com/About-Us.html (7 July 2012).

2

SOCIAL MEDIA AND SPORTS FANS IN AMERICAN CULTURE

THEY'RE NOT CRAZY, THEY'RE SPORTS FANS

Shortly before avid Pittsburgh Steelers fan James Henry Smith died, he requested that, instead of being on display at the funeral home in a casket, he wanted his lifeless corpse, dressed in his usual game-day attire and wrapped in a Pittsburgh Steelers blanket, to be positioned in his favorite recliner in front of a high-definition television playing a continuous loop of Steelers' highlights.[1] According to the undertaker interviewed in the film detailing the Pittsburgh Steelers fan's request, "He [James Henry Smith] wanted to look like he just fell asleep watching the game."[2] This is but one of the many remarkable anecdotes featured in the short documentary *Team Spirit* (2012), directed by Academy Award–winning director Errol Morris, which focuses on sports-themed funerals. Even the tag line of *Team Spirit*—"People say when you're a sports fan, you're a fan for life. But that might be a little shortsighted"—speaks to the intense devotion exhibited by many sports fans as enduring components of their identities, both in life and death.[3]

While these examples from the *Team Spirit* documentary illustrate some of the most extreme levels of sports fan dedication, many sports fans of varying degrees of devotion engage in peculiar behaviors in support of their favorite athlete or team that might seem equally strange to the casual observer. I carry out my own intense and irrational rituals when I watch my favorite college football team, the Nebraska

Cornhuskers, play on television. One of my most fanatical behaviors occurred during Nebraska's loss to Texas in the 2009 Big 12 Championship Game on December 5, 2009, when I decided to post my own play-by-play comments on Facebook. While I consumed alcohol before and during the game, which might help explain my irrational behavior, it was the rabid Husker fan inside me harboring an intense hatred for the Texas Longhorns that drove me to post 273 high-spirited and vituperative Facebook comments during the game's broadcast. This breaks down into approximately 1.52 posts per minute during the three-hour broadcast (3 hours = 180 minutes; 273 posts/180 minutes = 1.52 posts/min), an impressive and tiring feat, I have to admit. My flurry of posts during the game not only drove some of my Facebook friends to "unfriend" me that night, but also prompted the Facebook staff to send me the following message:

> David M. Sutera: Warning! You are engaging in behavior that may be considered annoying or abusive by other users. Facebook's systems determined that you were going too fast when posting on walls. You must significantly slow down. Further misuse of site features may result in a temporary block or your account being permanently disabled. For further information, please visit our FAQ page. December 5, 2009 at 9:39pm Like.

As a side note, one of my friends told me that if I used Twitter instead of Facebook, I would have been applauded by the website's administrator rather than admonished and might have even gotten more attention if other Twitter users shared information about my posts regarding the game.

Sadly, my behavior is common in the sports fan community. The eccentric activities of sports fans, either during the course of watching a game or in their everyday lives, have gained media attention that often positions them as operating on the fringes of normal behavior. Any person who devotes a significant amount of time and energy to what seems a frivolous activity, at least to an outsider, may, indeed, seem a bit off-kilter. Much has been written about what constitutes a fan of any persuasion. Henry Jenkins identifies the following stereotypes when describing the attributes of Trekkies (a group of devoted and eccentric *Star Trek* fans), which, I believe, can apply to any group of fans:

1. Brainless consumers who will buy anything associated with the [*Star Trek*] program;
2. Devote their lives to cultivation of worthless knowledge [about *Star Trek*];
3. Place inappropriate importance on devalued materials [autographs, etc.];
4. Social misfits who have become so obsessed with [*Star Trek*] that it forecloses other types of social experiences;
5. Are feminized and/or desexualized through their intimate engagement with [*Star Trek*];
6. Are infantile, emotionally and intellectually immature; and
7. Are unable to separate fantasy from reality.[4]

With the exception of sports fans being feminized or desexualized through their engagement with sports—the inverse is often true in that being a sports fan usually bolsters a male fan's perceived masculinity instead of calling it into question—these stereotypes appropriately describe the sports fan community.

Even though many sports fans engage in a wide variety of behaviors that call their sanity into question, most are unbothered by this perception and, in many instances, seek out some form of validation for their "crazy" exploits. Ranging from fans who have an intimate, near obsessive knowledge of their favorite team or athlete to those who attend games on freezing cold, snowy days painted in their team's colors wearing little more than shorts and sandals in the hope of catching the attention of live broadcast film crews, most sports fans actively seek recognition for their devotion. They key word here is *recognition*.

As I contend in Chapter 1, the desire for recognition is one of the most important motivating factors in our participation in sports, both as athletes and fans. Since most people will never have the chance to gain acknowledgement for their athletic performances or, at the very least, will experience only fleeting moments of athletic glory—usually in the form of high school sports—being a sports fan represents the best opportunity for nonathletes to gain widespread recognition in the world of sports. Sports journalism and sports broadcasting is another way nonathletes can play a more direct role in sports; however, these jobs are competitive and usually require a high level of education and a particular skill set, along with the fact that many of these positions are obtained through knowing someone already in the business who can vouch for you, and so forth. Therefore, sports fandom still offers the average citizen the most opportunities to have an active voice in sports.

MORGANNA THE KISSING BANDIT: MAJOR LEAGUE BASEBALL'S POSTER FAN OF THE 1970S AND 1980S

One of the earliest examples of a nonathlete using sports and mass media as a way to gain widespread recognition was Morganna the Kissing Bandit. During the 1970s and 1980s, while working as an exotic dancer, Morganna the Kissing Bandit (Morganna Roberts) became a popular fixture at many high-profile sporting events by running on the field wearing hot pants and an overly tight shirt to kiss famous athletes. What set Morganna apart from the other fans who tried to get on the playing field during games was not just that she possessed an impressive physique—Morganna's measurements were 60-23-39, all natural—but also because she had a flare for showmanship once she got on the field that endeared her to both players and fans alike. Even though she accentuated her prominent feminine features, her on-field exploits were quite tame in that she avoided performing overtly lewd actions on the field and always kissed athletes on the cheek, never on the lips. She indicated that the reason she would kiss athletes only on the cheek because "it was more sanitary and that way, their wives wouldn't get upset"; she also quipped that she did not want get "tobacco stains all over [her] teeth."[5] In addition, she was clever about how she positioned herself at the stadiums to be close enough to the playing field so she could easily and quickly run onto the field to perform her act. She also covered herself up with an oversized jacket, which allowed her to remain relatively anonymous without tipping off security guards as to her presence before she made her move onto the field.

Morganna Roberts first gained notoriety in 1971, when a friend dared her on a $10 bet to run out on the field at Riverfront Stadium during a Cincinnati Reds baseball game to kiss Reds third baseman Pete Rose, who was one of the most popular players in Major League Baseball (MLB) at that time. Even though she was tackled by a security guard, ejected from the stadium, and later charged with trespassing, judging by the applause and cheers her kiss prompted that night, she recognized that this might be a way to make a name for herself in the world of entertainment. She was correct. Soon after this event, she took her show on the road and successfully ran onto the field to kiss other prominent baseball players, including Cal Ripken Jr. (Baltimore Orioles), Johnny Bench (Cincinnati Reds), Steve Garvey (Los Angeles Dodgers), Don Mattingly (New York Yankees), and Nolan Ryan (Houston Astros), which prompted a Cincinnati sportswriter to give her the name Morganna the Kissing Bandit.[6]

Early in her career, Morganna developed somewhat of a good-natured "rivalry" with All-Star third baseman for the Kansas City Royals George Brett. It started in 1977, when Morganna ran onto the field in Baltimore during a game between the Orioles and Royals on August 22 and kissed George Brett as he waited in the on-deck circle to bat. In typical fashion, Morganna's exploits made it to the local newspapers, which featured a photo of her embracing and kissing a smiling George Brett. All in good fun and realizing this was a way for him to increase his profile early in his career, Brett vowed to get back at her for kissing him at his place of work. He got his revenge on September 12, 1977, when he attended a night club in Kansas City where Morganna was performing an exotic dance and jumped onto the stage in the middle of the performance to give her a kiss; while on stage, Brett was reported as saying to her, "Now we're even."[7] Of course, this only added to Morganna's celebrity status in the world of sports and earned her even more publicity in the mainstream press. Not to be outdone, Morganna later got back at Brett during the 1979 All-Star Game at the Seattle Kingdome, where she ran onto the field and kissed the Kansas City Royals All-Star third baseman on national television.[8]

Despite the fact she was arrested 19 times for her activities, Morganna became the unofficial mascot of MLB in the 1970s and 1980s. Ever the entertainer, even when she appeared in court, she managed to make light of the situation, which also earned her more positive publicity. For instance, she once had "colorful Texas attorney Richard 'Racehorse' Haynes argue the 'Gravity Defense' on her behalf, that she had leaned over a rail and had been naturally propelled onto the playing field because of her anatomy,"[9] and the charges against her were dismissed.

Along with being featured in *Playboy* magazine in the June 1983, April 1985, and September 1989 issues, she also appeared on national television several times with such prominent figures as Johnny Carson on *The Tonight Show* and David Letterman on his late-night program. During interviews with both high-profile talk show hosts, she proved to be a natural entertainer and displayed a quick wit. She held her own during interviews with Carson and Letterman and spouted some of the following one-liners when asked about her exploits, which drew laughter and applause from both hosts and their studio audiences:

- When asked about her physical measurements of 60-23-39, she responded, "Those are my baseball statistics."
- Responding to why Steve Garvey ran from her, she said, "I think he thought it was the start of a paternity suit."
- Explaining what happened when she kissed basketball star Charles Barkley, she indicated that, "He kept talking to my cleavage while I kissed him."
- In response to how she got started by kissing Pete Rose, she quipped, "I tell people my career started with a bet, and Pete's ended with one" (referring to Pete Rose's lifetime ban from the National Baseball Hall of Fame for betting on his team.)[10]

In reference to the last point, ironically, Morganna has been in the National Baseball Hall of Fame since the late 1980s, where she is featured in a photo of her attempt to kiss former Los Angeles Dodgers star Frank Howard.[11] She finished out her career by making appearances at Minor League Baseball games across the United States as the featured attraction, where she signed autographs and posed for pictures with fans before, during, and after each game.

After 20 years of running onto many playing fields throughout the United States and earning a permanent place in American popular sports culture, Morganna "retired" from public life. She decided to quit being the Kissing Bandit as of January 1, 2000, indicating that even though she had fun and everyone was wonderful, fans and players alike, she had enough. Today, she lives in Cincinnati, Ohio, with her husband of 35 years and seems to be enjoying her retirement, avoiding requests for interviews and public appearances.

Even though Morganna avoids public attention, various mass media and social media outlets still refer to her. Along with a cameo appearance in *Kingpin* (1996), she was also referenced in an episode of *The Simpsons* entitled "Homer, the Heretic" (the episode where Homer misses church to watch football on television). During the episode, Keith Jackson, famed ABC football announcer, lent his voice to the program where he mentions Morganna the Kissing Bandit. During the segment where Homer is watching the football game, Jackson exclaims in his typical high-spirited cadence, "Oh Doctor! A 98-yard triple reverse ties the score at 63–63! We've seen nothing but razzle-dazzle here today, three visits from Morganna the Kissing Bandit, and the surprising return of Jim Brown."

What makes Morganna's rise to stardom so amazing is that it occurred well before the Internet, let alone the existence of Twitter, Facebook, and other social media outlets. She managed to build her impressive and prolific celebrity just by gaining the attention of newspapers and television programs, and all without having videos of her posted on YouTube or Twitter posts instantaneously broadcasting her kissing activities to a worldwide audience. A fan by the name of Bill J. posted the following comment on the website mcgarnagle.com on June 28, 2011, which sums up what made her so appealing and why she would have a difficult time building her celebrity in contemporary society:

> Morganna is awesome! She sparked up the sometimes slow game of baseball. She always put a smile on my face. It took guts to run on the baseball field, knowing you'd probably be locked up and charged with a crime. Can you imagine the security after 9/11? . . . Morganna probably would have been shot! . . . lol."[12]

Morganna the Kissing Bandit has left an enduring legacy in American popular culture that would be difficult to match in today's hypermediated digital landscape, even with the aid of the Internet and social media.

ROLLEN STEWART, A.K.A. THE RAINBOW MAN: FROM JOHN 3:16 TO INMATE H87708

Another pre-Internet pop culture sports figure who rose to fame without the aid of social media whose story ended tragically in sharp contrast to Morganna's "feel-good" story is Rollen Stewart, a.k.a. the "Rainbow Man." He is best known for attending sporting events wearing an oversized rainbow Afro wig and holding up the religious sign "John 3:16." Stewart began his exploits during the 1977 NBA All-Star Game. During that contest, he danced crazily for camera crews and fans but without any reference to the biblical passage from the Book of John—a dimension he would add years later. From the attention he received during that game, he decided to continue his act at other high-profile sporting events. He felt his actions could eventually lead to a job as a product spokesman, claiming that his main goal was to be the "most famous person in the world no one knows about."[13]

With this in mind, Stewart continued to perform at various sporting events for several years, where he developed a reputation for himself as a spectacle attraction both at live sporting events and on national television. His act eventually earned him a spot on a Budweiser beer commercial, along with being hired to entertain guests at high-profile parties for Hollywood celebrities in Los Angeles and New York City. During this time in his life, Stewart admitted that he engaged in many decadent activities, going by the name of Rockin' Rollen. He claimed that his "life revolved around sex and drugs," and he once felt that "[he] was going to sail around the world in his waterbed."[14]

While he had already gained fame just for his rainbow hair act, it was not until he added the religious dimension to his persona that his celebrity really took off. Stewart came up with the idea to display the John 3:16 sign at sporting events after attending Super Bowl XVI in 1980. During the game, Stewart delivered one of his most lascivious performances, wearing nothing more than a loin-cloth, along with his trademark rainbow Afro wig. Stewart described his experience at the Super Bowl that day as shallow and unfulfilling, admitting that the "girls loved [his outfit]. Everywhere I walked, they were patting my butt. I could have held a thousand women in my arms that day but walked out of there sad."[15] In his hotel room after the game that night in Los Angeles, he watched a program hosted by televangelist Charles R. Taylor. After the broadcast, he decided to become a born-again Christian. He believed that God had spoken to him through the television and was calling him to use his sports celebrity to spread the teachings of Jesus Christ. Stewart decided that the best way to do this was by continuing with the Rainbow Man act at sporting events and adding a handheld sign and wearing a t-shirt reading "John 3:16."[16] Once he started flashing the John 3:16 sign at sporting events, obsessed with his purported divine mission, Stewart's activities gradually shifted from being merely amusing to somewhat unhinged as he began to conduct himself in an increasingly aggressive and invasive manner.

What helped elevate Stewart's profile was that he was adept at positioning himself at sporting events to consistently display his sign on national television broadcasts. By watching the live broadcasts, as he carried a battery-operated television with him at all live sporting events he attended, Stewart was able track what part of the stadium or arena the camera crews were filming and put himself in position to be seen by the camera. At football games, he frequently sat behind the goal posts, because he knew that every time a team attempted a field goal, the cameras would focus on that part of the stadium. This technique worked so well for him—transforming him into a cliché lacking its former novelty—that television networks tried to avoid filming him if at all possible. ABC's *Monday Night Football* former director Chet Forte told the *Los Angeles Times* in 1991 that, "Stewart became a great distraction . . . it was very annoying seeing this guy waving signs and all."[17] In addition, NBC's golf producer in the 1980s, Larry Cirillo, told ESPN that he asked his cameramen to refrain from showing Stewart, going so far as to threaten their jobs if they gave him airtime.[18] Despite the attempts of television networks to limit Stewart's visibility during sporting events, he continued on with his mission, becoming a high-profile fixture at many sporting events worldwide.

During the course of his career, Stewart claimed to have driven more than 60,000 miles a year to attend more than 100 sporting events in that same time frame, where he and his wife, Margaret Hockridge, spread their religious message.[19] Stewart was able to fund their journey by selling his ranch and, with the proceeds, purchase a van, which they used as both transportation and lodging. They sustained themselves by eating one meal a day, mostly at salad bars, according to Stewart, and they avoided having to pay admission to most games because many people sympathetic to his cause, mostly evangelical Christians, donated tickets to them for entry.[20] They focused their efforts on high-profile sporting events around the world, including the World Series, the Kentucky Derby, NBA and NCAA basketball finals, the NHL's Stanley Cup, and the World Cup soccer championship, the latter of which was viewed by more than 2.8 billion people worldwide.

At many of these events, the couple was often met with resistance in spreading their message. For instance, during the 1984 Winter Olympics in Sarajevo, local intelligence authorities believed Stewart was a spy and that the John 3:16 sign was a coded message indicating the location of strategic missile sites.[21] Stewart also claimed that they were forcibly removed from various sporting events by stadium security; however, he capitalized on the publicity from these ejections, which he claimed only helped to increase his celebrity profile and draw even more focus on his religious mission. Stewart and his wife expanded their reach outside the world of sports by posting their sign at the Republican and Democratic national conventions in the 1980s, as well as the wedding of Prince Charles and Princess Diana,[22] making him a fixture in American popular culture in the late 1970s and throughout the 1980s.

Stewart and Hockridge's prodigious efforts led to many subsequent cross-references in American popular culture. Stewart was featured on several popular television programs, including *Saturday Night Live*, *The Tonight Show with Johnny Carson*, and NBC's *St. Elsewhere*. Charles Schulz drew the Rainbow Man alongside the iconic Charlie Brown in a *Peanuts* cartoon in the 1980s. Further attesting to his popularity, Fox television's popular animated series *The Simpsons* depicted him holding up the John 3:16 sign wearing his rainbow wig in the episode originally broadcast on September 19, 1991, entitled "Stark Raving Dad."[23] In addition, a representation of the Rainbow Man appeared in past versions of several football video games as part of the background scenery.[24] Given the wide range of mass media outlets Stewart managed to influence and how many times his persona was mentioned on national television, he became one of the most popular nonathlete sports figures of all time.

Unfortunately, Rollen Stewart's sports celebrity story ends on a sour note. In the late 1980s, as his high celebrity status waned, so did his grip on sanity. While he always seemed a bit crazy, although in a comical way, his behaviors later in his career became more aggressive and violent. The first indication of this shift occurred when he allegedly choked his wife when she failed to hold the John 3:16 sign in the correct place during a nationally televised game.[25] Soon after this incident, his wife left him, which marked the beginning of his gradual downward spiral into depression, bankruptcy, and homelessness on the streets of Los Angeles. It was at this point that Stewart had another revelation as to how he should continue with his proselytism. He decided to take a more aggressive approach in spreading his message.

Claiming that, "God had given him a sign to use more negative tactics," Stewart decided that the best way to return to the spotlight was by setting off a series of stink bombs in public. One of his first attempts occurred during the 1990 American Music Awards in Los Angeles, where he attempted to throw skunk sacks into the audience, asserting that he wanted to show the public that "God thinks this stinks."[26] As Stewart intensified his tactics, he infiltrated other establishments, most notably by stink-bombing a Christian bookstore in Southern California and the main offices of the *Orange County Register* newspaper. He also made his presence known at the 1991 Masters Golf Tournament by sounding an air horn just as Jack Nicklaus was about to putt on the 16th green, while simultaneously setting off several stink bombs near the greens. In addition, he set off stink bombs during the first Evander Holyfield–Mike Tyson fight, causing a delay in the bout.

Stewart conducted his final public performance spreading his religious message in September 1992. Hoping to call attention to what he believed was the imminent apocalypse, he locked himself in a hotel room near the Los Angeles International Airport. Earlier that day, he brought two day laborers with him to the hotel, who later escaped, while a frightened maid locked herself in the bathroom after Stewart brandished an automatic handgun and two ammunition clips, each with 47 rounds of ammunition.[27] During the 8½ hour standoff in the hotel, Stewart plastered religious signs on the window and threatened to kill former president George H. W. Bush and President Bill Clinton. He also claimed he would shoot down planes from the airport if authorities refused him a three-hour press conference with all the major news networks to pronounce his warnings about the coming end of the world.[28] After his arrest, the district attorney offered him a plea bargain that would have put him in jail for 15 years. Stewart refused, opting for a public trial as one last major platform to spread his message. While he gained the publicity he wanted, Stewart was sentenced to three consecutive life terms in prison. After his sentencing, he refused to leave, still preaching his message about the coming of Jesus, while the police dragged him from the court kicking and screaming.

Now in his late 60s, Stewart comes up for parole every year but is repeatedly denied. Still determined to spread his message, he communicates with other born-again Christians, encouraging them to flash John 3:16 signs at public events around the world. While no longer at the forefront of attention, Stewart continues to make his presence known in popular culture. George Winter, who has been working on Stewart's biography and acts as his unofficial spokesman, created a blog to keep fans updated on Stewart's activities. On almost every post, Winter includes the following instructions to fans who want to support Stewart's cause:

> There are two ways that you can help Rollen.
>
> 1. Go to www.paypal.com and donate to the account set up for Rollen, rainbowman@gmail.com.
> 2. Make cheques or money orders out to "Rainbow Man" and send to "Rainbow Man," Box 131, 3353 Credit Woodlands, Mississauga, ON Canada L5C 2K1
>
> If you wish to leave messages for me and/or for Rollen, please use the same email address: rainbowman@gmail.com.[29]

In addition, filmmaker Sam Green produced the documentary *The Rainbow Man/John 3:16* (1997), and ESPN produced a short piece on Stewart in 2006; both works recount Stewart's rise to fame and gradual descent into infamy.

Both Morganna the Kissing Bandit and Roland Stewart, the Rainbow Man, are remarkable examples of average people making an extraordinary impact in the world of popular culture. Even more amazing is that they were able to create and maintain their celebrities without the existence of the Internet and social media. At that time in history, both Morganna and the Rainbow Man had to physically reproduce their on-the-field and in-the-stands activities if they wanted to continue to be noticed in mass media. As a result, this makes their respective accomplishments that much more astonishing because, unlike contemporary publicity hounds, they did not have the benefit of having a nearly unlimited number of people with the means to capture video footage on their smart phones or other portable viewing devices and disseminate it instantaneously to a widespread audience. Nevertheless, even with smart phones and Twitter, modern sports fans can no longer rely on shock value alone to garner interest from an increasingly inured public to spectacle forms of entertainment.

HOW DOES THE AVERAGE SPORTS FAN GET ATTENTION?

Unfortunately for the vast majority, because of the large number of sports fans in existence and their ubiquitous presence at most sporting events, it is difficult for the average fan to gain individual, far-reaching recognition for his or her actions. In fact, to obtain even the slightest mass media attention, sports fans must engage in bizarre, sometimes illegal activities. For instance, one of the surest ways to gain notice as a sports fan at a live game is to engage in the act of streaking, which is officially defined as the "nonsexual act of taking off one's clothes and running naked through a public place."[30]

Starting with 25-year-old Australian Michael O'Brien, the first documented streaker at a major sporting event, who on April 20, 1974, ran onto the field of an England versus France Rugby Union match at Twickenham naked,[31] to Mark Roberts, who streaked onto the field before a kickoff during Super Bowl XXXVIII and was tackled by New England Patriot's linebacker Matt Chatham,[32] streaking has a long and storied history at many live sporting events. Even though media outlets like ESPN avoid showing streakers during live broadcasts and on *SportsCenter* in the hope of discouraging such activities, streakers at sporting events often achieve a level of fame (and infamy) that most "well-behaved" fans never attain, as evidenced by the multiple websites and fan-made YouTube video posts that exist to call attention to streakers at sports venues around the world.[33]

While I never had the courage to run naked in public in support of my favorite football team (Nebraska Cornhuskers), one of my friends and fellow Nebraska football fans, Nick Aguilar, did. Soon after Nebraska's victory in the 1995 Orange Bowl against their hated rival, the University of Miami Hurricanes, on January 1, Nick ran naked down the busiest street in Omaha, Nebraska, that subzero, blustery night when thousands of other Nebraska fans were celebrating the team's first national championship since 1972. Despite the fact Nick spent the night in jail wearing nothing more than a police blanket and received an official criminal record for indecent exposure, his actions that evening earned him a great deal of respect from other Nebraska football fans, along with free drinks for the rest of his life from friends who witnessed the event. In contrast, even though I attended the game in Miami that night and was mentioned in a *Sports Illustrated* article following a group of Nebraska fans on a bus tour to the Orange Bowl as a "pony-tailed health inspector from Bellevue, Nebraska (pop. 30,982), about to chuck his job and take his chances as an actor in Hollywood,"[34] my recognition for participating in Nebraska's victory celebration pales in comparison to Nick's streaking exploits that night in Omaha as the more devoted Nebraska football fan.

To discourage fans from occupying the field during game time in any capacity, sharp lines of demarcation are drawn between the playing field and viewing areas at all live sporting events. These boundaries are specifically designed and implemented to exclude fans from getting too close to the athletes and on the playing field during games. One of the most comical examples of this occurred during a 1961 American Football League (AFL) game between the Dallas Texans (currently the Kansas City Chiefs) and the Boston Patriots, when a fan ran onto the field to break up a pass that helped secure the victory for the Patriots.[35] Starting from the center of the playing field and moving outward to the far reaches of the grand stands, the breakdown of boundaries that exists at most stadiums and arenas can be represented in the following manner:

1. Playing field/performative space: meant exclusively for athletes, referees, and other essential officials to facilitate game play;
2. Sidelines: place for coaches, bench players, trainers, side judges, scorekeepers, sports announcers, camerapersons, mascots, cheerleaders, off-duty police officers, stadium security, emergency medical crews, stadium maintenance/groundskeepers, and visiting athletes;

3. Premium seats/luxury boxes: limited to wealthy individuals, corporate sponsors, celebrities, former sports stars, specialized support staff (i.e., waiters, bartenders, etc.), and a few lucky "regular Joes" who either won a contest or are the guests of a wealthy friend;
4. General admission seats: along with concession vendors, stadium security, and stadium emcees carrying out promotional events, the space the majority of rank-and-file sports fans occupy; and
5. Parking lot: tailgating for all fans and those who don't have tickets to the game.

While there is some occasional overlap, these boundaries are strictly enforced at all live sporting events. Fans can only cross these lines when invited for some special event, for instance, singing the national anthem or taking part in on-field promotions like Dr. Pepper's halftime competition at college football games pitting two college students throwing footballs into oversized soda cans for a $100,000 grand prize. Otherwise, fans are expected to stay off the field and not interfere with the playing action of any live sporting event.

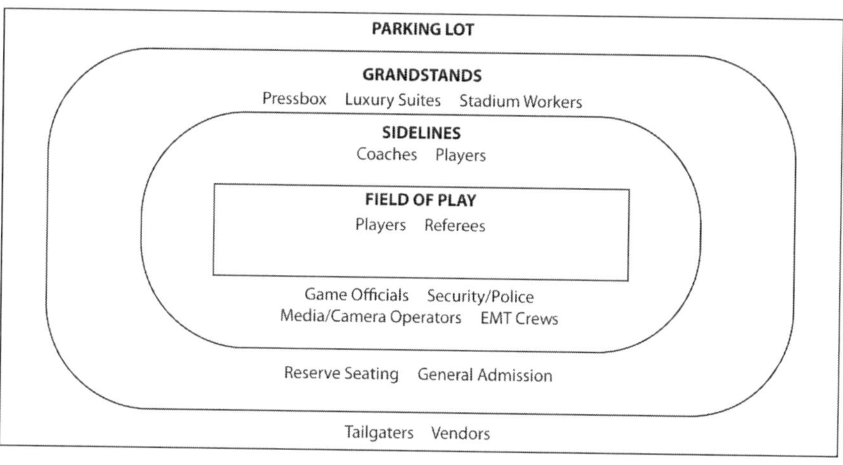

Figure 2.1. These are the traditional boundaries at most sports stadiums and arenas. With social media, fans can more easily cross over into the field of play and participate in the narrative of the sporting event without having to put themselves in physical danger or run the risk of arrest. ***Image courtesy of Richard Benak***

When fans do cross these lines without invitation and encroach on the playing field, these actions often result in fans being ejected from the stadium and, in some instances, arrested and potentially litigated. This occurs frequently at MLB games, where spectators are ejected for interfering with the game by simply trying to obtain a foul ball from the field of play. Take, for example, the well-publicized incident involving the fan interference of the Ichiro Suzuki impersonator at a Seattle Mariners game on August 2, 2011, which was replayed several times on *SportsCenter's* "Not Top 10 Plays" segment, and the video of which is currently featured on MLB's official website.[36] At least on the surface, it appears it was not the impersonator's intention to interfere with the game, preventing Dustin Ackley of the Mariners from getting a triple; however, soon after he mistakenly removed a fair ball from the field of play near the first-base side fence, thinking it was foul, he was summarily ejected from Safeco Field.[37] In addition, the infamous Steve Bartman incident during the 2003 National League playoff game between the Chicago Cubs and Florida Marlins is probably the most notorious example of unintentional fan interference that allegedly affected the outcome of the game.[38] While it is arguable that he cost the Chicago Cubs a chance at the World Series in 2003, nevertheless, he angered the Cubs fans in attendance so much that he was quickly removed from the stadium for his own safety, and he has endured prolonged harassment, including death threats from Cubs fans, long after the series ended.[39]

Because these examples garnered media attention, they help illustrate that, for fans to be recognized during the course of a game, they must perform acts that go beyond the bounds of what is considered acceptable fan behavior. Nevertheless, even though engaging in inappropriate behavior at games can result in widespread mass media attention, most fans will refrain from acting out at games to avoid unpleasant confrontations with stadium security, police, and enraged fans, along with potential litigation for trespassing or other more serious prosecutable offenses, including assault with potential jail time, costly fines, and a criminal record.

In spite of strict restrictions, many devoted fans have found ways to make their presence known during live sporting events without crossing these lines or breaking the law. For instance, the "Lambeau Leap," a long-standing ritual at the Green Bay Packers' home games at Lambeau Field, is one of the most prominent examples of "socially acceptable" player/fan game day interaction in American sports culture. The tradition started most unexpectedly late in the "1993 season during a game with the Los Angeles Raiders on the day after Christmas when the late Hall of Famer [defensive lineman] Reggie White picked up a fumble, ran it back for a touchdown, and then jumped into the crowd to celebrate."[40] Since then, the Lambeau Leap has become one of the most well-publicized sanctioned player/fan in-game interactions, and it frequently gainswide spread mass media attention, both during live broadcasts and on sports recap shows like *SportsCenter*.

Not only does the Lambeau Leap allow fans to get closer to their favorite athletes without running the risk of ejection or arrest, it also affords them a good chance of being noticed on national television as part of the team's touchdown celebrations. In fact, the desire to sit in this part of the stadium is so intense that the end zone tickets in the Lambeau Leap Zone are some of the most difficult to obtain, which drives up the demand for these tickets, allowing them to go for a much higher price than the face value of $250. Tickets in the Lambeau Leap Zone are so coveted that they are featured as key selling points in Green Bay Packers fan vacation packages and as the grand prize in Green Bay Packers' fan contests in remote locations as far away as Florida.[41] Attesting to the popularity of this ritual, players from other football teams, both at the professional and college levels, emulate the Lambeau Leap at their home stadiums. And even though some critics (mostly Packers fans) assert that imitative leaps at other stadiums pale in comparison to the Lambeau Leap, they are equally demonstrative of the passionate fervor for this type of player/fan interaction, often attracting the attention of camera crews at games, and are featured during live broadcasts, on the stadium's video board, and on sports news programs.[42]

While the Lambeau Leap and similar player/fan interactions are common and encouraged at most live sporting events, it is often difficult for the average fan to rely on these events as a way to get attention during the course of a game. Communal events at stadiums and arenas like this are highly capricious and offer fans little control over when and where they can interact with their favorite athlete or make their presence known during a live sporting event. Similarly, sports fans of the past had to be satisfied with being lucky enough to catch a foul ball at a game or meet up with their favorite athlete to get an autograph or some other bit of memorabilia (as seen in the 1979 Mean Joe Green Coca-

Cola commercial, where he gives his jersey to one of his fans).[43] However, with the advent of social media, sports fans are no longer bound by the physical restraints of the past and now have much more control over their expressions and level of participation in the world of mediated sports.

SOCIAL MEDIA AND SPORTS FANS AT LIVE SPORTING EVENTS

Before the existence of personal digital media devices and the expansion of social media, the following illustrative, rather than exhaustive, activities were some of the primary avenues through which sports fans could interact with the athletes or make their presence known during a live sporting event:

- Support their team through specialized cheers, waving signs or pennants, or using noise-making devices (e.g., "the wave" and vuvuzelas);
- Distract the opposing team using specialized jeers, signs, or noise-making devices (e.g., the wide range of free-throw distractions at basketball games)[44];
- Obtain team/athlete/game paraphernalia or other artifacts (e.g., autographs or foul balls at baseball games);
- Get close enough to the athletes to shake hands or establish some kind of physical contact (e.g., the Lambeau Leap);
- Throw items on the field in protest of an athlete or bad referee call (e.g., Philadelphia Phillies fans throwing batteries at J. D. Drew after he left the team to join the St. Louis Cardinals for more money)[45];
- Throw items onto the field to effect the outcome of a game (e.g., the "Snowball Game" between the Denver Broncos and San Francisco 49ers on November 11, 1985, when Bronco fans threw snowballs at 49ers field goal kicker, Ray Wersching, causing him to miss an extra point that won the game for the Broncos); or
- Run onto the field illegally, either naked or fully clothed (streaking, as explained in detail earlier in this chapter).

While some of these are more acceptable than others—many fans often express great distaste for the wave and vuvuzelas—for the majority of the history of live sporting events, these were the only ways fans could legally interact with the event in an appreciable manner.

The widespread availability of social media makes the aforementioned boundaries and restrictions at live sporting events seem much less constraining. Still able to perform all the previously listed actions at live sporting events, through the user-friendliness of specialized applications on their smart phones or other mobile devices, sports fans now also have the ability to make their presence known on a much wider scale without ever having to leave their seats. For example, instead of running the risk of ejection and arrest for streaking or throwing snowballs onto the field of play, fans can still get attention for these activities, albeit vicariously, by making a short video of other fans carrying out these events and then broadcasting it on the Internet (e.g., Philadelphia Eagles fans pummeling San Francisco 49ers fans with snowballs during a December 2009 game).[46] In this way, sports fans can help disseminate information about one of these illegal activities and provide commentary about it without running the risk of being arrested for crossing the boundaries between spectators and the field of play.

Another consequence of widespread social media employment is that fans now have much more control over the flow of information at live sporting events. Before social media, broadcast officials and mass media news agencies had tight control over the way fans received most sporting event game information. Television networks and radio stations were the only way fans not in attendance at the actual event could know what was happening while the game was still being played. As such, play-by-play announcers were the sole source for conveying timely comments about the game to a large audience, and camera crews monopolized the relay of visual evidence from the game itself. News agency photographers and reporters on the sidelines or in the press boxes controlled the chronicling of "newsworthy" aspects at a live sporting event. Now, with social media, the flow of information is more complex, and it operates as an intricate web of information exchange between media consumers and producers as opposed to the simple linear "trickle-down" model of the past. Sports fans can film certain events at the game or make comments and share them with anyone they choose by simply uploading their video to YouTube or posting Tweets using their smart phone or other similar devices immediately after these events occur with little mediation from outside influences like network censors through Standards and Practices.[47] Consequently, sports fans are no longer merely media consumers; with these tools at their disposal, they can now become producers and disseminators of unique and personalized images, sounds, and other information from live sporting events.

The number of social media outlets and options for fans to directly participate in the creation of the narrative at live sporting events is wide-ranging and relatively simple to execute. On the most basic level, fans can use their mobile devices to indicate that they are attending a sporting event on Facebook by updating their status, tagging themselves in photos they took while at the game, or using the "places" function on Facebook to feature their presence on a navigable Bing search engine map. Popular sites like Twitter and reddit often serve as continuous platforms for sports fans to communicate a seemingly endless stream of information regarding any aspect of a live sporting event, including ancillary scenarios that have nothing to do with the game itself. Fans sitting as far away as the nosebleed seats in huge stadiums or arenas can use their smart phones to take high-quality pictures or videos of game highlights and post them instantly on sites like Tumblr, imgur, YouTube, or Facebook. With all these social media options available to sports fans and the associated changes in behavior that accompany the proficient use of these applications, sports fans now have unprecedented control over how, when, where, and what they interact with at

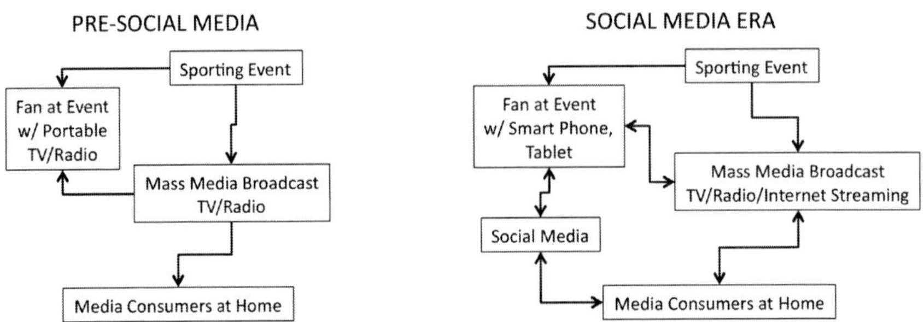

Figure 2.2. With social media, the flow of information takes on a much more complex dynamic that no longer adheres to the trickle down model of the past. ***Image courtesy of Richard Benak***

live sporting events. More importantly, social media gives fans vast potential in gaining recognition for their exploits to a nearly limitless audience. This recognition is not limited to the time or place in which the live sporting event occurred. Because social media sites serve as permanent records that exist in cyberspace in near perpetuity, anyone can access them at any time through an increasing number of personal digital devices and software applications; therefore, through sharing videos, pictures, or any other bits of sports-related information on the Internet, sports fans can have enduring legacies that have the potential to be viewed by incredibly large audiences worldwide.

CANDICE SORTINO, THE COLLEGE WORLD SERIES BUTT PINCHER

As I mentioned in Chapter 1 of this book, "Sports in American Society," the College World Series (CWS) was the highlight of my summers growing up in Omaha, Nebraska. From my perspective, the event has lost some of its folksy charm since it moved from its former home at historic Rosenblatt Stadium in a blue-collar neighborhood in South Omaha to the corporate-sponsored TD Ameritrade Park in gentrified downtown Omaha in 2010; however, the event is more popular than ever, and, as a result, finding tickets is much more difficult now that the series has entered the corporate era. My friend, Zach Ingle, and I foolishly tried to get tickets to the championship game of the 2012 CWS between the Arizona Wildcats and South Carolina Gamecocks on June 25, 2012. Since all reserved seat tickets were sold out—going for at least twice their face value with scalpers—and the line for general admission stretched more than a mile long, we had little chance of actually seeing the game in the stadium. Undeterred, Zach and I decided to try anyway, and, if we were unable to get tickets, we would at least mingle around the stadium to enjoy the energy of the game-day atmosphere.

Not surprisingly, we failed to get tickets for the game; however, we still had fun by taking part in some of the promotional activities at the various corporate-sponsored booths outside the stadium. We first attended the Capital One Credit Card baseball legends booth, where Barry Larkin (retired All-Star shortstop for the Cincinnati Reds and current ESPN baseball commentator) was signing autographs. Unfortunately, Zach was a few minutes too late to get an autograph from Larkin, and all he could do was watch as other fans got to interact with one of his childhood sports idols. Then, I took a turn in a batting cage sponsored by Buick, where they filmed my performance in super-slow motion and broadcast it on the Internet at the following website (which is still active as of the writing of this book at http://social-gen.com/cws_2012/index.php?e=19&id=1909&s=2). Finally, Zach and I watched the remainder of the game at the local art theater, Film Streams (www.filmstreams.org/), where they showed the ESPN broadcast of the championship game on the big screen in their main theater (free of charge, of course).

Meanwhile, as Zach and I putzed around the exterior of TD Ameritrade Park trying to get autographs from old baseball players and drinking free soda pop, a young, enthusiastic spectator was making CWS sports fan history inside the stadium. It all started during the seventh inning stretch, when fans in the bleacher sections in the outfield inundated the playing field with beach balls, a long-standing CWS tradition. While security and groundskeepers were in the process of clearing the beach balls from the field, several fans—all fully clothed, no streakers—ran onto the field in front of the capacity crowd. The first to run onto the field were two drunken young men who scrambled around until security caught up with them and tackled them to the ground. Once they were apprehended, a 17-year-old girl by the name of Candice Sortino suddenly hopped the fence and dashed out onto the field. Unlike the two young men who scurried aimlessly across the field, she had a more specific plan in mind: Her intention was to get close enough to some Arizona baseball players to "cop a feel" by touching their butts. As she snaked around the field performing her illicit act, invoking the spirit of Morganna the Kissing Bandit, she employed her youthful agility and quickness in eluding several security guards, all of whom fought back smiles as they halfheartedly chased her down. Before security finally caught up with her and placed her in the custody of the Omaha Police, she successfully patted the fannies of Arizona centerfielder Joey Rickard and his teammate, outfielder Joseph Maggi. After this, other fans ran onto the field, adding to the mayhem; however, at this point, no one could upstage Sortino. Consequently, she would be the individual most remembered for running onto the field during the 2012 CWS.

While Candice Sortino surely expected some attention for her butt-pinching incident, her exploits that night earned her a great deal more widespread attention than she might have originally anticipated. As might be expected, the crowd cheered as she scampered across the field dodging security guards on her way to touching the butts of the Arizona baseball players. Even though stadium camera crews avoided showing her on the Jumbotron, the video board featured the stadium's organist playing music in accompaniment to the people running on the field through the sound system. In addition, while Sortino performed her moderately salacious act, various news outlets, including the Associated Press, took pictures of her, many of which were published in local and national newspapers and posted on several mass media news websites during the course of the next few days. Sortino's first major press coverage came from the local NBC affiliate television news station in Omaha, WOWT. During her interview, Sortino indicated that she was not drunk and had no premeditated plans to run onto the field. She stated that she simply got caught up in the moment when she saw the other fans on the field, making her decision extemporaneously to jump onto the field and touch the butts of two Arizona players. When asked what seemed appealing about running onto the field, she replied, "I don't know because there [are] so many people watching and it's against the rules and then you get tackled, too."[48] The reporter continued, asking, "Did you want national face time; did you want the cameras to be on you? What did you want?" Sortino replied, "I didn't even think about that actually, I didn't realize it would such a big deal."[49] As it would turn out, her exploits became quite a big deal as the story made its way around the Internet.

In addition to the noteworthy mass media coverage Sortino obtained that night, she received even more exposure on the Internet through social media during the next few days and weeks. A slew of fans in the crowd took pictures and videos of the field dashers with their smart phones that night and posted them on popular sites, incluidng Twitter, Tumblr, YouTube, and Facebook. YouTube user "cocksevan" initiated the video sharing of the incident by posting a shaky, pixilated video of the field dashers in action. The video captured the scenario through a narrow horizontal frame of an extreme wide-angle shot that provided little detail of the perpetrators in action with the following description: "This is the group that started it all. College World Series, Championship Game 2. South Carolina vs. Arizona. Field running in the middle of the seventh inning. Enjoy."[50] While it was the first video to appear on the Internet about the incident, it obtained only 645 views, most likely due to its poor quality and limited description.

Soon after "cocksevan's" post, YouTube user "Amber Wood" posted a higher quality video of the field dashers, which featured more of Sortino's efforts on screen and had the following description that also called attention to the fact that one of the female fans who ran onto the field that night touched the butts of the Arizona baseball players (spelling and grammatical errors remain uncorrected):

> The mayhem at the 2012 College World Series Championship game ensued during the seventh inning stretch. BEACH BALL FURY! FIELD RUNNERS take their opportunity . . . three girls get in it. One girl fakes a surrender to fulfill her mission to tag the butts of AZ outfielders. Another runner tries the Lambo Leap escape route and fails! Fun times at the CWS.[51]

"Amber Wood's" post attracted 9,739 views, which is most likely attributed to its better quality and that fact that the YouTube user provided a more detailed description of the specifics on a girl pinching the butts of two baseball players.

Then, YouTube user "Eric Meyer" posted his video of the field dashers, which was where the video started to "trend" on the Internet, attracting nearly 24,000 views within the first 72 hours of being active. Adding to the drama of his video post, "Eric Meyer" added 1960s television and film composer Hugo Montenegro's song "Devil Woman" as mood music and spliced in textual commentary directing viewers' attention to specific dashers as they made their way around the field. At 22 seconds in the video, "Eric Meyer" overlays the following text calling attention to Candice Sortino jumping onto the field: "A girl begins her run:)." Since the video turns away from Sortino, focusing on a male fan being tackled to the ground by security, "Eric Meyer" overlays more text at 29 seconds indicating that "A girl touches a heinie," and soon thereafter, at 32 seconds, "A girl taps another one. . ." At 38 seconds, more text appears: "A girl is caught . . ." Then, at 40 seconds, the final text referring to Sortino states, "A girl is in big trouble now. . ." Along with augmenting the narrative components of the video with the audio and textual elements, "Eric Meyer's" following description of the incident on YouTube likely helped attract more attention than other videos depicting the goings-on:

> The shenanigans that ensued during the seventh inning stretch at the 2012 College World Series Game in Omaha, Ne. Arizona Wildcats vs. South Carolina Game Cocks. Lots of runners. June 25, 2012. Since this is my first You Tube upload ever I decided to mess around with it and add some music. Hope all you fans, on both sides of the borders, enjoy this little memory from the game :-) www.facebook.com/eforcewonder video is now up on Tosh.O's website too under Viewer Videos. http://toshcommunity.comedycentral.com/Video/CWS-2012-Seventh-Inning-Stretch. The original video from the runners themselves can be found here: www.youtube.com/watch?v=R5uBAVaFB1g&feature=plcp

He also used Facebook to publicize his post, which helped draw even more viewers. On his Facebook page, he indicated: "23,789 hits in 3 days . . . AND someone from Channel 6 News sent me a message asking if he could use it in a segment. How cool is that for my first YouTube video ;-). "[52] As noted in the description, "Eric Meyer's" video post was picked up by the Comedy Central Network program *Tosh.O's* website, where it gained even more views (an additional 6,000).[53]

The social media tracking website BuzzFeed.com took notice of Sortino's video and began to monitor its progress on the Internet. BuzzFeed.com devoted an entire page exclusively to Sortino's field dash at the CWS and the buzz surrounding it. The page features the headline, "A 17-Year-Old's Quest to Touch Two Baseball Players' Butts," along with four uncannily well-captured Associated Press photos of her touching the butts of the Arizona baseball players and a video post of her local television news interview.[54] The page also includes the Facebook conversation history of the incident, and it rounds out with an extensive comment section facilitated by BuzzFeed.com and links to all the major social media websites, including Twitter, StumbleUpon, reddit, and Facebook.

Once the video of Sortino's butt-pinching incident circulated on the Internet, a wide range of social media outlets picked up on the story and added steam to its popularity. One of the first social media sites that helped popularize the incident was Tumblr. Specifically, Tumblr user "mrlilymeow" was instrumental in this process by posting the four Associated Press pictures of Sortino with the following caption:

> Candice Sortino, age 17, ran out on the field during the seventh inning of the Arizona vs. South Carolina game at CWS on June 25th. She smacked two players' butts; the one shown here is center fielder Joey Rickard. Other fans posted their own on-site videos, adding to the buzz of Sortino's butt-pinching incident, which helped it become a popular Internet trend.[55]

The "mrlilymeow" Tumblr site alone attracted 92,933 views and generated numerous comments, many of which were rebloggings to a wide range of users on other social media sites. The following is a partial list of websites with their tag lines publicizing the incident:

- *The Inquisito.com* posted one of the butt-pinching photos with the title, "Crazed Fan Runs on the Field at College World Series to Cop a Feel."
- *Rich Kids Brand.com* posted the same photo with the caption, "17-Year-Old Girl Tries to Grab Asses at College World Series."
- *The Frisky.com*, again using the same photo, posted "Let's Be Friends: 17-Year-Old Girl Who Pinched Butts at the College World Series."
- *omgblog/omgsocialclub.com* posted all four pictures with the caption, "OMG, You Would Too: 17-Year-Old Girl's Baseball Field Butt Smack!"

These websites, along with several others, attracted numerous views and generated hundreds of comments and thousands of views.[56] According to the BuzzFeed.com statistics regarding the spread of the story and video of this incident within the first month of its occurrence, it received 3,896 Facebook referrals, 674 referrals on Twitter, and 492 on reddit, along with a total of 44,766 total views during that same time frame.[57] Considering that Sortino carried out her act in less than a minute on the field, she gained remarkable attention for her actions, attention that would be nearly impossible to attain before the existence of social media and the Internet.

Even though Sortino is now banned from all events at TD Ameritrade Park, the Century Link Center, and Omaha's Civic Auditorium for the next few years and faces criminal charges, she has the distinction of being the first person ticketed for running onto the field during the CWS at TD Ameritrade Park. As such, she has immortalized herself, albeit unintentionally, in the annals of sports fandom. Admittedly, past sports fans who have run onto the field—like Morganna the Kissing Bandit—have attained a higher level of fame than Candice Sortino; however, Sortino only had to perform her act once—spending less than a minute carrying out her act on the field—to gain considerable fame, while Morganna had to perform her act at multiple venues during the span of many years to get enough attention to attract a worldwide audience. Candice Sortino's rise to fame through the viral video coverage and social media chatter featuring her illicit activities is likely to encourage future sports fans to perform similar acts in an attempt to create their own crazy sports fan celebrity. In addition, it also shows how people outside mass media, for example, Eric Meyer publicizing his fan-made video of the incident on Facebook, can have a significant impact in spreading newsworthy events in the world of sports through the clever use of social media.

NOTES

1. "Steelers Fan Goes to Recliner in the Sky," *Seattle Times*, 7 July 2005, http://community.seattletimes.nwsource.com/archive/?date=20050707&slug=steelerfan07 (11 August 2012).
2. Tim Nudd, "Ad of the Day: Errol Morris Brilliantly Profiles the Craziest Sports Fans Around: Those Who Cheer for Their Teams Even in Death," *Adweek*, 1 August 2012, www.adweek.com/news/advertising-branding/ad-day-espn-142390 (1 August 2012).
3. Nudd, "Errol Morris Brilliantly Profiles the Craziest Sports Fans Around," www.adweek.com/news/advertising-branding/ad-day-espn-142390.
4. Henry Jenkins, *Textual Poachers: Television Fans and Participatory Culture* (New York and London: Routledge, Chapman, and Hall, 1992), 13.
5. Bob Fowler, "The Bandit: Morganna Kisses and the Victims Tell of Stolen Busses," *Spokane Chronicle*, 26 May 1986, http://news.google.com/newspapers?nid=1345&dat=19860528&id=HutWAAAAIBAJ&sjid=xfkDAAAAIBAJ&pg=5399,2637165 (7 October 2012).

6. Dan Raley, "An All-Star Memory Sealed With a Kiss," *Seattle Post-Intelligencer*, Seattlepi.com, 5 July 2001, www.seattlepi.com/news/article/An-All-Star-memory-sealed-with-a-kiss-1058973.php (6 October 2012).

7. "Brett Evens Score With Kissing Bandit," *Tri City Herald*, 13 September 1977, http://news.google.co.uk/newspapers?id=zok1AAAAIBAJ&sjid=rokFAAAAIBAJ&pg=3190,3272324&hl=en (6 October 2012).

8. Raley, "An All-Star Memory Sealed With a Kiss," www.seattlepi.com/news/article/An-All-Star-memory-sealed-with-a-kiss-1058973.php.

9. Raley, "An All-Star Memory Sealed With a Kiss," www.seattlepi.com/news/article/An-All-Star-memory-sealed-with-a-kiss-1058973.php.

10. Raley, "An All-Star Memory Sealed With a Kiss," www.seattlepi.com/news/article/An-All-Star-memory-sealed-with-a-kiss-1058973.php.

11. Fowler, "The Bandit," http://news.google.com/newspapers?nid=1345&dat=19860528&id=HutWAAAAIBAJ&sjid=xfkDAAAAIBAJ&pg=5399,2637165.

12. "Morganna the Kissing Bandit," *Springfield Historical Society @ mcgarnagle.com*, 24 June 2011, http://mcgarnagle.com/2011/06/24/morganna-the-kissing-bandit/ (7 October 2012).

13. Cecil Adams, "A Straight Dope Classic From Cecil's Storehouse of Human Knowledge, January 23, 1987 Archive: What's With Those 'John 3:16' Signs That People Hold Up at Football Games?" *Straight Dope.com*, www.straightdope.com/columns/read/457/whats-with-those-john-3 (8 October 2012).

14. Adam Gorightly, "'Somewhere Over the Rainbow,' Man," *Kooks Museum.com*, 1999, http://home.pacifier.com/~dkossy/rainbow.html (8 October 2012).

15. Gorightly, "'Somewhere Over the Rainbow,' Man," http://home.pacifier.com/~dkossy/rainbow.html.

16. Monte Burke, "John 3:16: Where Is He Now? The Original Sports-Event Proselytizer Strayed Severely From His Holy Ways," *Forbes*, 12 November 2009, www.forbes.com/2009/11/12/john-316-sign-lifestyle-sports-rainbow-man-today.html (8 October 2012).

17. Burke, "John 3:16: Where Is He Now?" www.forbes.com/2009/11/12/john-316-sign-lifestyle-sports-rainbow-man-today.html.

18. Burke, "John 3:16: Where Is He Now?" www.forbes.com/2009/11/12/john-316-sign-lifestyle-sports-rainbow-man-today.html.

19. Jerry Crowe, "Rainbow Man's Dark Side Keeps Him from Getting Out," *Los Angeles Times*, 19 May 2008, http://articles.latimes.com/2008/may/19/sports/sp-crowe19 (8 October 2012).

20. Suzanne Adelson, "Rockin' Rollen, Fan of God, Takes a Message to Every Game," *People Magazine*, vol. 29, no. 4 (February 1, 1988), www.people.com/people/archive/article/0,,20098186,00.html (8 Oct. 2012).

21. Adelson, "Rockin' Rollen, Fan of God, Takes a Message to Every Game," www.people.com/people/archive/article/0,,20098186,00.html.

22. Adams, "A Straight Dope Classic From Cecil's Storehouse of Human Knowledge," www.straightdope.com/columns/read/457/whats-with-those-john-3.

23. Al Jean, Commentary for "Stark Raving Dad," in *The Simpsons: The Complete Third Season* [DVD], 2003, 20th Century Fox.

24. Evan V. Symon, "5 Fans Who Ruined Sports," *Cracked*, 27 November 2011, www.cracked.com/article_19529_5-sports-fans-who-ruined-sports_p2.html (8 October 2012).

25. Burke, "John 3:16: Where Is He Now?" www.forbes.com/2009/11/12/john-316-sign-lifestyle-sports-rainbow-man-today.html.

26. Gorightly, "'Somewhere Over the Rainbow,' Man," http://home.pacifier.com/~dkossy/rainbow.html.

27. Burke, "John 3:16: Where Is He Now?" www.forbes.com/2009/11/12/john-316-sign-lifestyle-sports-rainbow-man-today.html.

28. Crowe, "Rainbow Man's Dark Side Keeps Him from Getting Out," http://articles.latimes.com/2008/may/19/sports/sp-crowe19.

29. George Winter, *The Rainbow Man Blog Spot*, http://therainbow-man.blogspot.com/2004_11_01_archive.html (17 October 2012).

30. "Streaking," *Streaking.org*, www.streaking.org/ (6 August 2012).

31. "Britain's First Streaker Meets His Match: It Was Cold. He Didn't Have Anything to Be Proud Of," *Guardian*, 21 April 2006, www.guardian.co.uk/sport/2006/apr/22/gdnsport3.sport (5 August 2012).

32. Wayne Drehs, "The Streaker Does Hollywood," *ESPN.com*, 26 January 2005, http://sports.espn.go.com/espn/page2/story?page=drehs/050126, (5 August 2012).

33. "15 Most Famous (or Infamous) Cases of Streaking in Sports," *Total Pro Sports*, www.totalprosports.com/2012/07/06/15-most-famous-or-infamous-cases-of-streaking-in-sports/ (6 August 2012); "Sporting Streakers (photos)," *TripleM.com*, www.triplem.com.au/melbourne/sport/photos/sporting-streakers (6 August 2012).

34. Hank Hersch, "Miami or Bust," in *Sports Illustrated Presents: That Championship Season, Nebraska 1994*, ed. David Bauer (Tampa, FL: Time, 1995): 74.

35. "Patriots Fan Runs Onto the Field and Wins the Game," *ebaumsworld.com*, 12 November 2011, www.ebaumsworld.com/video/watch/82033228/ (5 December 2012).

36. "'Ichiro' Interferes with Play," *MLB.com*, 3 August 2011, http://mlb.mlb.com/video/play.jsp?content_id=17595817 (8 August 2012).

37. Taylor Soper, "Fake Ichiro Unwittingly Gets Into the Action," *Official Website of the Seattle Mariners*, 3 August 2011, http://seattle.mariners.mlb.com/news/article.jsp?ymd=20110803&content_id=22690656&vkey=news_sea&c_id=sea (6 August 2012).

38. "The Steve Bartman Incident—Any Excuse Will Do," *The Chicago Cubs Suck.com*, http://chicagocubssuck.com/the-steve-bartman-incident-%E2%80%93-any-excuse-will-do.php (6 August 2012).

39. K. C. Johnson, "The Invisible Fan: The Scapegoat Bartman Has Managed to Stay Undetected for 8 Years," *Chicago Tribune*, 26 September 2011, http://articles.chicagotribune.com/2011-09-26/sports/ct-spt-0927-bartman-chicago--20110927_1_cubs-five-outs-scapegoat-bartman-alex-gibney (6 August 2012).

40. Chris Chase, "A Brief History of the Green Bay Packers' Lambeau Leap," *Yahoo! Sports*, 3 February 2009, http://sports.yahoo.com/nfl/blog/shutdown_corner/post/A-brief-history-of-the-Green-Bay-Packers-Lambea?urn=nfl-316361 (6 August 2012).

41. "Central Florida Packer Backers," *Central Florida Packer Backers Blog Spot*, October 2011, http://centralfloridapackerbackers.blogspot.com/2011/10/win-lambeau-leap-tickets-eat-free-brats.html (6 August 2012).

42. "Extremely Exciting Entertainment in NFL, Week 3," *Hartford Observer*, http://hartfordinformer.com/2011/09/sports/extremely-exciting-entertainment-in-nfl-season-week-3/ (9 August 2012).

43. "Coca-Cola Classic Ad: Mean Joe Green (full version) (1979)," *YouTube*, www.youtube.com/watch?v=xffOCZYX6F8 (9 August 2012).

44. "15 Impressive Free-Throw Distractions," *Total Pro Sports.com*, 12 March 2012, www.totalprosports.com/2012/03/02/15-impressive-free-throw-distractions/ (22 August 2012).

45. "They Were Throwing Batteries: Phillies Fans Hurl Insults, Projectiles at J. D. Drew," *CNNSI.com*, 11 August 1999, http://sportsillustrated.cnn.com/baseball/mlb/news/1999/08/10/cardinals_phillies_ap/#more (22 August 2012).

46. "Philadelphia Eagles vs. San Francisco 49ers Snowball Fight," *YouTube*, www.youtube.com/watch?v=2isksLw0jW8 (22 August 2012).

47. George Dessart, "Standards and Practices," *Museum of Broadcast Communications*, www.museum.tv/eotvsection.php?entrycode=standardsand (5 September 2012).

48. Chase Moffitt, "CWS Dasher Speaks Out," *Wowtv.com*, 27 June 2012, www.wowt.com/home/headlines/CWS_Field_Dasher_Speaks_Out_160632545.html (20 October 2012).

49. Moffitt, "CWS Dasher Speaks Out," www.wowt.com/home/headlines/CWS_Field_Dasher_Speaks_Out_160632545.html.

50. www.youtube.com/watch?v=R5uBAVaFB1g&feature=plcp (24 October 2012).

51. www.youtube.com/watch?v=vHkUn7aRquU (24 October 2012).

52. www.facebook.com/eforcewonder (24 October 2012).

53. www.youtube.com/watch?v=oRUfOJ1uJ8I&feature=related (24 October 2012).

54. Jack Moore, "A 17-Year-Old's Quest to Touch Two Baseball Players' Butts," *BuzzFeed.com*, June 2012, www.buzzfeed.com/jpmoore/a-17-year-olds-quest-to-touch-two-baseball-player (24 October 2012).

55. http://mrlilymeow.tumblr.com/post/25999356632/candice-sortino-age-17-ran-out-on-the-field (26 October 2012).

56. Many of the comments on these websites focus on gender issues, sparking a debate about whether a male perpetrator performing the same act on a female athlete would have been treated as kindly. While this is a significant component to the incident, it is outside the scope of this study.

57. www.buzzfeed.com/dashboard/jpmoore/a-17-year-olds-quest-to-touch-two-baseball-player#sort=views&user=jpmoore&uri=a-17-year-olds-quest-to-touch-two-baseball-player&time=2d (26 October 2012).

3

THE MERGING OF MASS MEDIA AND SOCIAL MEDIA IN SPORTS PROGRAMMING

THE JIM ROME SHOW: CROWD SOURCING BEFORE SOCIAL MEDIA

In the past, the primary way sports talk radio and television programs involved sports fans in their shows was through fan call-in segments, and they did so on a limited basis. Depending on the particular show in question, telephone lines were often overloaded with potential callers wanting to share their opinions, both positive and negative, to the hosts and broadcast audiences. As a result, especially with the most popular shows, fans had little control over their expressions, often relying on luck to beat out other callers in being selected for the show. And, if fortunate enough to actually get through on the phone, fans were at the mercy of the show screeners and hosts mediating what they could say on the air and how long they could express it. In addition, the few successful fans who managed to have their comments featured as part of the programs were bound by the strict time constraints of the actual show broadcasts, thus offering a small window of opportunity as to when they could appreciably contribute to the content of the sports talk programs. This top-down model was the common operating procedure used by television and radio broadcast networks in getting sports fans involved in sports talk shows for the vast majority of the format's history. In comparison to the avenues of expression contemporary fans have at their disposal through social media, these call-in segments seem archaic and provide almost no opportunity for sports fans to contribute to a topic of conversation during a live broadcast.

The Jim Rome Show radio and television programs of the early 1990s are quintessential examples of popular sports talk shows employing this type of top-down fan interaction. In 1994, Jim Rome was already well-known in sports talk radio; however, it was the infamous on-air fight with former Los Angeles Rams quarterback Jim Everett during an interview on ESPN2's television show *Talk2* that propelled him into stardom. Leading up to the interview with Everett, Rome repeatedly insulted Everett by calling him "Chris," in reference to female tennis star Chris Evert, on his talk radio program. This was a recurring bit of smack-talk lasting several months on the show where Rome used the Chris Evert comment to call Jim Everett's toughness into question for his alleged lack of courage in taking a hit on the football field in his career. During the nationally televised interview in April 1994, already aggravated by Rome's previous relentless taunts, Everett warned Jim Rome not to call him Chris again, implying he would strike back in physical retaliation if he continued with the insults. In typical Jim Rome fashion, he mockingly replied, "Okay, Chris." Immediately, Rome's derisive comment prompted an enraged Everett to "shove the table between them to the side and knock Rome backward in his chair,"[1] delivering a series of punches at Rome on national television in a *Jerry Springer Show*-like spectacle moment. While some cynics claim Jim Rome and his producers staged the incident as a publicity stunt,[2] it, nevertheless, earned Rome much respect with his audience and made him an instant sports celebrity. Soon afterward, Rome's already popular radio talk show, favored among mostly male sports fans for its smack-talking, caustic, and irreverent tone, gained national syndication on the Premiere Radio Network in 1996. Running from 9:00 a.m. to 1:00 p.m. on more than 200 radio stations nationwide, *The Jim Rome Show*, a.k.a. *The Jungle*, became one of the most popular call-in sports talk shows in the United States in the late 1990s and early 2000s.

During the high point of *The Jim Rome Show's* popularity, because of the sheer number of people wanting to talk on the air, it was difficult for fans to reach screeners on the busy phone lines. In addition, if callers managed to get through on the phone and survived the intense screening process, most calls were highly mediated by Jim Rome himself, as well as his production staff, and usually lasted only a few seconds. While Rome claimed on the air that he encouraged an "open format" during these call-in segments and was even quite friendly and welcoming with callers at first, he frequently cut off his call-in guests and often derided them for their poor performance or stupid comments on the air. Before fans were allowed to speak on the air, Rome warned them to make their comments worthwhile. His mantra for the call-in segment of the program, "more of me and less of you is better for the show," epitomized his marginalization of fans on the air during the program. "Bad calls" were interrupted in midsentence with a loud buzzer, and a short audio motif entitled "I Don't Like That Call!" followed Rome delivering a mocking final comment to further denigrate the caller. This became a popular feature of Rome's radio program, which now exists as a popular Internet meme on several websites, including YouTube[3], and is one of several popular cell phone ringtones featured on audiko.net.[4]

While his popularity has waned in recent years, Jim Rome is still a prominent figure in the world of sports broadcasting; however, even the hardnosed, controlling Rome acknowledges and understands the importance of social media in successfully engaging with contemporary sports fans. Through his current sports programs, he relinquishes at least some control over to his fans in how they can contribute to the content of the shows, which is a departure from the decidedly one-sided nature of his presocial media call-in sports talk show format. Even though Rome still controls what happens during the course of his current programs, disgruntled fans or fans who fail to make it on the show can post scathing rebuttals on his website, fan blogs, Twitter, and a wide range of other social media outlets with little interference from Rome and his production staff. This is a drastic change from the way sports fans could contribute to the narrative of Rome's previous program and marks a significant shift in the increase of fans having more control over expressing their own opinions and thoughts through social media.

THE CROWD SOURCING OF SPORTS FANS THROUGH SOCIAL MEDIA

Almost all mass media sports outlets recognize the importance of social media as part of the contemporary sports fan experience. Mass media companies initially viewed social media as a direct threat to their iron-fisted control over the flow of information; however, it did not take long for these same organizations to realize that social media could be easily incorporated into their programming strategies, which would allow them to attract large numbers of previously hard-to-reach viewers who engage with popular culture primarily through social media. In addition, show producers discovered that, through crowd sourcing, social media can be a cost-effective resource in generating new show content. As a result of social media, contemporary sports fans, along with all types of media consumers in other genres, are no longer held at the whims of capricious talk show hosts and their screeners if they want to express their opinions and comments in the world of sports media. Furthermore, as crowd sourcing becomes more common through social media, along with being able to more directly participate in the dialogue of topics during program broadcasts, sports fans are also helping determine the content of various programs by offering immediate feedback on what segments are popular and which ones are less engaging.

Even though ESPN has a strong grip on the flow of sports news information, they, too, recognize the importance of social media in attracting more viewers, and the network has adopted social media as an essential part of their programming strategies. Starting with ESPN's flagship program, *SportsCenter*, producers of the show actively develop many segments that allow fans to directly contribute to the show's content and engage in live on-air conversations through Twitter or Facebook. With social media in mind, *SportsCenter* segments are designed to provide fans with an ever-increasing amount of opportunities to contribute to the content of the program. For instance, while NFL analysts like Herm Edwards and Ron Jaworski provide expert commentary on the details of the New York Jets' 2012 quarterback controversy between Mark Sanchez and Tim Tebow, fans can post Twitter comments on the same issue, all of which appears simultaneously on the same screen during live programs. Incorporating viewer Tweets and Facebook comments as part of the visual reality of live programs is a clever strategy in attracting the increasing number of viewers who engage with sports mainly through social media. As a result, along with other common sports graphics, for example, scrolling updates of scores and sporting news across the bottom of the screen, Twitter comments have become a more common aspect of the screen geography of many sports talk programs and live sporting events.

"Snap Decision" is one of the latest *SportsCenter* segments that involves fans in determining the content and outcome of that part of the program. "Snap Decision" is designed to work in conjunction with the live *SportsCenter* program and the Facebook page, the latter of which has a direct link to the program that allows fans to vote on a debate topic conducted between two ESPN analysts on the air. As the debate ensues on live television, fans have three minutes to submit their votes through the *SportsCenter* Facebook page and Twitter at #SCLIVE. The results of the voting are constantly updated through a graphic showing the instantaneous changes in the fan-controlled voting, along with a clock graphic that counts down from three minutes at the top of the screen. Once the voting stops, a buzzer sounds, indicating that the three minutes are up, and the final results indicate which side of the issue in the debate has received the most votes as a percentage.

Judging by "Snap Decision's" first attempt on the August 30, 2012, broadcast of *SportsCenter*—more than 500,000 fans cast their votes during the three-minute-long segment of the live broadcast on Twitter, while the Facebook page obtained 2,795 comments and 9,225 likes in that same time frame—it appears that this segment has the potential to be a popular recurring feature on ESPN's well-liked daily sports news television show. On the December 3, 2012, *SportsCenter* broadcast, the "Snap Decision" segment posed the question, "Who is the NFL Rookie of the Year, Andrew Luck (Indianapolis Colts) or Robert Griffin III (Washington Redskins)?"As ESPN NFL analysts Ron Jaworski and Merril Hoge debated which of the two players is more deserving of the honor, nearly 1.4 million viewers cast their votes on Facebook in three minutes, giving Robert Griffin III a slight edge, at 51%, to Andrew Luck's 49%. The following are some of the fan comments in support of their candidate for the NFL Rookie of the Year Award, most of which were produced during the three-minute time frame of the segment (please note that all posts remain unedited for spelling and grammar):

Mateo Italiano: Luck is doing more with a lot less talent.

Rodney Shoemaker: Plain and simple, Griffin has done more with less, and being in the nfc east, I ' m a cowboys fan and still say he had a tougher time.

Erick Rivera: No argument here 68% completion, 104 Rating, only 4 yes 4 interceptions, RG3 is the Rookie of the Year.

Daniel Morales: Andrew luck for sure! The only reason luck has more interceptions is bc he throws the ball almost three times more than RGIII and Wilson! . . . Luck is making every person on that team better! Rookie of the Year: Andrew luck no doubt.

Bernie Holland: By framing all these polls as RGIII vs. Luck, you do a disservice to Russell Wilson, who is quietly doing great things in Seattle.

During the three-minute segment, the Facebook page also attracted 3,763 likes and generated 1,238 total comments. This kind of concentrated interest is remarkable because, since the segment ran during the 10:00 a.m. EST slot on a Monday, during a work week, this suggests that the majority of the 1.4 million fans who participated in the debate did so exclusively thorough social media, either through their personal computers or portable smart devices, rather than simply watching the live broadcast on television. In a relatively short period of time of its existence through Facebook, "Snap Decision" is one of the most popular and engaging segments on *SportsCenter*. Consequently, segments like this that directly involve fans during live broadcasts through social media are likely to become common features on *SportsCenter*. The success of program segments like "Snap Decision" will likely encourage other prominent mass media sports outlets the likes of NBC/Universal Sports, Yahoo!, and Fox to create similar features to attract more sports fans to directly participate in the execution of these program segments through social media.

These types of in-show fan contributions are becoming more and more frequent on *SportsCenter*, and more like it will emerge as producers explore the nearly limitless possibilities social media presents in generating fan interest and participation. The following is a partial list of some of the more popular past and present *SportsCenter* segments that incorporated and still incorporate fan participation through social media:

- "The Question of the Night": This ongoing segment poses a topical sports question, along with several choices, regarding a current sports event early in the show and encourages fans to vote on these choices using text messages, e-mails, and Tweets to determine the outcome of the poll, which is featured at the end of the program;
- "Bud Light Freeze Frame": This former segment showed prominent photos from the past week of sports, followed by viewer commentary on the images by sports fans through e-mails and such social media outlets as Twitter;
- "Coors Light Cold Hard Facts" (a.k.a. "Gatorade Cooler Talk"): In this segment, fans pose a "six-pack" of questions to analysts on various sports using e-mails, Twitter, text messaging, or Facebook, and the analysts respond to the various fan comments submitted through social media;
- "The Vent": This current segment features a sports journalist or sports commentator reacting to the results of a wide range of poll questions voted on by fans through ESPN.com and ESPN's Facebook page;
- "*SportsCenter* Home Video": This segment allows fans to submit their own videos from high school, recreational, or other small-scale sporting events and they are occasionally aired on the program;
- "Top 10 Plays of the Day:" This recurring segment appears at the end of each episode and features the day's top-10 sports plays and allows fans to send in their votes through Twitter at #SCtop10, *SportsCenter's* Facebook page, and other social media options to determine which plays are selected to the top 10; and
- "Not Top 10": This Friday segment gives fans the chance to vote on the worst plays of the week using many of the aforementioned social media outlets to help determine which not-top-10 plays are shown at the end of each episode.

What makes these segments so effective in attracting more viewers is the fact that they offer sports fans the opportunity to have their Tweets, e-mails, text messages, and Facebook posts displayed on *SportsCenter* during the broadcasts. For instance, during certain *SportsCenter* episodes, when fans help determine which plays make it to the top-10 list, various fan Tweets are displayed at the bottom of the screen with the person's Twitter name in full view while *SportsCenter* anchors read the fan's comments over footage of the potential top-10 play. While segments come and go, depending on sponsorships and fan interest, social media remains a vital component of *SportsCenter* in content and tone, and it will become even more important as the show incorporates social media in more and more future programs.

The social media component of *SportsCenter* has proven to be a highly successful means to not only produce fan-generated content for the program, but also an effective way to attract and engage more viewers and followers. One manifestation of this occurs through the *SportsCenter* section of ESPN's main Facebook page. Attesting to its popularity, this subsection of the Facebook page has more than 6 million "likes" and more than 260,000 "talking about it."[5] To put this in perspective, the *SportsCenter* subsection of ESPN's Facebook page alone has 12 times as many "likes" as the official Facebook page of the Democratic Party (504,099),[6] and more than 32 times the number of "likes" as the Republican Party's official Facebook page (183,968).[7] Along with the "Snap Decision" feature on Facebook, *SportsCenter's* Facebook page also allows fans to interact with almost any topic covered on *SportsCenter*. For instance, on December 5, 2012, Kobe Bryant of the Los Angeles Lakers became only the fifth player in NBA history to score more than 30,000 career points, joining the ranks of NBA legends Wilt Chamberlain, Kareem Abdul-Jabbar, Michael Jordon, and Karl Malone, who also attained this career points total. The following post initiated a heated conversation among NBA fans on Facebook: "Kobe Bryant becomes fifth player in NBA history to score 30,000 career points. LIKE if Kobe is the greatest scorer ever. COMMENT with your choice." Within 15 minutes after it was originally uploaded to Facebook, the comment drew 11,733 likes and generated 141 comments. Here are some of the comments from Facebook users in support of their favorite NBA player (please note that all posts remain unedited for spelling and grammar):

Phillip Reed: Obviously Kareem. Skyhook was unstoppable.

Harold Jason Rolle: Wilt, Kareem then MJ then Kobe then Iverson.

Joe Berrian: It Took Jordan less time and less shot attempts and Jordan had more assisst, steals, rebounds.

Randy Laird: Wilt chamberlain is the greatest period. Most points in a game. Most points in a season. Highest average in a season. It's not even close.

Tyler Nachazel: Mj does however have the most points per game, which if he played as long as kareem or karl, he would have scored the most, and lebron, he might have 20,000 points, but wait till he gets an injury it is bound to happen.

Chris Hernandez: Kobe is the greatest of all time. Jordan sucks.

Because a growing number of sports fans rarely watch live broadcasts of *SportsCenter* or any other mass media programs on television, sports show programmers need to find new ways to reach these media consumers. These types of sports fans are becoming more common in the contemporary media landscape, and social media operates as the perfect mechanism to engage this type of media consumer, enthusiasts who would otherwise go unrecognized or be outright excluded. Along with showing that opinions can vary widely about any given sports topic, these types of conversations are effective in drawing in a large number of followers who engage with the world of sports primarily through social media.

In the same way, Twitter has become a vital component of the *SportsCenter* program. The *SportsCenter* Twitter feed, which has almost 4 million followers,[8] also allows fans to interact more directly with almost every aspect of the program on a continual basis. At any given time, journalists, athletes, and fans can break emerging sports news through the *SportsCenter* Twitter feed. The instantaneous nature of the feed also allows fans to make comments on emerging stories before each show's broadcasts. This gives fans at least the perception of having the inside scoop on cutting-edge sports stories over sports fans who fail to take advantage of social media as part of their sports spectator experience. This also provides social media-savvy sports fans with a certain amount of independence over being held captive by mass media as to when and where they get their sports news. More importantly, this gives ESPN and their many sponsors a huge database of information in targeting specific demographics with advertisements.

There are many popular features that utilize Twitter in live broadcasts of various *SportsCenter* segments, including "Fan Forum" and "Numbers Never Lie." During live broadcasts, fans are encouraged to send Twitter comments to prominent *SportsCenter* personalities to have them comment on the air about the Tweet. A hashtag question is posted to the *SportsCenter* Twitter feed, and fans compete to have their Tweet displayed on the screen during the live broadcast while the analysts talk about it. For instance, during the live broadcast of *SportsCenter* on December 4, 2012, a "Numbers Never Lie" segment featured the following Twitter comment at the bottom of the screen while NFL experts Matt Hasselbeck and Damien Woody shared their views on the hashtag topic:

> @ROOKIEQBIMPACT – Rookie QB with the biggest impact this season.
> (Twitter Symbol)
> Michael Saunders @BigMikeSaunders
> #RookieQBImpact Russell Wilson. The top rated passer out of EVERY QB in the league since week 5. #NumbersNeverLie.

The graphic displaying this information remained on-screen as the two NFL analysts engaged in a lively conversation about which NFL rookie quarterback was performing the best up to that point in the 2012 season. Soon after the "Numbers Never Lie" segment concluded, the show's producers Tweeted the following comment to the Twitter feed:

> @BigMikeSaunders Thanks for your #ROOKIEQPIMPACT Tweet on Russell Wilson. It just aired on SportsCenter! -- > http://yfrog.com/721app (link to a screen capture image of the Tweet during the live broadcast).

In response to the Tweet from *SportsCenter* producers, Kristin Serio @krisserio posted the following comment:

> @sportscenter @BigMikeSanders Super cool to see your Tweet on air! Congrats, Mike!

This brief on-air segment and the Tweet from @krisserio recognizing and complimenting Mike Saunders's fortune at having his Tweet featured provided Mike Saunders (@BigMikeSaunders) a small moment of high-profile recognition on the premier sports news program on the top sports network in the United States and on one of the most popular social media websites worldwide. These types of fan interactions are made possible by the increased use of social media by both sports fans and mass media broadcasting outlets. As they become more popular with fans, these social media-driven segments will appear more frequently and further encourage sports fans to take a more active role in sports news and talk show programs like *SportsCenter*.

SportsCenter is not the only show on ESPN that employs social media as part of their programming strategy. In fact, almost all ESPN programs—sports news programs, sports talk shows, and many live broadcasts of sporting events—incorporate social media as a dimension of the broadcasts. *SportsNation* is one of the most prominent and successful social media-driven programs on ESPN. The show began in 2009 as a brief spot on *SportsCenter*, and it soon became one of the most popular fan interactive segments on the program. As a result, as of September 2011, *SportsNation* is now a fixture on ESPN2's weekday afternoon programming block.

As a matter of comparison between the two programs, while *SportsCenter* allows sports fans to contribute to the show's content, its format is ordered around a top-down dispersal of information from media producers to media consumers, as epitomized through the way sports anchors relay information on the air to viewers. On the other hand, *SportsNation* is designed more like a conversation between sports fans and sports commentators. According to the show's producer, Jamie Horowitz, "We want this to be the show the fans produce. . . . One of the goals of the program is to talk about things my buddies and I would talk about when we're hanging out at the bar."[9] The *SportsNation* webpage is specifically designed to bring in as much sports fan input to the program as possible, and the program has multiple links to a wide range of social media outlets. The primary content of the *SportsNation* program is derived through its website on ESPN.com, which results in more than 60% of the show's material coming directly from fans through video, Tweets, and online polling.[10] This is accomplished through a daily blog that allows fans to post comments on basically anything sports related, along with links to Facebook, Twitter, and YouTube, and e-mails pertaining to the world of sports.

The on-air execution of *SportsNation* directly involves viewers in almost all aspects of the program. Each episode begins with the segment "The A Block," which features several nationwide poll questions regarding a timely sports-themed question. Once fans submit their votes through Twitter, text messaging, and Facebook, a color-coded, state-by-state graphic illustrating the breakdown of the poll is featured on the following day's broadcast. Another popular segment on *SportsNation* is the "Did You Hear That?" spot. This segment presents a countdown of the best sound bites from the world of sports that have gotten fan buzz through social media. "Three Cheers/Jeers/Tears" occurs throughout the program, which presents the three most exciting sports moments of the day, for instance, a soccer bicycle kick or a diving catch in baseball (Three Cheers), the three most embarrassing moments in sports (two outfielders colliding with one another trying to catch a pop fly) (Three Jeers), and the three worst or most painful moments in sports that day (a vicious hockey fight or an athlete getting hit in the groin) (Three Tears). "Fake Calls from Fake Fans" allows sports fans to call in and impersonate a prominent sports figure. The impersonation is aired on the live broadcast of the program. "Weird Web Stores" features YouTube and other Internet videos, some not even related to sports, wherein the final video is paused right before its conclusion and fans are asked to vote on what they think might be the outcome. Finally, each *SportsNation* episode concludes with "What We Learned," which provides a wrap-up of the show and allows fans to add parting comments through Twitter and Facebook as a fan-generated capstone to the program.

The open format of the show, which allows fans to contribute to the content through social media, along with the way the content is generated spontaneously during the actual live broadcasts, makes *SportsNation* one of ESPN2's most popular programs. In its brief existence, the *SportsNation* Facebook page has more than 1,425,320[11] fans liking it, while the show's Twitter feed has 1,508,444 followers and counting.[12] Not only that, the show has made a celebrity out of one of the former cohosts, Michelle Beadle,[13] which resulted in her Twitter feed attracting 619,593 followers.[14] Beadle has become so popular through *SportsNation* that she recently left ESPN and took a job with NBC as host of *Access Hollywood*. Along with being the host of *Access Hollywood*, she conducts features on NBC's *Today* morning show and was involved in NBC's broadcast of the 2012 London Summer Olympic Games.[15] ESPN president John Skipper admits that even though losing Michelle Beadle to rival NBC is unfortunate, he is confident in the strength of the program without her presence. Skipper further suggests that finding a suitable replacement for Beadle internally will be a simple matter and take little time in that ESPN "has a deep bench of talent" to draw upon.[16] In fact, soon after Beadle left for NBC, ESPN auditioned various interim candidates from ESPN's on-air talent pool during live broadcasts of *SportsNation* as potential replacements.

Through this vetting process, which allowed for instantaneous fan feedback on their approval and suggestions for whom they wanted to see on the program through Twitter and Facebook, Charissa Thompson emerged as the full-time counterpart to cohost Colin Cowherd. Attesting to the continued strength of *SportsNation*, along with being one of ESPN's highest-rated television programs, the show has 1,697,009 followers on Twitter, 1,500,668 Facebook fans, and a Klout score of 85.9.[17] The success of *SportsNation* has prompted ESPN to design a large slate of fan-oriented shows that incorporate social media as both a way to obtain viewer-generated content and to more actively engage viewers in the execution of the on-air programs.

One such program structured around fan-generated content and participation through social media is the show *Audibles*. Like *SportsNation*, *Audibles* is a spin-off program that started in 2010 as a segment on another ESPN program, ESPN Radio's podcast of *ESPN: Football Today*. The segment started out as a simple way for sports fans to initiate conversation about various topics in the world of professional football through Twitter, Facebook, and text messaging. It grew in popularity, which led to ESPN developing the segment into its own spin-off half-hour show as part of ESPN's weekly programming schedule covering of the NFL.

In an attempt to simulate the living room setting of the average sports fan, the visual reality of *Audibles* features prominent NFL ESPN commentators and former athletes sitting in easy chairs around a coffee table surrounded by shelves with sports memorabilia. The composition and execution of *Audibles* is almost as simple as the studio set in which it takes place. This program takes its name from the way quarterbacks change plays at the line of scrimmage—or call audibles—to counteract an unexpected defensive formation or exploit an unforeseen weakness in the defense. This title is reflective of *Audibles'* spontaneity in that the program's commentators respond extemporaneously to questions and scenarios posed by fans through Twitter, Facebook, and the main ESPN website during the live broadcast of the show. According to ESPN, during the NFL season,

> *Audibles*, which debuted on a limited-run basis last year, will be a Thursday night staple on ESPN at 7:00 p.m. ET during the 2012 football season, and features new ESPN NFL analyst Jerry Rice, along with Steve Young, Keyshawn Johnson, Herm Edwards, and Trent Dilfer as the main players.[18]

ESPN executives are confident that *Audibles* will attract a significant number of viewers and participants by providing professional football fans the chance to directly interact and communicate through social media with former NFL stars and have their ideas and opinions expressed on national television by these prominent sports figures.

UNITE, ESPN's first late-night entertainment sports talk show targeted at college sports fans, adopts a format similar to that of *SportsNation* in using social media as a way for fans to contribute to the show's content and perform in its implementation. Producers of *UNITE* draw heavily from Internet conventions and iconography, and they actively employ the language of the Internet, including hashtags, textspeak, and other common abbreviations, in their mode of audience address. In addition, most of the segments are created with this Internet discourse and imagery in mind, resulting in fast-paced visual and audio bits intended for viewers accustomed to engaging with sports through the Internet and social media.

At the most basic level, *UNITE* performs similar segments as seen in *SportsNation*, for instance, displaying fan Tweets along with photos from their Twitter accounts in a large screen graphic, as the three co-hosts, Danny Cannel (the brash former Florida State quarterback), Reese Waters (the hip stand-up comedian), and Marianela Pereyra (the beautiful dancer and actress), respond to the Twitter comments in an animated and often irreverent and comedic fashion. "#GifoftheNite" or "#GifoftheWeek," for example, takes its name from a long-standing animated format, GIF (Graphic Interchange Format), which features a short repeating animation of a sporting event—often depictions of what they call athlete "fails"—submitted by fans through Twitter, which have the potential to be aired during the live broadcast of the show. Throughout the program, fans can vote on their favorite GIF through Twitter, email, text messaging, or Facebook to help determine which one is selected as Gif of the Night. For example, the winner of #GifoftheNite for the September 19, 2012, episode came from a Canadian Lingerie Football League game where the quarterback for the Regina

Rage, Nikki Johnson, flattened a defender from the Toronto Triumph on her way to a touchdown. After the GIF was announced as the fan favorite, it was left on the screen for several seconds as the hosts commented on it and mentioned the name of the viewer who originally submitted the GIF for consideration, while showing the fan's Twitter account on-screen. By displaying the fan's Tweets, along with the replay of the GIF, *UNITE* not only draws attention to the video itself, but also to the person who originally brought it to the attention of the show's producers. As such, segments like this offer fans a significant portion of on-air time, calling attention to their participation as "clever" sports fans in the execution of the program.

UNITE also broadcasts fan-produced videos throughout the program. These crudely made videos feature the editing and camera style similar to what is common on YouTube, again included to appeal to contemporary fans who employ social media as a major part of their sports entertainment experience. Viewers are encouraged to submit their homemade videos to the program, which can range from depictions of fans going crazy watching their favorite team play on television to footage they shot from their smart phones from live sporting events, all of which are potential visual fodder for the broadcast. For instance, on the September 19, 2012, broadcast, a segment showed the end of the Brigham Young University versus Utah football game from the previous weekend, where Brigham Young lost the game after missing a last-second field goal. The segment was designed as a mashup of ESPN's broadcast footage from the game intercut with fan-shot footage captured on smart phones at the game, along with videos of fans watching the climax of the game on television at home. In addition, right after the mashup video of the game, cohosts interviewed Jon Hays, Utah's starting quarterback, using Skype, and they talked extensively about the dramatic ending to the game, accompanied by an activity update on his Twitter account after recently being named the Utah starting quarterback.

Another *UNITE* segment that features fan-made videos is "Battle of the YouTube Fans." The format of "Battle of the YouTube Fans" follows a simple plan of comparing two fans talking to their personal computer onboard cameras about their favorite team in a highly animated fashion and often in an inebriated state. The "Battle of the YouTube Fans" segment featuring a standoff between Clemson and Florida

State football fans ranting and raving at the camera in support of their teams was one of the highlights of the September 21, 2012, broadcast, and it drew much interest from fans, as evidenced through the immediate influx of Twitter comments regarding fan videos in the segment.

Judging by some of the initial responses from various fan blogs, the show has gotten off to an inauspicious beginning. The following is just a sample of some of the scathing criticisms of the show from ESPN's website (please note that all posts remain unedited for spelling and grammar):

"Bobby," August 21, 2011: "That was the most BORING hour I have ever spent watching ESPN in my 29yrs. I know its late night so most wont see this show but its a total rip off of SportsNation but a thousand times worse. SN is the varsity and UNITE the freshman team. Id be embarrased to work for that show";

"george Quinn," August 31, 2012: "You guys lost me when the marianette called u of m Ann arbor comm college so long, and good luck with ur mediocre personalities that r not engaging and r even less knowledgeable. Word of advice, don't pick a fight during your first show with a college that has more alumni than almost any school in the country you won't win or improve your ratings";

"Kopliverpool," September 6, 2012: "This show looks destined to be the next TMZ, and TMZ is an absolute pile of filth. Nobody likes pop culture. We watch sports on ESPN, not 29 year old dorks that sit in front of the tv screen and try and fail to make college kids laugh. "Swagger, epic, gangster" ??? So is UNITE intended for 15 year olds? come on now. . . . My mind is numb after 25 minutes of this garbage and it continues for 1 1/2 more hours! Nope, won't be watching ESPNU until Saturday and definitely won't watch this show again";

"KenPNelson," September 12, 2012: "This show is really really bad. Please air something else. Anything. Bowling reruns would be more entertaining";

"gatorrick101," November 23, 2012: "Possibly the worst show I've seen on ESPN"; and

"tailg8er2000," November 27, 2012: "I am watching this show right now and I like it. Some real haters here."

Another indication of *UNITE* being poorly received by fans is that it has a relatively low number of Twitter followers, at a little less than 4,500,[19] as compared to *SportsNation*, which has more than 1.5 million followers.[20] Admittedly, as of the writing of this book, *UNITE* is still in its infancy; therefore, these early unfavorable responses may be a knee-jerk reaction to a show that has potential but needs to fine-tune some of its elements to have the same appeal as *SportsNation*. Regardless, one thing that social media offers ESPN with this program is instant feedback on audience reception of the show. It remains to be seen if *UNITE* will catch on with audiences, and, even if the show ends up being canceled, the method by which ESPN developed, implemented, and tracked the progress of the show is likely to set a model in developing new programs with social media as both a content-producing tool and an audience response testing mechanism.

"RICKRATT" ON *MIKE AND MIKE IN THE MORNING*

ESPN's *Mike and Mike in the Morning* is an exemplary program that actively engages a massive audience on a nearly instantaneous basis across multiple media platforms. Starting out as a radio program in the late 1990s and due to its burgeoning popularity, *Mike and Mike in the Morning* was later simulcast on ESPN2 in direct competition with the network's flagship program, *SportsCenter*. *Mike and Mike in the Morning* appeals to their male-oriented audience by presenting the gibing banter common among sports fans as a major component of the show, as personified through the sarcastic but good-humored exchanges between the cohosts, Mike Goldberg and Mike Golic. Another feature that gives this show such popular appeal is that the hosts allow viewers to engage in this banter as part of the live program through all types of social media, including e-mails, text messages, Twitter, and Facebook, along with the occasional phone call.

Mike and Mike in the Morning engages listeners and viewers on many levels through audience-centered segments. Along with fan polls, game predictions, Twitter comments, and e-mails read on the air, fans are allowed to participate in the show in several ways. For example, the segment "Grill Golic" features phone calls or e-mails from fans asking Mike Golic various questions, usually about football, because he is a famous NFL veteran, which is one of the few times viewers' and listeners' voices are actually heard on the air. Another key segment, entitled "Man Up Question of the Day," features Mike Golic, the macho guy in the comedic pair, along with fans, usually through e-mails, text messages, and Tweets, instructing Mike Greenberg, the nerdy, nonathletic persona of the duo, how to be more manly.

Using Twitter technology, *Mike and Mike in the Morning* attempts to engage viewers by directly involving the audience through their mode of address and the fact that social media is such a crucial part of the program. For example, a popular fan interaction segment entitled "What Makes You a Sports Doofus?" allows fans to Tweet or e-mail their description of what makes a person a sports doofus, which has resulted in some of the following fan suggestions:

- Wearing baseball pants to play in a slow-pitch softball game;
- As an adult at a Major League Baseball game, muscling out a five-year-old kid for a foul ball and then holding the ball over your head as if you just won the World Series;
- Having an intense fantasy sports discussion while attending a live game;
- Getting a team- or player-oriented tattoo;
- Putting team flags on your car;
- Wearing a sponsor-festooned jersey while riding your bike; and
- Wearing an official team jersey with your name on the back while attending the game of that team (the favorite of both hosts).

Mike and Mike in the Morning is a testament to the power of involving audiences in the execution of their show in gaining widespread popularity. More importantly, the show is an astute implementation of encouraging fans to participate more directly in the content and execution of the program. The ratings of the show attest to the success of *Mike and Mike in the Morning*, which reaches millions of listeners and viewers each day; furthermore, the fact that other talk shows on ESPN and other sports networks, for example, ESPN's follow-up morning program *First Take* and Fox Sports Network's late-night program *The Best Damn Sports Show, Period*, have adopted similar strategies in appealing to their audiences is further proof of the efficacy of the emphasis on audience interaction as exemplified by *Mike and Mike in the Morning* and its use of social media. Moreover, an important benefit of this active engagement with the audience is that the producers have an immediate and ongoing measure of audience reception that allows for subtle adjustments in programming that meets audience demands and preferences.

While fans are able to participate in many of the live broadcasts of popular sports programs like *Mike and Mike in the Morning*, because of the huge number of sports fans vying to have their opinions aired on television or radio, even with the aid of social media, it is difficult for fans to make a significant impression on these shows. Although producers encourage viewers to participate in the content and execution of the program, the show is still focused on the interactions between the hosts and main sports celebrity personalities as the main content; therefore, when fans manage to make an impression on the hosts and have their contributions affect the program, it is a remarkable achievement that requires significant effort on the part of the viewer, along with a great deal of luck in catching the attention of show producers, who are the primary screeners of fan-generated comments.

Take, for instance, my friend and fellow sports fanatic Rick Benak, a.k.a. RickRatt, who managed to help determine a small aspect of the set design on a broadcast of *Mike and Mike in the Morning*. On July 7, 2009, the *Mike and Mike in the Morning* program featured a 1980s theme day, which included decorating the set with such 1980s pop culture icons as Smurf dolls, the gopher action figure from the film *Caddyshack* (1980), several Rubik's Cubes, a handheld Coleco electronic football game, and a series of album jackets from prominent musicians of the time (e.g., Michael Jackson's *Thriller* and Journey's *Escape*). It was the Journey *Escape* album that caught my friend's attention while watching the program.

Along with being an avid sports fan, Rick is also a music snob. As such, he considers Journey to be an overrated musical group undeserving of the acclaim they received throughout their history. On the other hand, he is one of those fans that considers Rush to be the greatest band of all time and is quite militant about it. Upon seeing the Journey album on the set of *Mike and Mike in the Morning* that day, he decided to voice his displeasure with its inclusion in the visual composition of the day's show by sending the following email:

From: Richard Benak [mailto:benakr@cox.net]
Sent: Tuesday, July 07, 2009 07:08 AM
To: ESPN Morning Show
Subject: 80s shirt
They just showed a group of your workers on ESPN2 and I don't know who he was, but the young man in the Rush Signals concert t-shirt should be given a huge raise. That was my first of 16 Rush concerts. I still have that shirt (and matching hat).
Rick
Omaha

Not expecting much of a response from the show, Rick was surprised by what ensued. Soon after he sent his e-mail, the person who wore the Rush t-shirt, Paul Ryan (no relation to the Wisconsin Congressman), replied to Rick's email:

From: "Ryan, Paul J." [Paul.J.Ryan@espn.com]
Date: Tue, 7 Jul 2009 07:18:47 -0400
To: Richard Benak [benakr@cox.net]
Subject: RE: 80s shirt
I brought in all the Rush 80s records permanent waves hold your fire as well but they're off set next to liam!

After the next commercial break, Paul Ryan was responsible for replacing Journey's *Escape* album cover with Rush's *Moving Pictures*, and it remained for the rest of the show.

Proud of his accomplishment, Rick then posted the following on the Power Windows website to brag about his ability to have an impact on *Mike and Mike in the Morning* '*s* visual environment:

From: Richard Benak [benakr@cox.net]
To: pwrwindows@yahoo.com
Sent: Tuesday, July 7, 2009 09:26 AM
Subject: Power Windows Website
On ESPN's Mike and Mike in the Morning, they were having an 80s day. There was a scan of the workers on the show, and one was wearing a Signals concert t-shirt (my first Rush show in '82). I sent an e-mail to the show about it (suggesting that the employee wearing that should get a raise). I got an e-mail back from the guy (Paul Ryan), and he said that he brought in all Rush albums from the 80s but they were off-screen in Liam's area. I e-mailed him back that

> Moving Pictures should take the place of Journey's Escape on the main set. The next time they came back on the air, MP was there. I've attached a screen shot.
> Rick
> Omaha

Soon after Rick made this post, word reached fans on one of Rush's fan websites, "Rush Is a Band," and it became a topic of discussion on the website's blog. The activity on the website about how Rick's e-mail had encouraged producers of *Mike and Mike in the Morning* to switch out the Journey album cover for the Rush album cover resulted in 28 comments in the thread and even got one like on "Rush Is a Band's" Facebook page. The following is a comment on the "Rush Is a Band" website that directly references Rick Benak's contribution to the *Mike and Mike in the Morning* program:

> EPSN posted a preview archived video clip and photos of the Mike & Mike 80s Day episode from today. The story with the appearance of the Moving Pictures album goes like this. The following is from the Power Windows website:
>
> It was 80s day on today's Mike and Mike in the Morning on ESPN. When the show began, resting on their desk were album covers of Michael Jackson's Thriller, Journey's Escape, and Poison's Look What The Cat Dragged In. Rush fan Rick Benak noticed one of the crew wearing a Signals concert t-shirt and sent an email to the show suggesting that the employee wearing the Rush shirt should get a raise! He then received an e-mail back from the ESPN crew member, Paul Ryan, who stated that not only had he worn his Rush shirt, but that he had in fact brought in all Rush albums from the 80s but they were off-screen. Rick replied that Moving Pictures should take the place of Journey's Escape. The album switch was apparently done during the commercial of the show.[21]

The original e-mail my friend sent to *Mike and Mike in the Morning* regarding a small detail about a set-prop that day set in motion a series of information-sharing events, propagated by social media among sports fans and fans of the musical group Rush, that resulted in my friend getting far more recognition than I am sure he could have anticipated.

Although my friend Rick's activities did not go viral, his accomplishments through the effective use of social media did not go unnoticed among both fans of *Mike and Mike in the Morning* and Rush (the band). Before e-mail, Twitter, and other social media outlets, my friend would have had to rely on being lucky enough to call in to the show to inform them that they should replace the Journey album with the one from Rush. Now with social media, all it took was for him to send a short e-mail message to catch the attention of show producers. Moreover, what makes this occurrence even more remarkable is that this experience took place well before the recent trend of incorporating social media as a crucial part of almost all sports show programming, which is standard operating procedure in today's media landscape. As a result, my friend's level of recognition on such a high-profile mass media program is quite an accomplishment. In addition, this minor event also speaks to the power of social media in not only getting fans more directly involved in the execution of radio and television programs, but also the fact that media producers have accepted the reality that social media is an important component in helping build content and attract more viewers and listeners.

NOTES

1. Mike Reilley and T. J. Simers, "Irritated by Insults, Everett Goes After Cable Talk Show Host: Media: Former Rams Quarterback Attacks Jim Rome After Being Called 'Chris Evert' During an ESPN2 Interview," *Los Angeles Times*, 4 April 1994, http://articles.latimes.com/1994-04-07/sports/sp-43089_1_talk-show-host-jim-rome (25 August 2012).
2. "Was Jim Rome vs. Jim Everett Staged?" *DanOnTheStreet.com*, 30 July 2012, http://danonthestreet.com/news/2010/07/31/was-jim-rome-vs-jim-everett-staged/ (25 August 2012).
3. "Jim Rome Manual Buzzer," 27 June 2010, www.youtube.com/watch?v=NQxT7ab07jk (25 August 2012).
4. http://audiko.net/ringtone/Jim+Rome (25 August 2012).
5. www.facebook.com/SportsCenter (26 August 2012).
6. www.facebook.com/democrats (26 August 2012).
7. www.facebook.com/pages/Republican-Party/107891235905850 (26 August 2012).
8. https://twitter.com/#!/SportsCenter/followers (26 August 2012).

9. Richard Huff, "Fans Rule on ESPN2's *SportsNation*," *New York Daily News*, 4 July 2009, www.nydailynews.com/entertainment/tv-movies/fans-rule-espn2-sportsnation-article-1.425807 (26 August 2012).

10. Huff, "Fans Rule on ESPN2's *SportsNation*," www.nydailynews.com/entertainment/tv-movies/fans-rule-espn2-sportsnation-article-1.425807.

11. www.facebook.com/sportsnation (26 August 2012).

12. https://twitter.com/SportsNation (26 August 2012).

13. Michael Rothstein, "How *SportsNation* Became an ESPN Staple and Developed an Emerging Star in Michelle Beadle," *Ann Arbor.com*, 23 September 2010, www.annarbor.com/sports/um-football/how-sportsnation-became-a-espn-reality-and-developed-an-emerging-star-in-michelle-beadle/ (26 August 2012).

14. https://twitter.com/MichelleDBeadle (26 August 2012).

15. Michael McCarthy, "ESPN: Beadle Gone, Is Erin Andrews Next?" *USA Today*, 15 May 2012, http://content.usatoday.com/communities/gameon/post/2012/05/espn-announces-that-michelle-beadle-will-leave-network/1#.UDrTNEQls7A (26 August 2012).

16. McCarthy, "ESPN: Beadle Gone, Is Erin Andrews Next?" http://content.usatoday.com/communities/gameon/post/2012/05/espn-announces-that-michelle-beadle-will-leave-network/1#.UDrTNEQls7A.

17. http://fanpagelist.com/user/sportsnation (20 February 2013).

18. "ESPN, NFL Agree to Eight-Year Deal," *ESPN.com*, 8 September 2011, http://espn.go.com/nfl/story/_/id/6942957/espn-nfl-television-deal-keeps-monday-night-football-network-2021 (26 August 2012).

19. https://twitter.com/UNITE (25 September 2012).

20. https://twitter.com/SportsNation (25 September 2012).

21. "Rush *Moving Pictures* Sighting on *Mike and Mike in the Morning*," *Rush Is a Band*, 7 July 2009, www.rushisaband.com/display.php?id=1895&p=3&n=10&o=DESC#comments (3 December 2012).

4

AMATEUR SPORTS ANNOUNCING AND SOCIAL MEDIA

SO EASY, ANYONE CAN DO IT, RIGHT?

For those who hold occupations in which public speaking is not a major part of their work, sports announcing might seem ridiculously simple and nothing but a frolic. To the average person, commenting on live sporting events or providing recap analyses of the day's top sports plays for a living might appear to require little more than a decent speaking voice and a basic knowledge of sports. Based on what I have observed while watching games on television with friends and family—depending on the amounts of alcohol consumed—many sports fans mercilessly berate sports announcers for even the slightest error. And, in the same breath, many of these same critics of sports announcers loudly suggest that they could do much better than the "bums" on television.

Unfortunately, I had the displeasure of enduring one such incident during the 2012 NCAA college football season at a sports bar with friends while watching the Nebraska game against Michigan on October 27, 2012. Since it was an afternoon kickoff and there was a lag between the end of the morning game and the start of the Nebraska game, many of the bar televisions displayed ESPN's college football recap program hosted by Rece Davis and featuring Lou Holtz and Mark May as expert analysts. After Lou Holtz gave his opinions about the performance of several athletes from games that ended earlier in the day, one of my slightly inebriated friends, a hypercritical college football fan, suddenly blurted out, "If a mumbling idiot like Lou Holtz with a lisp worse than Sylvester the Cat [from the Warner Brothers' cartoons] can be one of ESPN's main college football commentators, how hard can it be?"

Even though I avoided debating my friend in response to his question, hoping to steer clear of further attention and embarrassment for his public outburst, I wanted to inform him that, based on personal experience, as it is with most public speaking occupations, sports announcing is much more difficult than it looks. After holding two jobs as a part-time sports announcer myself, I learned the hard way that operating as an effective sports announcer requires much more skill and experience than it appears on the surface. My first sports broadcasting job was as a dog track announcer at Bluff's Run Casino Greyhound Park in Council Bluffs, Iowa, in 2006. I unexpectedly got the job after I applied for a bartending position to supplement my income as a high school biology teacher. During the interview, I was informed that the current announcer had just quit and that they wanted me to consider taking the position. Having no experience as an announcer, I was a bit hesitant; however, I knew this was a chance of a lifetime, so I accepted the job offer. While it took me a while to get the hang of calling the dog races, I became pretty good at it. When my friends attended the races, they were amazed that I could rattle off all those complicated, polysyllabic names in such a short period of time without stumbling over my words. Announcing at the dog track was truly one of my favorite jobs, and I would have gladly made a career out of it if they had paid me more than $9.00 an hour and offered some benefits.

My next sports broadcasting job did not turn out as well. After hearing about my experiences with the dog races, one of my professors at the University of Kansas asked me to announce local high school football games in the Kansas City area as part of a new podcast network he was establishing. In my mind, I felt confident that I could easily perform the work. I figured since I watch plenty of football on television and am a huge football fan, along with my dog track announcing experience, I would have no trouble making the transition as a color commentator for high school football.

It did not take long for me to realize I was terribly wrong in my initial assessment. Even though I was a successful dog track announcer, it was quite a different matter when it came to announcing football games. As I quickly learned, the scant knowledge of football that I obtained by watching the sport on television left me largely incapable of making intelligent or timely remarks during the fast pace of a live game broadcast. In retrospect, I cringe at my ineptitude as a football announcer. In trying to improve my performance by infusing some of my comments with humor, much like what I had seen on countless live sports broadcasts executed by professional football announcers, all I did was further embarrass myself as I failed to keep up with my play-by-play partner. Based on my poor performance and the unfavorable comments I received from the audience, my professor asked me not to return the following season. So mercifully ended my ignominious and brief career as a football announcer.

Based on a wide range of misconceptions and lack of firsthand experience, some spectators might consider sports broadcasting an uncomplicated occupation. As I previously mentioned, when I watch sporting events with friends and family, I am often annoyed at the criticism I hear about the alleged ineptitude of the sports commentators from many of these unreasonable and irrational "arm chair" announcers. At an early age, I was made aware of this perception among sports fans regarding how many high-profile sports announcers were unqualified for their jobs. For example, in my childhood in the late 1970s and early 1980s, since ESPN had yet to exist and ABC was the only network that covered college football on the Omaha television stations, watching Nebraska football games on television was a rare event. As such, famous ABC announcer Keith Jackson called most of the games. I actually liked his announcing, but many of my irate elders did not share this opinion. I recall hearing from many of them during Nebraska games, especially when they were losing, that Keith Jackson was a terrible announcer. That's right, Keith Jackson! Arguably one of the best college football announcers of all time, and they were ridiculously spouting off about how bad he was. For those who were fortunate enough to experience him in action during his long and illustrious career, just hearing Keith Jackson shout "fumble" in the midst of a live broadcast through his mellifluous baritone voice was enough to add a heightened sense of drama to even the most boring games. Those geezers had no idea what they were talking about when it came to Keith Jackson. Referring to Keith Jackson as a bad college football announcer is like suggesting that Michael Jordan was better at baseball than basketball.

This is not to suggest that all sports announcers are exceptional at their craft. Some obviously perform better than others; however, even the supposed worst sports announcers possess much greater skill as broadcasters and exhibit a more extensive knowledge of sports than most spectators are willing to admit. After watching ESPN personalities like Stewart Scott or Mike Greenberg effortlessly deliver sports news on *SportsCenter* or hear play-by-by legends the likes of Al Michaels or Bob Costas call a live game, the average fan might believe that being a sports announcer requires little more than a slight mastery of the language, coupled with a strong love of sports and good sense of humor. In reality, the road to success in sports announcing is a long, difficult, and highly competitive process. The profession requires not only a specific set of natural skills and intensive education, but also many years of experience before announcers even at the lowest level of broadcasting at local news stations can become proficient at their craft, let alone reach the heights of sports announcing celebrity through the major networks.

Regardless, many sports fans hold to this misperception of what it takes to be a sports announcer and are highly critical of even the slightest mistake made by even the most accomplished in the field. With this in mind, several Internet websites are devoted solely to offering fans a widespread forum to voice their displeasure with sports announcers. Bleacher Report, one of the most popular sports fan Internet sites, has several pages devoted to highlighting the shortcomings of some prominent sports talk celebrities. Paul Grossinger, a featured columnist for Bleacher Report posted "The Worst Sports Announcers" on August 12, 2012, which includes a slideshow of the 20 worst sports announcers with a breakdown of why they are so bad, along with an embedded video illustrating a prominent example of each announcer's on-air mishaps. He began by commenting on the sad state of sports announcing with the following statement: "Some Sportscasters, like [the] immortal John Madden and Harry Caray, manage to combine interesting commentary with a love of the sport that actually enhances the fan's experience. Sadly, those announcers are few and far between."[1]

The following are some of his scathing evaluations of prominent contemporary sportscasts as represented in the website's slide show:

- Dennis Miller: "Miller may have been a comedy star on *SNL's* "Weekend Update," but he was never meant for football. Insecure with the promotion, he tried too hard with every line and just wasn't funny."
- Tony Siragusa: "He constantly tries to showcase himself when he is on-screen, thinks he is the centerpiece of the game, and is, frankly, pretty boring."
- Collin Cowherd: "After Redskins safety Sean Taylor was brutally murdered by two robbers in his home, he actually blamed it on his past and said 'sometimes you've got stains, stuff so deep, it never, ever leaves.'"
- Brent Musburger: "Famous for his days alongside 'Jimmy the Greek' while dinosaurs still roamed the earth, Brent Musburger has become quite the dinosaur himself."
- Cris Collinsworth: "I know, it's hard to replace John Madden. Cris Collinsworth suffers so strongly by comparison that he ranks as one of the worst announcers in sports."
- Joe Buck (number 1 on the list): "Is it even possible to create a complete 'Joe Buck list' of things he does to make baseball fans mute the television? Is it the rank lack of enthusiasm with which he calls the game? Or perhaps it is the rank bias against certain teams and players that colors every game he covers? It's all of the above that make Joe Buck the worst announcer in sports."

This website provides an entertaining evaluation of prominent sportscasters that encourages fans to participate in the conversation through social media. In the short existence of the webpage, posted on August 12, 2012, more than 100 fans have voiced their opinions through the comments section, with more sure to come as the need arises among fans to criticize other sports announcers.

While some comments reinforce Paul Grossinger's assessments, many fans have provided contradictory positions in support of certain vilified sportscasters and offer alternative suggestions to add to the list. The following is a sample of some of those contradictions (please note that I maintain the spelling and grammatical errors in fan posts):

- Zach White: "'Sportscasters like the immortal John Madden?' John Madden was the worst, said the stupidest things."

- Nathan Gianfortune: "Wow. This columnist lost all credibility from the begining, after praising Harry Carey . . . who is one the worst know comentators in the history of sports, (and I'm a Cubs fan)."
- M. K.: "Skip Bayless MUST be on this list!!!"
- "chi4life": "Mark Jackson and Brent Musburger should be no where near on the list, both are some of the best in sports."
- Zach Volpi: "How could you not include Lou Holtz[?] "
- Jordon D'Atri: "Apparently you don't watch much hockey . . . Pierre Mcquire??"

Obviously, judging by the gamut of sportscaster evaluations, both by the columnist and fan responses in the comment section, there seems to be a wide range of qualities that sports fans factor into their opinions regarding what it takes to be a good sports announcer. And this is not the only website that allows and even encourages fans to offer harsh appraisals of sports announcers. Awful Announcing (www.awfulannouncing.com), whose tag line is "Putting announcers on notice since 2006," offers some of the most scathing criticism of sports announcers. For whatever reason, the website takes great exception to the alleged ineptitude of former ESPN college football announcer Pam Ward. In fact, their disdain for her is so great that, along with featuring her image as the leading figure on the Mount Rushmore of Bad Sports Announcers on the masthead of the website, they provide a weekly mocking column listing the worst sportscasters of the week called the "Pammies."[2] By providing visitors with complete schedules of the bad announcers from each week who they classify as prime targets, the website encourages fans to help determine which sportscasters make it on the list through Twitter and other social media outlets. Each list features examples of stupid comments made by sports announcers, accompanied by the Twitter name of the fan who first sent in the comment to the website. The following is the top-10 list from the week of September 17 through 24, 2012, counting down from 10 to 1 following the pattern set by David Letterman on his popular late-night talk show franchise:

10. "Timeout, errrrr, end of the first quarter."—Beth Mowins (via jl711)

9. "There's grass between the knee and the ground."—Andre Ware (via ufchomp)
8. "They've lost five games by a total of an average of three points."—Lee Corso (via sctvman)
7. "Steve Spurrier will go for the Juggler here."—Gary Danielson (via NJ_Ryan91)
6. "Young man is from Flowery Branch, Florida, not that far outside of Atlanta."—Verne Lundquist (via AbeGordon)
5. "I don't think he purposely did that, but he just got his hand on there. Possibly could have been a five-yard penalty instead of a 15."—Eric Crouch, still not aware that the five-yard facemask penalty was abolished prior to the 2008 season (via devsfan30)
4. "He started his tackle in bounds, didn't hit him until he got out of bounds."—Matt Millen (via AA)
3. "It's a gimme throw as long as the QB puts it on the money and the WR catches it."—Glen Mason (via mattgray81)
2. "Never bet against the Catholics."—Lee Corso (via AA)
1. "Let's update you on Auburn vs. LSU. The Tigers lead it 9–0."—Wendi Nix (via ZackTN).[3]

Although almost all of these criticisms are ticky-tacky, the top-10 feature serves at least two functions that benefit both the producers of the webpage and the people who visit the site in a recursive pattern. This segment benefits the producers because the crowd source from fans helps generate much of the website's content through their Twitter comments and blog entries. At the same time, when the website acknowledges fans who help determine the top-10 list by posting their Twitter handles after each comment, it operates as a subtle encouragement to other fans, prompting them to send in their comments in the hope that they will have their names published on the website. This pattern repeats itself as fans and producers generate the list for the following week and so on.

The truth behind the harsh criticisms and unreasonable appraisals levied by sports fans is that most sports announcers perform remarkably well during the heat of live broadcasts. Sports fans are notoriously critical of all aspects of sports, even to the point of irrationality, and their evaluation of sports broadcasters is no exception. Regardless, many sports fans fail to appreciate the fact that even though sports announcers go through much preparation and research before each broadcast, sports announcing is conducted extemporaneously. As a result, this leaves little margin for error during live broadcasts and often results in many on-air blunders. Sports fans often have unrealistic expectations of sportscasters and mistakenly believe that they could perform just as well, if not better. With this perception in mind, certain social media outlets have sprung up that cater to fans wanting to take a shot at sports announcing. This might seem like the perfect opportunity for sports fans to display their skills and upstage their professional counterparts on a widespread platform; however, what most often occurs through these scenarios is that sports fans realize the genuine rigors of sports broadcasting. As such, any sports fan who has the opportunity to announce a game under the pressures associated with a live broadcast might reserve such harsh judgments in the future and gain a new appreciation for professionals in the field.

SOCCER FANS GET THEIR CHANCE AT ANNOUNCING THROUGH THE FANZONE ON SKY SPORTS

The old saying "never judge a person until you walk a mile in their shoes" should be kept in mind when fans criticize sports announcers. And, as certain sports fans are learning when they get the opportunity to engage in sportscasting through unprecedented opportunities afforded to them by various mass and social media outlets, it is not as easy as it looks.

Sky Sports, a prominent English and Irish sports broadcasting network, created an opportunity for fans to actually call the action of live Premier League soccer matches a few years ago, and the promotion remains intact, at least to a certain extent. I learned about this feature through my friend Brenda Sieczkowski, a devoted soccer fan and active participant on online forums for many international soccer leagues. Brenda mentioned that she saw a live broadcast featuring soccer fans announcing various Premier League matches, but she could not recall on which website it took place. She went to one of her most trusty soccer fan forums, Total Football Forums, to ask for assistance in identifying the source of the broadcasts through the following post:

> Posted 20 May 2012 04:59 PM

> Hey football fans,
> I'm trying to get more information about a feature I remember watching a few years back where fans from different clubs were actually doing the play-by-play announcing for games. Does anyone else remember this? Was this a regular feature or a special promotion? How did the league select the fans who got to announce? If you have more information, please respond.
> Thanks! Brenda.

Within approximately 15 minutes, "Wez 17" responded with, saying,

> Posted 20 May 2012 05:16 PM
> This?
> www.youtube.com/watch?v=Nv0kRS2Fn1I&feature=player_embedded
> [Featuring the highlights from the Fan Zone broadcast of Manchester United 3 Liverpool 1]

Later that evening, "Lady-in-Red" posted the following response, followed by "tide":

> Posted 20 May 2012 10:49 PM
> Fanzone used to be class! loved watching that, so much better then Andy Grey!

> Posted 20 May 2012 11:50 PM
> I remember watching the Fanzone when it was West Ham vs. Tottenham, and Tevez scored for West Ham to keep them in the league and the guy was going crazy. It was pure class!

The following day, Brenda responded:

> Posted 21 May 2012 12:47 AM
> Thanks! That's exactly what I was talking about.[4]

So, along with learning what the soccer fans on the website meant by their usage of the term *class*, which is how soccer fans express that something is very good or "cool," I also learned that, in 2008, the Sky Sports Network created an online program through Fanzone that involves soccer fans as commentators for live Premier League matches. For the first few years of its existence, Sky Sports gave fans the chance to announce a wide range of Premier League matches through the main website; however, as of the 2012 season, this option now exists only for Super Sunday matches.[5] All fans have to do if they want to announce for their favorite team is fill out a brief online registration form, and they immediately go into the sports announcer "talent pool." After an initial audition and screening process, fans are given the opportunity to announce a game. Based on their performance and feedback from other fans, some announcers are asked to return, while others are not. Once a fan announcer establishes himself as a regular, Sky Sports features each of them on the Fanzone website with their own profile and an option for other fans to leave comments and rate each fan announcer through an online poll.

The physical setup of the program is simple. The set consists of a sparse studio space wallpapered with Fanzone logos, where two fans from opposing teams, both of whom wear the jerseys of their respective teams, sit next to each other watching a live soccer match on television.[6] The fan announcers offer spontaneous commentary as the games unfold, which usually comes in the form of uncontrolled yelling and gesticulating as their team either scores a goal or fails to capitalize on various scoring opportunities. The program's informal tone is meant to approximate how average fans from opposing teams might interact with one another while watching a game together either at home or in a pub, with an emphasis on good-natured banter as a major component of the show. Even one of the most critical sports fan websites, Awful Announcing.com, praises many of the announcers on Fanzone by indicating that, "Sky Sports Fanzone is one of the best ideas as far as broadcasting goes. You get two fans to do commentary for the network, talk trash, and hilarity ensures."[7]

Although I never had the chance to see one of the live broadcasts, I witnessed several reposts on YouTube that feature the highlights of certain matches, along with a few postmatch recaps provided by the same fan announcers. Even though none of these fans have professional announcing experience, for the most part, they perform quite well, although I imagine watching an entire match of these fans rambling on for two hours might be a bit monotonous. Regardless, judging by some of the YouTube comments, the program seems to work well as a form of spectacle entertainment, and it has attracted a great deal of interest from fan announcers and those who want to watch these fan announcers call the soccer matches.

The YouTube component of Fanzone, usually shortened versions of each broadcast featuring the highlights of the game, often gets a large number of views, along with many high-spirited comments by other fans, who provide their own opinions about the fan announcers. The Fanzone YouTube repost of the Liverpool versus Manchester City 1–1 match from November 27, 2011, is one of my personal favorites. In the repost, along with the team's red jersey, the Liverpool fan wears a plastic tiara and sits in front of the Liverpool team flag, while the Manchester City fan, also dressed in his team's jersey, wears a light blue and white (Manchester City team colors) knit cap in the shape of a rooster's comb on his head. The seven-minute recap of the game's highlights features a great deal of gibing between the two fans, punctuated by intense bursts of excitement when each fan's team scores a goal. The Liverpool fan gets so excited when his team scores that he rips off his jersey, knocks off the tiara, and gesticulates around the cramped set, to the obvious consternation of the Manchester City fan. At one point in the match, after a near goal, the Liverpool fan jumps up in excitement and accidentally hits the Manchester City fan with his microphone, giving him a bloody nose. Even though this was an accident and the Liverpool fan apologizes, the Manchester City fan is clearly angry and strikes back at the Liverpool fan immediately afterward.[8] This particular exchange, along with the rest of the interactions between the two fans, seems like an incident that might have occurred if the two were watching the match together at a pub, which has the potential to erupt into a knock-down, drag-out brawl. In this way, the Fanzone soccer announcing program achieves the proper tone in appealing to quintessential soccer fans, which is a close approximation of how average fans engage with live soccer matches, while also allowing these fan announcers to contribute to the production of each program.

Along with getting soccer fans directly involved with the broadcast of live soccer matches, another significant aspect of the Fanzone soccer fan announcing program is that it encourages fans to interact with one another through such social media outlets as YouTube and Twitter. While many of the comments pertain specifically to the playing action in the soccer matches, many fans leave specific comments about the

Fanzone announcers. The following are some of the fan comments regarding the Fanzone announcers from the YouTube repost of the Liverpool versus Manchester City 1–1 match from November 27 (please note that I maintain the spelling and grammatical errors in fan posts):

- "crazynathan552": "best fanzone yet."
- "MrOzzie94": "LMFAO!!! Even though we should of won (Liverpool), I've never seen such funny fans in my life!!!" and "Looooooooooooooool these two are the funniest 'fan zone pundits' ever!!!"
- "ornfree" (in reference to the moment when the Liverpool fan accidentally struck the Manchester City fan in the nose): "That Liverpool fan is hysterical. 'I've just knocked the city fan out. It was going to come at some point, he's been doing me 'ead in all day.'"
- "NexLevel123" (calling attention to the Liverpool fan's derision of Manchester City's tradition of singing during matches): "'we've won nothing, we'll sing about the moon' LMAO."

This is one of many YouTube reposts of Fanzone broadcasts of Premier League soccer matches that features only the highlights of each match. Almost all of those I saw had more than 10,000 views and at least four pages of comments, many directed either in support of or criticizing the fan announcers. Even though Sky Sports has scaled down the sports fan announcing segment to just Super Sunday matches, it remains a popular feature with soccer fans.

This type of fan-oriented segment seems like it would have great potential with almost all American sports, even though nothing like this exists at the same level as it does with Sky Sports through the Fanzone. It seems unlikely that Roger Goodell, commissioner of the NFL, and ESPN would team up to allow the average NFL fan to perform in a similar manner with coverage of even a preseason game; however, a similar program like this has great potential in the United States to attract fans who might otherwise be disinterested in sports. Reality television is one of the most popular genres, and a show structured around sports fans announcers would likely draw in fans just for the spectacle quality of these highly capricious broadcasts alone, regardless of the outcome or details of the featured sporting events. It might take a smaller American sports broadcasting network to experiment with this format, but, regardless, given the increasing interest sports fans have in wanting to participate in the sports narrative and broadcast networks using crowd sourcing as a way to generate new content, it appears likely that a similar sports fan announcing program will inevitably emerge in the world of American sports broadcasting. If so, despite my past failings, I might muster up enough courage to take another chance at becoming a sports announcer.

THE EPIC SPORTS BROADCASTING FAIL: "BOOM GOES THE DYNAMITE"

As a kid, I loved watching a show called the *Football Follies*, produced by NFL Films legendary filmmaker Steve Sabol. The show consisted of such popular NFL figures of the 1970s as all-star Pittsburgh Steelers running back Franco Harris and Pro Bowl Dallas Cowboys quarterback Roger Staubach, normally two of the most graceful and accomplished players of that era, making fools of themselves by either accidentally colliding with teammates or tripping over their own feet in the open field, thwarting an easy touchdown. Augmenting the comedic value of this show was the addition of Mel Blanc, famed voice-over artist for some of the most beloved animated cartoon figures in history, including Bugs Bunny, Porky Pig, and Daffy Duck, who provided the narration using many of the same silly voices he used in the Warner Brothers' cartoons. Cashing in on the popularity of the NFL Films' *Football Follies*, Johnny Carson, from NBC's *The Tonight Show With Johnny Carson*, aired the films as a weekly segment during the football season, which became a fan favorite.[9] I remember asking my parents if I could stay up late for *The Tonight Show* just long enough to watch the *Football Follies*. It got to the point where my father enjoyed watching the segment as well, which was one of the earliest father–son moments I can recall from my childhood.

Judging by the number of sports fail programs both on television and the Internet, contemporary sports fans still love seeing normally graceful athletes being clumsy or making fools of themselves, both on and off the field. Many ESPN sports talk programs feature segments devoted solely to athlete and sports fan fails, which are shown both on television and on the Internet. As previously indicated, some websites exist solely to call attention to sports announcer mistakes. As seen on Awful Announcing and many others, these websites provide brutal coverage of even the slightest on-air sports announcer mistakes. Whenever a sports announcer utters an expletive during a live broadcast, even if the announcers manage to cut themselves off before they say the full word on the air, it is almost certain that it will reappear somewhere on the Internet. Finding examples of this requires a simple Google search for "sports announcers cursing," and hundreds of instances will pop up.

For instance, during a St. Louis Cardinals versus New York Mets game on July 28, 2010, ESPN's Anish Shroff said live on the air, "Let's take you back to Shitty Field as the Mets threaten in the eighth,"[10] a slip in reference to the name of the New York Mets' home stadium, Citi Field. Another prominent example occurred during a *Monday Night Football* broadcast on September 12, 2011, when ESPN announcer Ron Jaworski uttered the following analysis of Miami Quarterback Chad Henne's performance in the game: "That's one Chad [Henne] would love to have back. He knew he had the one-on-one matchup going down the right sideline. Shit, you have to get rid of this ball just a split second quicker."[11] Almost immediately afterward, sports fans and even some NFL athletes went to Twitter to post their comments about Jaworski's on-air gaffe, which quickly became a trending topic. Larry Fitzgerald, all-star NFL wide receiver for the Arizona Cardinals, posted the following within minutes of the comment: "LOL Ron Jaworski. I thought I was the only one who caught that." Soon after Fitzgerald's Tweet, NFL.com football analyst and podcast personality Dr. William "Funny" Dave Dameshek Tweeted: "Just rewound it to confirm, but yeah, Jaworski just said (re: Henne's bad pass), 'Sh*t, you have to get rid of the ball a split sec earlier.'"[12] Within five days, the *Huffington Post's* story of the incident alone drew 25 pages of comments, and it was shared 291 times on Facebook, 24 times on Twitter, and 90 times through e-mail.[13] These are only two examples of sports fans taking professional sports announcers' gaffs and circulating them through social media to the point where the mistake becomes a popular Internet trend.

That is exactly what happened to Brian Collins, who, as a freshman journalism student at Ball State University, performed one of the worst sports broadcasts in sports television history. The incident occurred in March 2005, when Collins volunteered to replace the regular sportscaster on Ball State University's student television station. Coupled with the fact that Collins had no on-the-air experience as a broadcaster, the person operating the teleprompter was also inexperienced and advanced the text too fast, making it nearly impossible for Collins to keep up during the live broadcast. Adding to that, Collins had the typed script pages in his hands, but they were out of order. As a result, most of his broadcast consisted of jumbled sentences, long pauses, and frustrated sighs. Completely flustered, at one point during the live broadcast he can be seen "mouthing to someone off camera 'I'm sorry.'"[14] To his credit, Collins tried to improvise his way through several highlights but only exacerbated his situation by fumbling over his words as he botched the descriptions of a college baseball game highlight and a NBA game recap between the Indiana Pacers and New Jersey Nets. Out of frustration, he delivered the following line when describing a three-point jump shot by Indian Pacers guard Fred Jones that would earn him perpetual and widespread notoriety in American popular culture: "Later . . . he gets the rebound . . . he passes it to the man . . . shoots it and boom goes the dynamite."[15]

From there, Collins sputtered on a few more seconds about the first team All-American selections, mispronouncing both Kansas forward Wayne Simien's and Syracuse's Hakim Warrick's names. After a few final scores from the NIT Basketball tournament, the lead anchor mercifully cut him off by saying, "thank you, Brian, for that look into sports, Brian."[16] In the three minutes and 54 seconds it took to deliver his inept performance, Brian Collins unwittingly left an indelible mark in sports broadcasting that would extend beyond the world of sports and eventually influence many aspects of contemporary American popular culture.

Without the existence of social media, the "boom goes the dynamite" incident most likely would have failed to reach anyone outside the student news room at Ball State University; however, soon after the original broadcast, someone from the student television station at Ball State took the clip and uploaded it to eBaumsworld on April 1, 2005.[17] From there, the Collins video gained nearly 100,000 views soon after it was posted, but that was only the beginning of its eventual spread. Since the eBaumsworld website offers visitors a sweeping choice of social media sharing options, including Facebook, Twitter, StumbleUpon, Read It, LinkedIn, Tumblr, and YouTube, Collins's video quickly spread throughout the aforementioned social media outlets, which led to the video going viral. The "boom goes the dynamite" phrase became a popular trend on Twitter and was the fodder for chatter on various social media blogs that spread the details of Collins's video to a worldwide audience. For example, since the video was initially shared on YouTube by "nuzzle77" on December 23, 2005, it has attracted 7,534,259 views, 15,598 likes, and 866 dislikes and generated 14,971 viewer comments.[18] Putting this in context with other viral videos, the "Boom Goes the Dynamite" video ranks 14th on Urlesque.com's list of 100 Most Iconic Internet Videos, topped only by other popular viral videos, including the Star Wars Kid, Sneezing Panda, Numa Numa, Michael Richard's Racist Rant, and Rickrolling involving the hit song "Never Gonna Give You Up."[19] In addition, ESPN *SportsCenter* announcer Scott Van Pelt used "boom goes the dynamite" during the program and even e-mailed Collins to help assuage his embarrassment by indicating that, "[i]f this is the worst thing that ever happens to you, life will be good."[20] Within a short period of time, as the video spread like wildfire through social media, Brian Collins and his "boom goes the dynamite" catchphrase became a widespread Internet sensation that would later have an unexpected enduring impact on American popular culture outside the world of sports.

The attention Collins received from the spread of his sports broadcast on YouTube and other social media video websites alone was enough to propel him and his on-air mishap to a level of unprecedented notoriety in the history of sports journalism. Collins admits that he would have been happy to put the botched broadcast behind him and maintain his anonymity; however, fate had other plans for this mild-mannered college freshman. After several months of the video spreading on the Internet and its development into an Internet meme, David Letterman of CBS's *Late Show*, a Ball State University alumnus, invited Collins to appear on his show. For the June 9, 2005, Thursday night broadcast, Collins was planted in the audience "for a planned yet spontaneous meeting and exchange with [David Letterman]."[21] In typical David Letterman fashion, the sarcastic and acerbic host teased Collins for the majority of his segment of the show for his on-air mishap, yet applauded his efforts in at least having the courage to finish the broadcast without walking off the set. According to Collins, Letterman treated him with great respect—even though Collins was the butt of many jokes during the broadcast—and when he talked with Letterman, Collins indicated that, "he [Letterman] was friendly and it almost felt like he was talking with one of his neighbors."[22]

Even though appearing on one of the most popular late-night talk shows on American television opened Collins to even greater scrutiny on a nationwide scale, appearing on David Letterman's show would prove to be cathartic for Collins. Not only did his appearance on the show help him deal with the relentless derision he endured for several months after the on-air incident, putting it in a more comedic and lighthearted perspective, but is also allowed him to embrace it as a chance to expand on his fame as a potential sports fan celebrity. Collins openly admitted that he was completely mortified by his failed broadcast and tried, albeit unsuccessfully, to distance himself from the incident. In addition, according to some people who were classmates of Collins at Ball State University at that time, Collins was adversely affected by his bungled sports broadcast. Soon after his Letterman appearance, some of his fellow classmates posted on the website wizbangblog.com their observations of how Collins dealt with the repercussions of the embarrassing incident. "P-Town Princess" posted on June 19, 2005, the following scathing assessment of the way Collins handled himself (please note that I keep all spelling and grammatical errors intact):

> Here is the thing. I am a tcom [telecommunications] student at BSU as well and I think he is a big baby. What the nation doesn't realize is that after this happened, Brian cried like a little school girl. All the while I knew it would get him so much publicity. Publicity that someone who wants to be an anchor would kill for. He was embarassed, whined, and tried to disappear when the whole time he should've embraced it as a mess up and moved on . . . and cashed in on his ebaumsworld.com success. This kid is a complete tool and makes me very angry by acting like he loves his clip on national tv and that he didn't hate it. After fellow students repeated his famous mantra in one of my tcom classes over and over, one student yelled at them telling them it was so horrible what happened. Well I think he got great publicity and he should stop being a big baby.

Supporting Collins, "msb68" posted the following on June 22, 2005, in direct response to "P-Town Princess":

> What makes Brian Collins someone people are interested in is the exact thing you lack. He doesn't think he knows everything. He has humility and sincerity. He responded genuinely to a situation that was upsetting, and didn't think how he could profit from it. Had he responded as you would have, like a pompous jerk, no one would have wanted to see him on Letterman. Seems to me like someone is jealous.

Putting the incident in perspective, Eric Sohn posted on June 10, 2005:

> Here's the thing. He did end up on Letterman. Fifteen minutes of fame is more than I've had. Collins is a footnote, not a laughingstock. When he's 65 and talking to his grandkids, he'll be able to look back and laugh. Heck, look at William Hung. He made a couple of shekels from Cingular ads, etc . . . and all because he embarassed himself on national TV. Not a bad swap. And now we're writing about them.

Expressing that Collins may have benefited from his Letterman appearance, "Fort Wayne's Finest" posted the following on June 10, 2005:

> I am a Telecommunications major at Ball State University and friend of Brian Collins. He lived on my floor this past school year. It was great to see Brian on Letterman last night (Thursday, June 9, 2005). I'm glad he finally became a good sport about it. For so long, he would hope that it would all just go away. Last night, Letterman helped him out big time. From the ashes of live television infamy, Brian Collins has morphed from laughing stock of Generation Y message boards to household name for the entire country. WAY TO GO, BC! "BOOM GOES THE DYNAMITE!"

Regardless of how Brian Collins dealt with the psychological and emotional effects of his on-air mishap, the attention he received from "boom goes the dynamite" has made him a pop culture celebrity, and his catchphrase has influenced an incredibly wide range of both mass and social media. The number of places where "boom goes the dynamite" appeared in American popular culture outside the world of sports is staggering. The following is a partial list of instances where celebrities have used the "boom goes the dynamite" phrase on various television shows, video games, and films, and even in music:

- During the 81st Academy Awards broadcast, Will Smith made an on-air mistake during the live broadcast and uttered the phrase "boom goes the dynamite" out of frustration, which was met with much laughter and applause.[23]
- Steven Colbert used the line on the October 15, 2008, episode when providing commentary on a boring chess match on his segment "Sport Report."
- Chris Pratt's character, Barry, from the film *Wanted* (2008) uttered the line to taunt James McAvoy's character, Wesley, in one of the early office scenes.[24]
- The character Cleveland Brown from *Family Guy* and *The Cleveland Show* uses "boom goes the dynamite" as an ongoing catchphrase to signify when he reaches sexual climax.
- In the *Veronica Mars* episode "Welcome Wagon," Veronica speaks the line after the police open a garage full of stolen goods.
- The video game *Borderlands* has an achievement called "Boom Goes the Dynamite" when players kill 50 enemies with a cluster bomb.
- The 2010 *NBA Jam* video game features the catchphrase when players make a basket or slam dunk over an opponent.
- In the November 22, 2010, episode of *House M.D.* entitled "Small Sacrifices," Dr. Gregory House (Hugh Laurie) says, "Boom goes the dynamite, scores are tied, and we are even Steven!" when catching a colleague in a lie.
- On May 24, 2011, Brian Collins made an appearance on Comedy Central's *Tosh.O* in his segment "Web Redemption" where host Daniel Tosh interviewed Collins about the details of his newfound celebrity.

Given the sheer number of times Brian Collins's catchphrase has been referenced in so many different forms of mass media entertainment, along with its existence as an Internet meme and viral video, "boom goes the dynamite" has become an iconic idiom in American culture with enduring appeal and influence. While Collins's sports broadcast is considered one of the worst performances in the history of broadcasting, and journalism schools use it as a prime example of what to avoid in executing a proper broadcast—now referred to in professional broadcasting circles and many journalism and communications textbooks as the "Collins Incident"—Brian Collins has become a celebrity. More importantly, the Collins Incident is not only an example of what can go wrong during a live broadcast, it is also a prime case study of how any moment captured on video can become a form of spectacle entertainment through its spread on the Internet and through social media. The one thing the incident most certainly shows is that there really is no such thing as bad publicity and that, in the contemporary mediascape, widespread publicity, even when it is unfavorable, is one of the surest ways that anyone, regardless of talent or position, can become a celebrity.

NOTES

1. Paul Grossinger, "The Worst Announcers in Sports," *Bleacher Report.com*, 12 August 2012, http://bleacherreport.com/articles/1294448-the-worst-announcers-in-sports (27 September 2012).
2. Matt Yoder, "The Pammie Awards," *Awful Announcing.com*, 26 September 2012, www.awfulannouncing.com/pammies/pammy-awards/ (28 September 2012).
3. Matt Yoder, "Your Week 4 Pammies Winners and Updated Standings," *Awful Announcing.com*, 26 September 2012, www.awfulannouncing.com/pammies/pammy-awards/your-week-4-2012-pammies-winners-updated-standings.html (28 September 2012).
4. *Total Football Forums*, www.totalfootballforums.com/forums/topic/78172-fan-announcers-for-premier-league-games/#entry1146838 (1 October 2012).
5. "What Happened to Sky Sports Fanzone?" *Digital Sky.com*, 3 March 2012, http://forums.digitalspy.co.uk/showthread.php?t=1636781 (2 October 2012).
6. The Fanzone broadcasts program occurs simultaneously as an adjunct to the traditional television and radio broadcasts of the game called by professional announcers.
7. "Sky Sports Fanzone Gets Feminine for a Day," *Awful Announcing.com*, 28 April 2009, http://awfulannouncing.blogspot.com/2009/04/sky-sports-fanzone-gets-feminine-for.html (3 October 2012).

8. "Fanzone: Liverpool vs. Manchester City 1–1," 27 November 2011, www.youtube.com/watch?v=uwC-HS38Xco&feature=relmfu (3 October 2012).

9. Joe Posnanski, "His 21,038,400 Minutes of Fame: Give It Up for Steve Sabol, Who Over 40 Years Has Transformed the NFL With Pop Art," *SI.com*, 8 February 2012, http://sportsillustrated.cnn.com/vault/article/magazine/MAG1165530/index.htm (3 October 2012).

10. David Helene, "Watch: ESPN Announcer Accidentally Calls Citi Field 'Shitty Field,'" *SportsGrid.com*, 29 July 2010, www.sportsgrid.com/mlb/watch-espn-announcer-accidentally-calls-citi-field-shitty-field/ (3 October 2012).

11. Michael McCarthy, "ESPN's Ron Jaworski Curses Live on *Monday Night Football*," *USA Today*, 12 September 2011, http://content.usatoday.com/communities/gameon/post/2011/09/live-tv-sports-blog-new-england-patriots-vs-miami-dolphins/1#.UGyjyxgls7A (3 October 2012).

12. "Ron Jaworski Gaffe: ESPN Announcer Says 'Shit' On *Monday Night Football* (video)," *Huff Post Sports*, 13 September 2011, www.huffingtonpost.com/2011/09/13/ron-jaworski-verbal-gaffe-shit_n_959710.html (3 October 2012).

13. "Ron Jaworski Gaffe," www.huffingtonpost.com/2011/09/13/ron-jaworski-verbal-gaffe-shit_n_959710.html.

14. Gene Wojciechowski, "Despite 'Worst' Sportscast, Collins Says He'd Try Again," *ESPN.com*, 6 March 2007, http://sports.espn.go.com/espn/columns/story?id=2785830 (5 October 2012).

15. "Boom Goes the Dynamite," *Hark.com*, www.hark.com/clips/bprtkbsfvy-boom-goes-the-dynamite (3 October 2012).

16. "Boom Goes the Dynamite," www.hark.com/clips/bprtkbsfvy-boom-goes-the-dynamite.

17. William Wei, "Where Are They Now? The 'Boom Goes the Dynamite' Kid Is Now a Real Reporter," *Business Insider*, 19 May 2010, http://articles.businessinsider.com/2010-05-19/tech/29969850_1_newscast-shooting-video-sportscenter (4 October 2012).

18. www.youtube.com/all_comments?v=W45DRy7M1no (4 October 2012).

19. "The 100 Most Iconic Internet Videos," *urlesque.com*, 7 April 2009, www.urlesque.com/2009/04/07/the-100-most-iconic-internet-videos/ (5 October 2012).

20. Gene Wojciechowski, "Despite 'Worst' Sportscast, Collins Says He'd Try Again," http://sports.espn.go.com/espn/columns/story?id=2785830.

21. Kevin Burke, "Letterman Perceptive, Friendly, Reports Ball State Senior, " Ball State University, 5 September 2007, www.bsu.edu/news/article/0,1370,--54420,00.html (5 October 2012).

22. Burke, "Letterman Perceptive, Friendly, Reports Ball State Senior, " www.bsu.edu/news/article/0,1370,--54420,00.html.

23. Joyce Eng, "Top Oscar Moments: Tears for a Joker, Million-Dollar Babies, and More," *TV Guide*, 23 February 2009, www.tvguide.com/News/2009-Oscar-Moments-1003234.aspx (5 October 2012).

24. "Memorable Quotes for *Wanted* (2008)," *IMDB.com*, www.imdb.com/title/tt0493464/quotes (5 October 2012).

5

SOCIAL MEDIA AND SPORTS MEMES

ORIGINS OF PRE-INTERNET MEMES: "KILROY WAS HERE," "FRODO LIVES," AND ALFRED E. NEUMAN

In his 1989 text *The Selfish Gene*, Richard Dawkins lays the foundation for the modern definition of the term *meme*. In the book, Dawkins draws an analogy between a gene—the hereditary mechanism by which genetic traits in the biological world are passed on from one generation of organisms to the next—and a meme—the cultural equivalent to the biological gene—as the entity through which ideas are spread from one individual to another. According to Dawkins:

> Examples of memes are tunes, ideas, catchphrases, clothes fashions, ways of making pots, or building arches. Just as genes propagate themselves by leaping from body to body via sperms and eggs, so memes propagate themselves in the meme pool by jumping from brain to brain via a process which, in the broad sense, can be called imitation.[1]

From this concept, the main vehicle fueling the dissemination of ideas on a cultural level resides in a deliberate form of mimesis (or imitation) on the part of social actors and media consumers. Much like the way specific traits evolve as biological organisms commingle genetically through their cellular hereditary units, so do cultural ideas and concepts as they are copied in memes, either deliberately or by accident, and passed on from one source to another in a social setting. Through various forms of imitation, reproduction, and permutation of an original idea, popular culture memes can spread based on a wide range of nuanced social contexts and modes of transmission during long periods of time. Without anticipating the Internet, Dawkins points out that memes transmit from one person to another at a much faster pace than biological evolution by asserting that the meme "is achieving evolutionary change at a rate that leaves the old gene panting far behind."[2] Now, with the Internet as the cultural environment and social media as the driving mode of transmission, memes evolve exponentially faster than pre-Digital Age memes, and they can change and change drastically in a matter of days or minutes rather than years or decades.

Before the Digital Age, transmission of memes relied primarily on mass media outlets driven mostly by pundits, along with word-of-mouth transmission among media consumers through verbal conversations, coupled with such print media as handbills, flyers, posters, and graffiti. By today's standards, this method of spreading information appears to move at a glacier's pace. While the modes of transmission of cultural ideas that existed before the Internet and social media required much more time and effort to establish and spread a meme, there are many historical examples that show the power of a popular idea spreading in society through simple word of mouth. Such concepts as "Kilroy Was Here," which originated from American servicemen using graffiti to spread the simple drawing of a person with a large nose peering over a wall, was a popular post-World War II pre-Internet meme. "Frodo Lives," which arose from the 1960s counterculture appropriating the phrase from *The Lord of The Rings* novels as a protest to the Vietnam War, also rose to prominence without the assistance of digital technology and online social networking.[3]

Another prominent meme that spread in popular culture long before the Internet existed is the image of the Alfred E. Neuman character. Most contemporary media consumers likely primarily associate the iconic image of this gap-toothed, redheaded buffoon with the satirical comedy publication *Mad* magazine; however, the Alfred E. Neuman image, in its earliest and most rudimentary manifestations, has its origins dating back to the late 1800s as a derogatory illustration of Irish Americans in mass media. Even in its crudest forms, this image exhibits many of the disparaging features, for example, the oversized ears, gap-toothed grin, and disheveled red hair, that remain intact with *Mad* magazine's contemporary mascot. Building on the unfavorable stereotype of the Irish as uncouth drunken brutes—often referred to as "Paddys" and "Bridgets" in colloquial circles—numerous unflattering illustrations of Irish Americans were common in the mainstream press in the 19th century. Famous illustrators from that time, including Thomas Nast, Frederick Opper, and Joseph Keppler, all produced derogatory cartoons depicting Irish Americans as apelike humanoids with unintelligent grins and large, misshapen ears, and they portrayed these figures in an overtly racist manner to reinforce the popular culture stereotype of the Irish as lazy, drunken, and idiotic.[4]

For example, Thomas Nast created the illustration entitled "The Day We Celebrate: St. Patrick's Day, 1867," which features a motley group of Irishmen, represented as drunken monkeymen dressed in top hats and suits, savagely beating policemen with broken bar stools.[5] John E. Hett, publisher of the fanzine *The Journal of Madness*, suggests that the "What Me Worry?" motto also has its roots in Irish American stereotype folklore.[6] Along with featuring a rudimentary image of Alfred E. Neuman on the cover, the 1911 satirical Irish folklore book *Wurra-Wurra: A Legend of Saint Patrick at Tara* tells the tale of the Irish praying to their primitive Wurra-Wurra (worrying) god in times of dire need.[7] During the next 30 years, appearing in various mass media advertisements ranging from 7-Up soft drink ads to anti-Franklin D. Roosevelt political campaign posters and postcards with such phrases as "Sure I'm for Roosevelt" and "Me Worry?," the images in these commercial and political ads were strikingly similar to the gap-toothed, redheaded fool that would eventually become the long-standing mascot of *Mad*.

After making his first appearance on the December 1956 cover of *Mad*, the Alfred E. Neuman character has been appropriated, transformed, and utilized as the grist for low-brow, popular culture humor to fit the satirical needs of many generations. More importantly, the creation, transformation, and dissemination of the Alfred E. Neuman image serves as a quintessential example of a pre-Internet meme that spread without the aid of social media and, despite its quaintness, remains a well-known icon in contemporary American popular culture with lasting widespread appeal.

INTERNET MEMES: WHERE DO THEY COME FROM AND HOW DO THEY SPREAD?

In the Digital Age, contemporary memes have the capacity to arise spontaneously from a nearly limitless number of outlets and original sources. Internet users can appropriate existing images and concepts from films, television programs, or any other audio/visual source and transform these media fragments to support or augment whatever inside joke or bit of Internet gossip they want to spread from person to person. The original source of a meme can come from any aspect of popular culture.

Issues raised in politics often serve as excellent starting points for memes. A perfect example of this is the viral backlash against Papa John's Pizza chief executive officer John Schnatter's claim during the 2012 presidential election that the Affordable Healthcare Act (Obamacare) would force him to reduce his employees' hours to avoid providing them with health insurance.[8] Soon after he made these comments, multiple memes arose in protest on such sites as Reddit and Mashable, resulting in one of the most popular with the tag line "Better Ingredients. Better Pizza. Better find a second job," which is an appropriation of the company's official advertising slogan.[9]

Memes can take on a variety of forms, ranging from viral videos to clever alterations of pop culture colloquialisms. Some of the most common are appropriations of a popular phrases changed to fit a particular situation or context, known as snowclones. Economics professor Glen Whitman coined the term *snowclone* as a neologism that fits a particular linguistic formula where different concepts can be inserted into the phrase to express new ideas, usually in a comedic or satirical manner. One example is the line "I'm not a doctor, but I play one on television," derived from a much-copied Vick's cough syrup commercial from 1989,[10] where simply replacing the term *doctor* with any other noun can make a snowclone of this popular phrase.

Internet memes can spring from quirky photographs of unsuspecting celebrities, for instance, the "Sad Keanu" meme, which originated from a photo of Keanu Reeves sitting in a slouched position on a park bench,[11] or the average citizen posting a video of an unusual event or image, like the "Numma Numma" video, which simply features a teenager sitting in front of his computer lip-synching the words to the song

"Dragostea Din Tei" by the Moldovan pop group O-Zone.[12] More importantly, with the use of social media, Internet memes can spread at a breakneck pace and undergo meteoric transmutations as the concepts make their way through popular culture. The following is a partial list of popular culture references that have undergone numerous alterations and permutations as they establish themselves as Internet memes:

- LOLcats: images of cats with semiliterate captions like "I can haz cheezburger."[13]
- Condescending Wonka: a screen capture of actor Gene Wilder in the 1971 musical *Willy Wonka and the Chocolate Factory* with patronizing and such sarcastic captions as "Oh, you just graduated? You must know everything."[14]
- Star Wars Kid: an amateur video of a teenager performing a bit of high-spirited but clumsy lightsaber choreography, which has undergone numerous alterations, that ranked at the most viewed Internet viral video at more than 900 million views.[15]
- "The Rent Is Too Damn High": a political slogan coined by New York state gubernatorial candidate Jimmy McMillan during the 2010 debate that now serves as a snowclone template "The ____ Is Too Damn High" to complain about a variety of frustrations.[16]
- Chubby Bubble Girl: a photo fad meme based on a photograph of a girl running through a yard with a bubblemaker in her hand, which, after its introduction, underwent more than 200 derivatives in the span of two months and remains a popular Internet meme.[17]

While varying wildly in content and style, these Internet memes follow a similar pattern regarding the way they were introduced and spread on the Internet. The popularity of Internet memes illustrates how media consumers are eager to participate in popular culture. Today, average citizens not only have the capacity to create their own memes through a wide range of high-powered personal computing devices, but also the ability to distribute their ideas to worldwide audiences through the skillful deployment of social media on the Internet.

TEBOWING: THE ULTIMATE SPORTS MEME THAT BRINGS SPORTS FANS AND ATHLETES TOGETHER

Sports serve as the inspiration and springboard for a wide range of Internet memes. Devoted sports fans are passionate about their favorite teams, and they actively seek ways to express their opinions on a public platform in the world of sports. Before the Internet, sports fans had few ways to express themselves outside the limited number of outlets under the tight control of mass media conglomerates. For many sports fans, the best way to get any attention aside from running onto the field and disrupting the game was to display handwritten signs expressing some pithy statement in the hope that the television cameras would capture the image for broadcast. Now, with the aid of social media as the means of dissemination and the Internet as a ubiquitous platform, sports fans can participate in the creation of the sports narrative through a wide array of channels and have the potential to attract vast audiences worldwide instantaneously. (For a more detailed discussion, see Chapter 2, "Social Media and Sports Fans in American Culture.") As media consumers become savvier in negotiating the Internet and utilizing social media, sports memes are becoming an effective avenue through which sports fans can leave a lasting impression on popular culture. As with other types of memes, some sports memes rise to prominence, while others fail to gain much recognition beyond their original sources. Regardless, all sports memes rely on the skillful employment of social media to spread; however, many unpredictable factors outside the direct control of those who initiate a meme determine its popularity and potential viral spread, and only time will tell if a sports-themed concept will catch on with the public.

In 2011, I attempted to create my own Internet sports meme. The idea came to me after observing an incident that occurred during the Thanksgiving Day broadcast of the game between the Detroit Lions and the Green Bay Packers, when an enraged Ndamukong Suh of the Lions was ejected for stepping on Green Bay offensive lineman Evan Dietrich-Smith during an on-field altercation. After seeing replays of the incident during the rest of the game's broadcast and later on *SportsCenter*, along with continual analysis from sports pundits about the event, I found the basis for what I thought had the potential to become a trending sports meme. I thought that creating an image of Suh stepping on a baby seal in place of the Green Bay offensive lineman might work as a noteworthy sports meme with the potential to get some attention on the Internet.

Unsure of how to go about the process of introducing an Internet meme, let alone how to alter the original image of Suh stepping on his opponent to fit what I had imagined, I asked one of my colleagues, Isley Unruh, a media scholar who specializes in blogging and is a skilled Photoshop user, for help. After a brief explanation regarding the details of what I had in mind, Isley put together a seamless Photoshopped image of Suh stomping on a cute baby seal instead of Dietrich-Smith and assigned the title "Suh Stomping" to the meme. We then went about the process of introducing it on the Internet. After I uploaded the image to my Facebook page with a link to Isley's blog, which contains an extensive and comedic analysis of the potential meme (worth reading in full at www.isleyunruh.com/?p=5222), we were confident that "Suh Stomping" had a good chance of sparking interest.

Despite our best efforts, the "Suh Stomping" meme failed to gain much recognition beyond the few friends who saw it on my Facebook page—which received a total of 10 likes and 6 comments and was reshared 15 times—and Isley's personal blog, which only had three comments directed at the meme (one of them from me). Perhaps it was unsuccessful because we did not post it on the proper social media channels, like Reddit, 4chan, or Tumblr. Most likely, the original idea itself was not as clever as I imagined, and an image of a person stepping on a helpless baby seal is just not that amusing and might even be offensive and off-putting. Regardless, the experience was a clear illustration that the success of any meme depends on much more than a "clever idea" coupled with an expertly Photoshopped image posted on someone's Facebook page and personal blog to catch on with Internet audiences.

In sharp contrast to the "Suh Stomping" meme Isley and I failed to get off the ground, around that same time, during the 2011 football season, an ingenious sports meme known as "Tebowing," featuring Tim Tebow, one of the most high-profile NFL players, became an Internet sensation. According to Know Your Meme.com, "Tebowing" is a photo fad named after [NFL quarterback Tim Tebow] [that] involves getting down on one knee, placing one's elbow on the knee and fist on the forehead, similar to prayer or Thinker's pose named after the famous

Rodin statue."[18] The Tebowing image originated from a photograph of Tim Tebow dropping to one knee in the aforementioned pose after he led the Denver Broncos to a come-from-behind victory against the Miami Dolphins on October 23, 2011. The first sports fan to appropriate the image was Jared Kleinstein, a New York real estate agent and Denver Broncos fan. To celebrate the victory, Kleinstein and several friends took a picture of themselves in the now-famous Tebowing position outside the Sidebar in New York City, a gathering place for Denver Broncos fans where they had just watched the game. Kleinstein then posted the image to his Facebook page, and it received an inordinately high number of likes and comments within hours of the posting.[19] Based on the popularity of the image on his Facebook page, the following day, Kleinstein decided to start a Tumblr site devoted to the image and bought the rights to the domain Tebowing.com. Along with posting the image on the Tumblr site, he also defined the act of Tebowing as "to get down on one knee and pray, even if everyone else around you is doing something completely different."[20] Within two days of the site's launch, Kleinstein's original Tebowing image obtained more than 175,000 views.[21] Numerous visitors then shared the image on Twitter and other social media outlets, which led to it gaining immediate widespread attention in American popular culture.

Soon after Tebowing.com launched on October 27, 2011, the act of Tebowing attracted attention in several popular mass media outlets, including ESPN, Yahoo! Sports, *Huffington Post*, *Wall Street Journal*, and *New York Daily News*, which greatly intensified the popularity and eventual spread of Tebowing on the Internet.[22] That same day, Tebowing became a trending Twitter topic and even had the approval of Tim Tebow himself when he posted the following Tweet on his personal Twitter account: "#Tebowing – to get down on one knee and start praying, even if everyone else around is doing something completely different. Love it!" Tebow's Tweet about Tebowing was then re-Tweeted by more than 10,000 Twitter users and marked as "favorite" by nearly 2,000 others, a sure indication that this image was fast approaching official meme status.[23] The fact that Tim Tebow himself embraced the Tebowing image favorably instead of being outraged by what could be perceived as a tacit insult to his alleged lack of skill as a quarterback and unabashed religious devotion not only allowed the meme to more rapidly spread but simultaneously helped increase Tebow's already prolific sports celebrity status beyond the world of sports and with a worldwide audience.

Based on the information provided by Kleinstein on the website regarding the proper way to Tebow, media consumers now had the simple template to create their own Tebowing images to share with other Internet users. By taking pictures of themselves striking the now-iconic Tebow pose, which could occur anywhere and involve a nearly limitless number of potential set ups, fans could directly participate in the spread of this meme involving a high-profile sports celebrity figure with broad appeal both within and outside the world of sports. Many fans quickly followed suit and produced their own Tewbowing images at numerous locations around the United States and worldwide, featuring a wide range of creative scenarios and interesting subjects within the frame. The Tebowing website has so many entries and postings that it must organize the submissions into the following categories: Top 10, Toddlers, Global, Patriotic, Celebrity, and Holiday. A year after Tebowing was first introduced, people have taken pictures of themselves in the pose at numerous high-profile sites in the United States, including in front of the Lincoln Memorial in Washington, D.C., atop the Empire State Building in New York City, at the base of the Gateway Arch in Missouri, and with the Golden Gate Bridge in San Francisco, California, in the distant background. In addition, tourists have produced Tebowing images at international landmarks in more than 80 countries, including the Egyptian pyramids, Stonehenge in England, the Eiffel Tower in Paris, Machu Picchu in Peru, the Great Wall of China, and even at the South Pole in Antarctica. Celebrities have also created their own Tebowing images, including the following:

- Miss Delaware's Outstanding Teen 2012 and Miss Delaware 2012 Tebowing at an appearance.
- Warren Buffett Tebowing with a fan at Piccolo Pete's, an Omaha restaurant.
- Robert Downey Jr. Tebowing outside the 2012 Academy Awards ceremony in front of the Dorothy Chandler Pavilion.
- Rep. Robert Bell Tebowing at the Virginia House of Representatives after passing the "Tim Tebow Bill" allowing homeschooled students to play at their local high schools.

- Actress Maria Menounos Tebowing on the red carpet before the Golden Globe Awards in Beverly Hills, California.
- Ellen DeGeneres Tebowing backstage on the set of her popular daytime television program, *Ellen*.

Even noncelebrities posting to the site can achieve fame by making it to the top-10 list through extreme or unusual enactments of Tebowing. The following are a few examples:

- High school students Tebowing en masse at various proms and homecoming events.
- Wedding parties striking the Tebowing pose in churches and wedding reception halls.
- "Enormous Snowman Tebowing," which consists of a 15-foot snowman of Tim Tebow in the pose with a little girl striking the same pose in front of her house.
- In-flight Tebowing, featuring enough airplane passengers Tebowing to fill the entire aisle inside a Boeing 737.
- A doctor Tebowing after surgery with the tag line, "Taken immediately after saving this patient's life."
- Beatles Tebowing, with one person in a line of four Tebowing in a crosswalk emulation of the iconic Beatles' album cover *Abbey Road*.
- A preteen child Tebowing in his hospital room while connected to an intravenous device delivering chemotherapy (obviously one of the most touching images on the website).

The immediate popularity of Tebowing is a testament to the direct participatory aspect of this meme, driven by the ability of media consumers to spread it through social media on their personal computing devices. These qualities of the meme and the logistics of its dissemination allowed Tebowing to spread in popular culture in a manner that has ultimately involved both sports fans and people who would otherwise be disinterested in sports.

One of the most significant aspects of Tebowing is that the meme allows media consumers the chance to place their physical bodies into the image, by striking the Tebow pose, which forges a close connection to the original subject of the meme, Tim Tebow himself. The act of Tebowing allows anyone with a camera and the ability to bend down on one knee to take part in spreading the meme in a wide range of scenarios and contexts. More importantly, the Tebowing meme's spread may have been one of the driving forces responsible in skyrocketing his popularity, both in the world of sports and popular culture in general, beyond what he might have been able to attain with mass media coverage of his performance on the field and activities off the field alone.

On December 13, 2011, a further testament to the popularity of the Tebowing meme manifested when Yahoo! Sports reported that the *Global Language Monitor*, a publication that tracks and analyzes trending terms on the Internet, indicated that the term *Tebowing* had been accepted into the English language. While established dictionaries like *Merriam Webster's* and the *Oxford English Dictionary* have yet to recognize Tebowing as an official word, the *Global Language Monitor* indicated that "Tebowing" showed up in enough mass media and social media outlets to allow the term to qualify, at the very least, as an official meme. The *Global Language Monitor* "has been recognizing new words once they meet the criteria of a minimum number of citations across the breadth of the English-speaking world, with the requisite depth of usage on the Internet, social media, and 75,000 global print and electronic media."[24] Based on this analysis, Tebowing is a popular term that is being used with increased frequency, both within and outside the world of sports, and it is likely to remain as a permanent term in the English lexicon.

Concurrent to the meteoric rise of the Tebowing meme, ESPN writer Bill Williamson posted an article decrying Tim Tebow's ineptitude at the quarterback position, which sparked yet another meme related to Tim Tebow known as #OccupyTebow, in reference to the ongoing Occupy Wall Street protests in the United States. The article focuses on the idea that Tebow is not equipped to operate as an effective NFL quarterback, summed up in the following statement: "I hate to jump to early conclusions, but it is safe to say Tebow currently is far from being a competent NFL quarterback and that the Broncos have arguably the worst quarterback situation in the NFL."[25] The article set off a "lengthy chain of comments . . . naming a wide range of things that are better than [Tim] Tebow."[26] According to Know Your Meme's analysis, the #OccupyTebow snowclone meme spread to Twitter, where comments and Tweets follow the simple format of mathematical inequality of "X is greater than Tebow," or "X > Tebow," for short. As of November 2,

2012, Bill Williamson's original article had attracted more than 5,000 comments following the aforementioned formula. The following is a brief listing of some of the most recent #OccupyTebow comments as of the writing of this book:

- Ramen noodles instead of stuffing at Thanksgiving > Tebow.
- Ken Burns firing Peter Coyote and hiring Dan Dierdorf to narrate his next documentary > Tebow.
- The smell of burning teeth when the dentist uses that drill > Tebow.
- Not being deaf at a Yanni concert > Tebow.
- Grown men who watch professional wrestling > Tebow.
- Uploading a new picture on Facebook and waiting for people to like it > Tebow.
- Working at Wal-Mart during Black Friday > Tebow.
- Posting here for the first time, more than a year after this thing started > Tebow. [27]

The sheer number of negative comments regarding Tim Tebow's failings as a quarterback is staggering, and more are added to the website every day. Regardless, this level of attention only augments Tim Tebow's celebrity status. The #OccupyTebow meme, while not as good natured as Tebowing, still allows fans to participate in the creation of the sports narrative, even if it is only by writing a pithy insult directed at Tim Tebow's alleged inadequate quarterbacking skills. Furthermore, as the #OccupyTebow meme suggests, if sports pundits and fans considered Tim Tebow more talented as a NFL quarterback, he would not have gained a level of attention in popular culture that rivals that of some of the most highly skilled active NFL quarterbacks, the likes of Peyton Manning, Drew Brees, and Tom Brady. Paul Payack, president and chief word analyst of the *Global Language Monitor*, indicates the importance of sports in popular culture in stating that, "Sports have become significant generators of new cultural trends and memes that transcend the athletic arena."[28] The memes that sprang from Tim Tebow are a testament to Payack's statement, as well as proof of the power sports have in general in attracting interest from a widespread audience in pop culture. This is likely to increase as new generations of media consumers come up with innovative methods and performances to gain attention in the world of sports and discover new avenues in promoting themselves to the general public through social media.

JACK BLANKENSHIP, THE ALABAMA FACE GUY: A MEME OR NOT A MEME?

Predicting which ideas in popular culture will become Internet memes seems to follow no definite formula. Internet memes often rise to prominence arbitrarily and capriciously. Also, based on the unpredictable whims of pop culture, Internet memes can explode on the scene instantaneously and then disappear from the public eye just as quickly. One website that helps provide some context in qualifying and tracking Internet memes is Know Your Meme (www.knowyourmeme.com). This website offers a wide range of categories for Internet memes, ranging from photo fads, for instance, the Chubby Bubble Girl, to viral videos, like the Star Wars Kid. In addition, the website features a comprehensive breakdown and classification of each meme based on the following categories:

- About: provides a general description of the content and details of the meme.
- Origin: provides the source of the original popular culture reference of each meme and its first appearance on the Internet.
- Spread: explains how the meme originally spread and the media consumers who helped spread the meme.
- Notable Examples: lists the various permutations of the meme that occurred as the idea was transmitted on the Internet.
- Search Interest: displays, using Google Trends, data regarding the number of search queries during the life of the meme and, in some cases, provides a region-by-region listing of search queries regarding the meme worldwide.
- External References: usually provides links to other meme-oriented websites that also track the creation and evolution of Internet memes, including Quickmeme, 4chan, and Reddit.

- Meme Determination: based on the previously listed criteria, provides an evaluation indicating whether a trending Internet concept attains meme status.
- Recent Videos/Recent Images: tracks emerging permutations of the meme in question and provides links to each new permutation.
- Comments: provides links to Facebook discussions on the meme, along with a comment section sponsored by Know Your Meme.

This system of classification and tracking might not be the official standard in qualifying Internet memes, but it serves as a good starting point in understanding what it takes for an idea to become an Internet meme and, more importantly, how it spreads and changes during its lifespan. Referring to Know Your Meme's classification system, along with drawing information from other Internet meme websites, will help determine whether a sports-themed trend originating from a rather unique method of distracting free-throw shooters at basketball games perpetrated by University of Alabama basketball fan Jack Blankenship (a.k.a. "the Alabama Face Guy") during the 2011–2012 college basketball season meets the criteria as a meme.

As previously touched upon, one way that sports fans try to make their presence known at sporting events is to create distinctive and innovative signs with clever statements or display silly images to get noticed by the athletes and television film crews. One of the more popular methods to get attention from both athletes and the media at basketball games is to sit in fan zones behind the basket and perform crazy acts to distract the opposing team's players while they are shooting free throws. These free-throw distractions are widespread rituals at almost all live basketball games, and they usually involve fans waving their hands back and forth or holding up a sign to distract the shooter.

Jack Blankenship, a freshman from the University of Alabama and an avid basketball fan, achieved remarkable and long-lasting fame for his specialized free-throw distractions during the 2012 college basketball season. Blankenship's rise to prominence originated during a game between Alabama and Ole Miss on February 4, 2012. During the broadcast on ESPN2, Blankenship caught the attention of ESPN camera crews when they noticed him making an odd facial expression—with nostrils flared, eyebrows raised, eyes bulging, and jaw thrust outward—

and holding up a huge cutout of his face with the same expression to distract players on the opposing team. One of the announcers, Pam Ward, drew even greater attention to Blankenship by asking incredulously, "This guy . . . who does that? I mean, who makes a picture of themselves?"[29] Regardless of Ward's derisive comments, as a result of this brief mentioning on national television of his actions that night, Blankenship gained instant popularity the following day when a screen capture of the ESPN2 broadcast, posted on imgur, received more than 680,000 views within 24 hours (to date, 715,481).[30] This mass media coverage, along with the screen capture image from the ESPN broadcast, was the first incident that Blankenship utilized in launching his Alabama Face Guy shtick (through social media) into a popular trending topic on the Internet.

Know Your Meme's breakdown of the Alabama Face Guy starts with the following brief description: "Jack Blankenship's face, also simply referred to as 'The Face,' is an oversized cutout of University of Alabama student Jackson Blankenship's contorted face, which he uses during college basketball games as a distraction to the opposing team."[31]

Figure 5.1. Getting the student body at the University of Alabama involved in the face guy distraction. ***Image courtesy of Jackson Blankenship***

The website then provides information regarding the initial spread of the original screen capture image of Blankenship at the February 4, 2012, Mississippi versus Alabama basketball game, which was posted to Reddit and entitled "Distraction Done Right." To provide some context regarding the features on Reddit, images posted there have an extensive comments section where fans can assign a number of quality points that help rank the image's popularity, along with an option that allows fans to give the photo entry either an up vote or down vote. Soon after the original screen capture of Blankenship with his oversized image at the Mississippi versus Alabama basketball game was posted on February 4, 2011, the "Distraction Done Right" Reddit picture drew 11,475 up votes and 9,600 down votes, and received an overall score of 1,875.[32]

Know Your Meme identifies Blankenship's routine as a "photobomb"[33] meme and provides the following history of past oversized image photobombings in sports: "The tradition of bringing oversized heads to sporting events was started . . . by a group of students at San Diego State University in 2002, featuring an oversized cut out of Michael Jackson. The practice was first documented in the December 19, 2005, issue of *ESPN the Magazine*."[34] Since that time, using the oversized cutout of a person's head as a free-throw distraction has spread nationwide, and it is a common practice among fans at high school, college, and professional basketball games. Know Your Meme points out that a crucial difference between Blankenship's distraction and those previously described is that he was one of the first to use his own face rather than that of a public figure. The website displays a photo from *ESPN the Magazine*, along with an explanation that past free-throw distractions featured large cutouts of celebrities' heads, including Conan O'Brian, Michael Moore, and Emilio Estevez, among others, scattered throughout the stands behind the basket. In this way, by mimicking an already established ritual in popular culture and applying his own unique and inventive slant to it, Blankenship performed one of the most important operations to initiate a potential Internet meme.

While Jack Blankenship has already attained more recognition than most fans will ever get in their entire lifetimes with his appearance on ESPN2 and the subsequent attention he received from his Alabama Face Guy routine screen capture on the Internet, it wasn't until *Birmingham News* photographer Hal Yeager captured an image of Blankenship making the same face while holding up the same large cutout of his face at an Alabama versus Florida game on Valentine's Day 2012 that his fame really took off. Demonstrating the ability to promote himself through social media, on the night of February 14, 2012, Blankenship re-Tweeted the photo from the February 4, 2012, Mississippi State game, telling his followers to look out for him during the upcoming game against the University of Florida with the following Tweet, "Get ready world. We return at 6:00 on @espn pic.twitter.com/JmZ6MuA1." As with the screen capture of Blankenship on Reddit, soon after the *Birmingham News* posted the photo of Blankenship, it became a popular Internet trend, appearing on multiple mass media sites, including ESPN, Yahoo! Sports, and the Hollywood Gossip website. In addition, Blankenship gained more than 200 Twitter followers the day the photo was first published on his personal account.[35] The following day, the *Birmingham News* image was posted on Reddit under the title "My New Favorite Sports Fan." Within the first five days it appeared, Blankenship's second photo from the *Birmingham News* received 41,617 up votes, with an overall score of 2,812, almost 1,000 more points than the score of the first Reddit photo of Blankenship posted the week before.[36] Also, on February 15, 2012, Tumblr user "cajunboy" reposted the second image, and it drew nearly 25,000 comments in five days.[37]

Blankenship's exposure didn't stop with the initial coverage he received from the first ESPN game. After a few weeks of his images, videos, and Tweets circulating on the Internet, on February 21, 2012, NBC's *Today* and *Late Night With Jimmy Fallon* invited Blankenship to appear on their shows in New York. On both nationally televised shows, Blankenship had segments devoted solely to him and the details of his free-throw distraction ritual, which had become a popular Internet trend. During his *Today* segment, Blankenship explained the history of his facial expression, while cohost Ann Curry indicated that the YouTube video of him had received more than 1 million views in about two weeks. Later in the segment, producers featured archival footage of Blankenship photo bombing[38] *Today* years earlier, when he stood behind famous weatherman Al Roker making a similar funny face on national television.[39]

Later that evening on *Late Night With Jimmy Fallon*, Fallon conducted an interview with Blankenship lasting nearly four minutes. The interview featured Blankenship providing Fallon with the following five steps outlining how to properly execute his unique facial expression:

1. Flare your nostrils;
2. Frown;
3. Raise your eyebrows;
4. Make your eyes big; and
5. Inhale deeply to exaggerate the other expressions.

As Blankenship explained these five steps, Jimmy Fallon performed them in sequential order for the audience, which resulted in thunderous laughter and applause. Fallon ended the segment by saying, "I'm a big fan of you, buddy, we appreciate anyone who has fun in life, so thanks for being here.[40] Fallon's comments regarding Blankenship's approach in gaining widespread attention as a sports fan is a testament to the power of an average person who, using creativity and ingenuity through social media, now has unprecedented control over creating their own celebrity, all without having to resort to the extreme measures of someone like Rainbow Man (Rollen Stewart) referenced in Chapter 2, "Social Media and Sports Fans in American Culture."

Even though Blankenship's profile has subsided a bit since the original media coverage surge of his Alabama Face Guy routing during the 2011 college basketball season, he remains a sports fan celebrity. Funny or Die, the Internet comedy website sponsored by Will Farrell and Adam McKay's production company, produced a tribute video about Blankenship and his Alabama Face Guy distraction routine, where he is seen performing his act at various Los Angeles landmarks, including Venice Beach, the Santa Monica Pier, and Le Brea Tar Pits, along with him photobombing a performance by aging pop singer Rick Springfield and posing with Darth Vader and a Stormtrooper from *Star Wars* in front of Grauman's Chinese Theatre.[41]

Now calling himself a "distraction artist," Blankenship has carved out a niche for himself in creating his own celebrity and has indicated that his ambitions include eventually becoming a stand-up comic. He even made a mock video of himself campaigning for the presidency of the University of Alabama. The video features him making comedic campaign promises, including that, if he is elected, he will place wishing wells all over campus and allow "no more Nickelback [rock group] music to be played on local radio stations."[42] As of November 2012, even though his bid to become the University of Alabama's president was unsuccessful, Blankenship's mock campaign video has received 398,072 hits and generated 711 viewer comments, most of them complimentary, indicating that viewers appreciate his style of humor.[43]

In addition to producing the University of Alabama presidential campaign video, he also appeared in a promotional video produced by the Paul "Bear" Bryant Museum at the University of Alabama. In the video, entitled "So Many Trophies, So Little Space," Blankenship performs his comedic Alabama Face Guy routine as a janitor who accidentally breaks the crystal football atop the National Collegiate Athletic Association (NCAA) Division I national championship trophy, only to replace it with another one from a box labeled "spare crystals" (www.youtube.com/user/bryantmuseum). Through all these high-profile appearances, Blankenship appears to understand how to go about promoting his celebrity through his Alabama Face Guy routine and is savvy about finding new avenues through which to increase his exposure.

With all this media hype, along with the positive feedback Blankenship received through his public appearances, it might seem a foregone conclusion that the Alabama Face Guy is a widely accepted meme, but a consensus is lacking among the many social media outlets that provide analysis and tracking of memes regarding the Alabama Face Guy's qualification as an "official" Internet meme. Unlike the Tebowing or #OccupyTebow memes, which have both been declared official memes by Know Your Meme, doubt remains among Internet users and the various websites devoted to meme coverage as to whether the Alabama Face Guy trend meets the requirements to be called a meme. Know Your Meme is currently researching and evaluating the Alabama Face Guy meme, and, as of the writing of this book, the site has yet to make a determination either assigning it official meme status or declaring it "deadpooled"—a colloquial term indicating that an Internet trend failed to make it as a meme; however, the tremendous amount of interest Blankenship has obtained through the Internet and social media suggests that the Alabama Face Guy routine meets many of the characteristics of Richard Dawkins's definition of a meme.

Examining Internet search interest using Google Trend analysis of searches for "Jack Blankenship" helps show that his image and variations of his image underwent viral spread. The Google Trends website interface consists of three main elements: a graph measuring search

Figure 5.2. Do you think this qualifies as a sports meme? *Image courtesy of Jackson Blankenship*

interest dating back to 2004 to the present where the number 100 represents the peak search volume at any given point in time; an animation of a map of the world showing changes in views during that same time period; and a section listing search terms related to the original concept. According to the breakdown of the search interest for "Jack Blankenship" on Google Trends, the graph remains at zero consistently from 2004, until it makes a sudden spike to 100 in February 2012, the month when Blankenship performed his first free-throw distraction.[44] Search interest tapered off the following months, at 47 in March 2012, 31 in April 2012, 18 in May 2012, 8 in June 2012, and 3 in July 2012. A small boost occurred in August 2012, at 7, and the graph fell to 5 in September 2012, 4 in October 2012, and up again slightly to 5 in November 2012. Related Google searches like "Alabama Face Guy" and "Jack Blankenship's Face" both exhibited similar patterns on their respective graphs.

The Google Trends graphic provides another visual representation of search interest on a topic by indicating changes throughout time on a map of the world's countries that changes color when search interest peaks at certain points in time. With the three aforementioned search options regarding Jack Blankenship, the map remains pale blue for the majority of the animation and then suddenly produces a quick burst of dark blue in the U.S. map when the progress bar reaches February 2012. It then returns to light blue for the remainder of the animation. This data from Google Trends indicates that Jack Blankenship was anonymous in popular culture prior to his current level of fame and that his rise to prominence occurred, as indicated on the Google Trend graphs and maps, in direct relation to the time frame in which he first performed his basketball distraction routine. Consequently, even though search interest spiked at the maximum for a brief moment, it indicates that there was an enormous amount of interest in Jack Blankenship from a significant portion of the U.S. population, which occurred through Internet users exchanging information about his Alabama Face Guy routine. As a result, this pattern suggests that the trend underwent viral spread on the Internet in early 2012, thus fulfilling a primary requirement of a pop culture reference attaining meme status.

Along with the attention Blankenship received in mass media, the widespread circulation of Blankenship's photos through social media has led to the Alabama Face Guy becoming a popular Internet trend with lasting power. Many of these images are featured on a wide range of websites, including multiple repostings on Facebook, Dead Spin, Cheez Burger, and Funny Junk. Blankenship now has 4,972 followers on Twitter, and his Tumblr site displays numerous photobombs of people, many not even sports fans, posting images of themselves emulating his facial expression at many locations outside of numerous sporting events.[45] A simple Google search for "Jack Blankenship" results in numerous examples of his visage combined with other popular culture references in new images and scenarios. The following are just a few examples of people Photoshopping Blankenship's image from the *Birmingham News* in mashup photobombings of high-profile historic scenarios:

- Amid a crowd of protesters during the 2011 Egyptian Revolution.
- Blankenship photobombing Alfred Eisenstaedt's iconic *VJ Day in Times Square* photograph of a sailor kissing a woman in a white dress in New York's Time Square at the end of World War II.

- Inside the Situation Room of the White House with President Obama, Vice President Biden, and Secretary of State Hillary Clinton on the day U.S. forces killed Osama bin Laden.
- Among a group of appalled spectators watching a police officer pepper spray Occupy Wall Street protesters.
- In the background of Eddie Adams's famous Vietnam War photo depicting the South Vietnamese police chief executing a Viet Cong prisoner at point-blank range with his pistol.
- In front of the Capitol Building in Washington, D.C., during President Obama's 2008 inauguration.

The following are additional examples from the same Google search that produced remixes of Blankenship combined with numerous past and present popular culture figures and celebrities:

- Alongside Ken Jennings on the set of the game show *Jeopardy*.
- A side-by-side comparison of Blankenship making his silly face and the *Muppet Show* character Beaker, lab assistant to Dr. Bunsen Honeydew.
- A Photoshopped image of famous British pop singer Adele cradling a cutout of Blankenship's oversized head at a music awards ceremony.
- Appearing alongside Megan Alexander from the television program *Inside Edition*, where both make the funny face.
- J. D. Crowe's cartoon caricature entitle "The Budget Face" of Alabama governor Robert Bentley holding an oversized cutout of his own grimacing face as a criticism of his mishandling of the state's budget.[46]
- A Lego toy model depicting a Lego figure of Blankenship holding up a larger Lego head image of himself photobombing a Lego hockey game entitled "Lego Jack Blankenship Goes to a Hockey Game."

This level of ubiquitous imitation by a wide range of Internet users in combining it with other popular culture references is a key component to Blankenship's Alabama Face Guy routine reaching Internet meme status. Another important aspect to all these permutations indicates that Blankenship's Alabama Face Guy image has widespread popularity outside the world of sports and invades other aspects of American popular culture, just like the memes associated with Tim Tebow (Tebowing and #OccupyTebow). Whether or not the Internet community accepts this as an official Internet meme, based on the number of times his original image, and permutations and remixes of his image, have been shared through social media, Jack Blankenship's Alabama Face Guy routine adheres to Richard Dawkins's definition of a meme, both in terms of mimesis and viral spread.

While Blankenship is an exceptional case study of a sports fan gaining widespread acclaim for his silly exploits, it is likely that future sports fans will emulate his example and attempt to become just as popular. More importantly, potential Blankenship imitators will employ many of the same techniques using social media to gain attention with mass media. In fact, more and more mass media outlets no longer view social media as a threat. Many mass media entities embrace the surge in popularity with social media as a way to provide media consumers with some input in the creation of news stories and attract a demographic of potential viewers who are driven by the desire to gain their own 15 minutes of fame.

NOTES

1. Richard Dawkins, *The Selfish Gene*, 2nd ed. (New York: Oxford University Press, 1989), 192.
2. Dawkins, *The Selfish Gene*, 192.
3. Jacopo della Quercia, "7 Memes That Went Viral Before the Internet Existed," *Cracked.com*, 11 April 2011, www.cracked.com/article_19119_7-memes-that-went-viral-before-internet-existed.html (14 November 2012).
4. Tahree Lane, "Mad for Alfred: A New Exhibit Shows *Mad* Magazine's Poster Boy Has a Checkered Past," *Toledo Blade*, 20 January 2008, www.toledoblade.com/Art/2008/01/20/Mad-for-Alfred-A-new-exhibit-shows-Mad-magazine-s-poster-boy-has-a-shadowy-past.html (13 November 2012).
5. Lane, "Mad for Alfred," www.toledoblade.com/Art/2008/01/20/Mad-for-Alfred-A-new-exhibit-shows-Mad-magazine-s-poster-boy-has-a-shadowy-past.html.
6. Lane, "Mad for Alfred," www.toledoblade.com/Art/2008/01/20/Mad-for-Alfred-A-new-exhibit-shows-Mad-magazine-s-poster-boy-has-a-shadowy-past.html.

7. Curtis Dunham and John Innes, *Wurra-Wurra: A Legend of Saint Patrick at Tara* (New York: Desmond Fitzgerald, 1911), 13.

8. Harry Bradford, "Papa John's Anti-Obamacare Meme Goes Viral (photos)," *Huffington Post*, 14 November 2012, www.huffingtonpost.com/2012/11/14/papa-johns-obamacare-boycott-meme_n_2129800.html?1352910915&ncid=edlinkusaolp00000009 (15 November 2012).

9. Todd Wasserman, "Papa John's Gets Bludgeoned by Memes for Obamacare Stance," *Mashable.com*, 13 November 2012, http://mashable.com/2012/11/13/papa-johns-memes/#101181-2 (15 November 2012).

10. Paul McFedries, "Snowclone Is the New Cliché," *ieeeSpectrum.com*, February 2008, http://spectrum.ieee.org/at-work/education/snowclone-is-the-new-clich (15 November 2012).

11. Dave Mellisy, "20 Top Memes of 2010: The Internet Has a Mind of Its Own, and That Mind Has Some Odd Interests," *About.com Web Humor*, December 2010, http://humor.about.com/od/bestofthebest/tp/top_memes_2010.htm (15 November 2012).

12. The "Numma Numma" video is a remarkable example of an Internet meme. The original video, posted by Gary William Brolsma on 6 December 2004, has been viewed by nearly 50 million viewers and parodied multiple times, and it is even the subject of an ongoing online amateur video contest at www.youtube.com/watch?v=60og9gwKh1o (14 November 2012).

13. "What Is an Internet Meme?" *Tech Target.com*, February 2009, http://whatis.techtarget.com/definition/Internet-meme (14 November 2012).

14. "Condescending Wonka," *Know Your Meme.com*, http://knowyourmeme.com/memes/condescending-wonka-creepy-wonka (14 November 2012).

15. "Star Wars Kid Is Top Viral Video: A Two-Minute Clip of a Teenage Boy Pretending to Wield a Lightsaber Has Become the Most Popular Viral Video on the Internet," *BBC News*, 27 November 2006, http://news.bbc.co.uk/2/hi/entertainment/6187554.stm (14 November 2012).

16. "The Rent Is Too Damn High," *Know Your Meme.com*, http://knowyourmeme.com/memes/the-rent-is-too-damn-high-jimmy-mcmillan (15 November 2012).

17. "Chubby Bubbles Girl," *Know Your Meme.com*, http://knowyourmeme.com/memes/chubby-bubbles-girl#fn6 (15 November 2012).

18. "Tebowing," *Know Your Meme.com*, http://knowyourmeme.com/memes/tebowing#fn16 (17 November 2012).

19. Ben Cohen, "The Godfather of Tebowing Tells All," *Wall Street Journal Blogs*, 27 October 2011, http://blogs.wsj.com/dailyfix/2011/10/27/the-godfather-of-tebowing-tells-all/ (17 November 2012).

20. "Tebowing," http://tebowing.com/ (17 November 2012).

21. "Tebowing," http://knowyourmeme.com/memes/tebowing#fn16.

22. "Tebowing," http://knowyourmeme.com/memes/tebowing#fn5.

23. https://twitter.com/TimTebow/status/129728076203565056 (18 November 2012).

24. "Tebowing Accepted Into the English Language: Six-Week Rise of the Global Phenomenon," *Global Language Monitor.com*, 11 December 2011, www.languagemonitor.com/new-words/tebowing-accepted-into-english-language/ (19 November 2012).

25. Bill Williamson, "Time for Elway to Think Post-Tebow," *ESPN NFL, AFC Blog*, 30 October 2011, http://espn.go.com/blog/afcwest/post/_/id/34680/time-for-elway-to-think-post-tebow#comments (19 November 2012).

26. "Tebowing," http://knowyourmeme.com/memes/tebowing#fn18 (19 November 2012).

27. Williamson, "Time for Elway to Think Post-Tebow," http://espn.go.com/blog/afcwest/post/_/id/34680/time-for-elway-to-think-post-tebow#comments.

28. "Tebowing Accepted Into the English Language," www.languagemonitor.com/new-words/tebowing-accepted-into-english-language/.

29. Dave Wilson, "Alabama Fan Uses 'the Face' to Distract Opponents," *ESPN.com*, February 2012, http://espn.go.com/espn/page2/index?id=7578845 (21 August 2012).

30. Wilson, "Alabama Fan Uses 'the Face' to Distract Opponents," http://espn.go.com/espn/page2/index?id=7578845.

31. "Jack Blankenship's Face," http://knowyourmeme.com/memes/jack-blankenships-face (21 November 2012).

32. "Distraction Done Right," www.reddit.com/r/pics/comments/pbeis/distraction_done_right/ (21 November 2012).

33. The *Urban Dictionary* defines photobombing as "The fine art of ruining other people's photos, usually involving someone with an awkward smile or open-mouthed attempt," www.urbandictionary.com/define.php?term=Photo%20bombing (25 August 2012).

34. "Jack Blankenship ' s Face, " http://knowyourmeme.com/memes/jack-blankenships-face#fn8.

35. "My New Favorite Sports Fan," *Meme Center.com*, www.memecenter.com/fun/152799/my-new-favorite-sports-fan (5 September 2012).

36. "My New Favorite Sports Fan," www.reddit.com/r/funny/comments/pr018/my_new_favorite_sports_fan/ (21 November 2012).

37. "Make This Alabama Basketball Fan a Meme," http://cajunboy.tumblr.com/post/17664894840/make-this-alabama-basketball-fan-a-meme-internet (22 November 2012).

38. It should be noted that when Blankenship photobombed on *Today* years earlier, he did not have a large cutout of his own face. He merely made the facial expression behind Al Roker. See Matt Scalici, "Jack 'the Face' Blankenship Appears on the *Today Show*," *Alabama Live.com*, 21 February 2012, www.al.com/sports/index.ssf/2012/02/jack_the_face_blankenship_appe.html (25 August 2012).

39. "Alabama Face Guy Jack Blankenship Stops by *Late Night With Jimmy Fallon* to Talk Basketball (video)," *Huffington Post*, 22 February 2012, www.huffingtonpost.com/2012/02/22/alabama-face-guy-jack-blankenship-jimmy-fallon-video_n_1293456.html (25 August 2012).

40. Josh Wolford, "Alabama Face Guy Starts Viral Campaign for Presidency of the University," *WebProNews.com*, 30 March 2012, www.webpronews.com/alabama-face-guy-viral-campaign-for-president-2012-03 (25 August 2012).

41. "The Alabama Face Guy: Los Angeles," *Funny or Die.com*, www.funnyordie.com/videos/a5cf524f12/the-alabama-face-guy-los-angeles (24 November 2012).

42. "Jack Blankenship for UA [University of Alabama] President," *YouTube*, 29 March 2012, www.youtube.com/watch?v=-XOfoxg4Glo&feature=player_embedded (25 August 2012).

43. "Jack Blankenship for UA [University of Alabama] President," www.youtube.com/watch?v=-XOfoxg4Glo&feature=player_embedded.

44. www.google.com/trends/explore?hl=en-US#q=%22jack+blankenship%22 (23 November 2012).

45. www.tumblr.com/tagged/alabama-face-guy?before=1331601409 (21 August 2012).

46. J. D. Crowe, "Budget Face," *Alabama.com*, 23 February 2012, http://blog.al.com/jdcrowe/2012/02/budget_face.html (24 November 2012).

6

TWITTER'S IMPACT ON SPORTS: BRIDGING THE GAP BETWEEN SPORTS FANS AND ATHLETES

Of all the social media outlets on the Internet, Twitter is the premier microblogging website in existence. As of the writing of this book, Twitter has more than 100 million active users worldwide who generate 230 million Tweets per day.[1] Twitter chief executive officer Dick Costolo's statement that "We . . . offer simplicity in a world of complexity" epitomizes the company's intent to provide users with an efficient application to communicate quickly and easily with one another.[2] Another important factor contributing to the popularity of Twitter is that the 140-character limit encourages users to post, for the most part, lighthearted and trivial comments. This was likely the intended use of Twitter from its very inception because, according to Twitter founder Jack Dorsey, perplexed about what name they should chose for their new website, he and his colleagues came across the term *twitter* in the dictionary, which is defined as "a short burst of inconsequential information, and chirps from birds, which was exactly what the product was."[3]

Adding to this, a 2009 study conducted by the market-research firm Pear Analytics found that, after analyzing 2,000 Tweets during a two-week period, they were able to classify the content of the Tweets into the following six categories:

1. pointless babble 40%

2. conversational 38%
3. pass-along value 9%
4. self-promotion 6%
5. spam 4%
6. news 4%[4]

Microsoft researcher Danah Boyd contests Pear Analytics' assignment of these six categories and offers a more nuanced qualification, stating that "[Tweeting] is fundamentally a mix of social grooming and maintaining peripheral social awareness. They want to know what the people around them are thinking and doing and feeling, even when copresence isn't viable."[5] Regardless of how social media analysts choose to qualify the ways in which people use Twitter and the content of most Tweets, it primarily involves an exchange of trivial, colloquial information that occurs through short, concentrated textual bursts.

Anyone who is either a sports fan or spends a great deal of time with one can attest to the claim that sharing trivial information is an apt description regarding the way sports fans communicate with one another, where most conversations involve simple recollections of past games or comments on player statistics. This also epitomizes the way athletes and fans communicated with one another in the past, which usually occurred through brief autograph sessions with a few inane pleasantries exchanged and a simple signature on a piece of paper or other sports artifact as physical evidence proving that a fan actually made contact with an athlete. Now with social media, and most especially Twitter, sports fans can engage in substantial communication with their favorite athletes across great distances with remarkable efficiency. In the same way, athletes have unprecedented opportunities to increase their fan base beyond the pre-Internet bounds, which were often limited to a concentrated geographical region and whose publicity was held captive at the whims of mass media outlets in broadcasting an athlete's activities to the general public. Now, athletes have the capacity to reach out to potential fans worldwide at any time of their own choosing and make their mark not just in the world of sports, but also in popular culture at large.

ATHLETES REACHING OUT TO FANS THROUGH TWITTER: THE CHAD JOHNSON EXPERIMENT

One of the first athletes to recognize and exploit the potential of social media to increase his fan base and popularity was NFL wide receiver Chad Johnson (Chad Ochocinco). Johnson achieved notable success as a player during his 11-year NFL career, mostly with the Cincinnati Bengals, where he set many franchise records for receiving yards and touchdowns, was chosen as an All-Pro three times, and made the NFL Pro Bowl six times. Even though his on-the-field accomplishments are impressive and worthy of acclaim, Johnson is better known for his off-the-field activities, most notably through his prolific use of social media, especially Twitter.

Soon after Twitter became an Internet sensation, Johnson was already utilizing it to reach out to fans, where he attracted more than 1 million followers. Before the start of the 2009 NFL season, he announced that he was going to Tweet fans during games the following season.[6] The NFL wasted no time in quashing Johnson's intention, stating that, "league policy prohibits players from using sites such as Facebook and Twitter 90 minutes before kickoff up until the conclusion of the postgame media session."[7] Undeterred, Johnson (who then went by the last name Ochocinco) devised a clever way to circumvent these restrictions. During a podcast on UStream, he announced that he was going to sponsor a weekly fan contest where he would provide travel to the game and lodging for a different fan each week, and while at the game, he would send the fan hand signals in the stands. The fan would then post the Tweet by proxy for Johnson during the game.[8] Johnson created an unprecedented situation for fans to directly participate in the weekly NFL sports narrative by having fans operate as virtual carrier pigeons in clandestinely relaying information from a prominent athlete while on the field of play to fans on the Twitterverse to avoid detection by NFL officials.

During the 2010 preseason, Johnson took the plunge and disobeyed the NFL's ban on social media during games and Tweeted two texts during Cincinnati's game against the Philadelphia Eagles on August 20, 2010 (please note that I retain the language and grammar in the original Tweet). At 6:50 p.m., he tweeted, "Just talk with Kelly Washington, Desean Jackson, Geoff Pope, Hank Baskett and I caught a ball from

Mike Vick, I love prw-game warm up." At 9:53 p.m., this was followed by, "Man Im sick of getting hit like that, its the damn preseason (expletive)! 1day I'm gone jump up and start throwing hay makers. "

True to their word, the NFL's response was swift and harsh. Days after Johnson's willful act of defiance, NFL executive vice president of football operations Ray Anderson levied a $25,000 fine on him for violating two NFL policies of "possessing an electronic device on the sidelines during a game and posting messages on social media sites during a game."[9] In response, Johnson Tweeted, "I've been fined by the league a substantial amount of money for tweeting, 1st time twitter hasn't made me money but cost me money." He later added, "Dear NFL I apologize for tweeting during the game but that was 2 months of my Bugatti payments you just took from me, I won't do it again."[10]

After the incident, Johnson turned the NFL fine to his advantage in earning sympathy from fans who applauded his defiance of authority and willingness to reach out to fans through social media during live games. Undeterred, Johnson continued to interact with fans through Twitter, all off the field, which led to him being named the "most influential sports personality in the online world."[11] Even though his playing skills waned as he moved from the Cincinnati Bengals to the New England Patriots and later the Miami Dolphins, through his skillful and persistent use of Twitter and other social media outlets, Johnson remained a prominent figure, not just in the world of sports, but in popular culture at large.

In spite of Chad Johnson having the reputation of being arrogant, selfish, and irreverent on the field, during press conferences and interviews, he has shown the capacity for great empathy, consideration, and generosity with his fans. He established many relationships with his fans through Twitter, but one of the most remarkable was with an avid Cincinnati Bengals fan by the name of Chris Kernich. Adopting the Twitter handle #the_man-CK, Kernich Tweeted Johnson on multiple occasions, usually to congratulate him on a good performance during a game. His connection with Johnson remained at a casual level until a personal tragedy struck Kernich. On the night of November 15, 2009, assailants attacked Kernich and two of his friends, and Kernich suffered life-threatening injuries. Doctors told family and friends that even though Kernich had lapsed into a coma, he could still hear people talking to him. After starting a Facebook page in support of Kernich, which drew support from 3,000 people, some of his friends thought that a visit from his idol, Chad Johnson, might help with his recovery.[12] A few days later, on November 19, 2009, two of Kernich's friends Tweeted Johnson's Twitter feed, texting, "@OGOchoCinco URGENT!! — we are asking for some of your support to help @the_man_CK survive this hard time. This would mean so much! PLZRESPOND. (Katrina Polansky)." This was followed by, "@OGOchoCinco Chad please come visit my friend Chris Kernich at Akron City Hospital. He suffered a bad head injury and he is your #1 Fan!! (Zack Siegrist)."

Given the fact that Johnson, at the height of his popularity, received hundreds of Tweets per minute, it came as no surprise that Kernich's friends did not hear back from him right away. Determined to reach Kernich's sports idol, his friends went to Facebook looking for a way to contact the Cincinnati Bengals to get word to Johnson to visit him in the hospital. Through a long series of contacts, they eventually got word to Bengals defensive line coach Jay Hayes through the following e-mail (please note that I retain the language and grammar in the original e-mail):

> To Whom It May Concern: One of my very close friends, Christopher Kernich, is at the Akron City SUMMA Hospital in Akron, OH in critical condition in the ICU. . . . He follows OchoCinco all day everyday. He even pays for his app on his phone to get updates about Cinco constantly. There is never a day that goes by when I don't hear something about him. WHO DEY!!!! is his favorite saying and he always has something to say about the Bengals. We all see Chad as kind of a role model for Chris, he plays the same position and Chris follows his every move.
>
> Now we're asking you to help us out. Maybe a phone call from the head coach or even Cinco himself would be amazing. We know if Chris heard either voices that it's going to help. There is nothing further we can do right now except pray for a miracle. We are asking from the bottom of our hearts for you guys to help us out.—Chelsea Groom[13]

Soon after Jay Hayes received the message, he contacted Johnson, confident that he would respond to this plea for help. Johnson indicated that he remembered seeing Tweets about a fan in trouble, but he was unaware of the details, stating that, "On Twitter you can only write so much. So when my coach explained it to me, I called the next day."[14] The following day, Johnson called the hospital to speak with Kernich on the phone. Kernich's sister, Stephanie Paynter, answered the phone and, after realizing who he was, informed Johnson that her brother had just died a few minutes earlier. Johnson recalls the situation saying, "I was sad, I was really sad. All I remember is saying, 'I'm sorry.' There's not much I can say in a situation like that."[15] Soon after Kernich's funeral, his friend, Kirk Stivers, sent the following Twitter message to Johnson: "@ogochocinco @the_man_CK was buried today with your jersey! A great person was laid to rest today. His memory will always be alive! RIP CK." Within five minutes of Stivers's Tweet, Johnson, who was scanning through the hundreds of messages the night before his game between the Cincinnati Bengals and the Cleveland Browns on November 29, 2009, responded with the following message: "@the_man_CK bruh I love you man, RIP, you'll never be forgotten, I'm playing for you tomorrow."[16]

This small act of kindness on the part of Chad Johnson obviously would have been much more unlikely to occur without the aid of social media. In the past, the best way fans could contact their favorite athletes was through autograph sessions or to find some obscure connection with an athlete to facilitate contact. Now, fans have any number of channels to interact with athletes through social media, especially Twitter, which seems to be the primary mechanism that allows for these types of interactions to take place more frequently and with less effort.

While many athletes shy away from the spotlight during their personal time, Chad Johnson not only encourages fans to talk with him if they see him in public, he actively creates events where he directly interacts with fans in a public setting. For instance, during the 2009–2010 and 2010–2011 seasons, before each away game, Johnson made it a regular practice to treat 85 fans (his jersey number) from the opposing team to dinner. Before the game against the Cleveland Browns on October 3, 2012, he sent out the following Tweet inviting Browns fans to dinner: "@ogochocinco #OCCNImHungryNews 1st 85 folks meet me at XO Prime Steakhouse for dinner. See you there, dinner starts at 6, drink till i get there #1Luv." Johnson had no problem filling up the XO Prime Steakhouse, and he brought a camera crew along to chronicle the event.[17] The video features a quick pace indicative of the Twitter style and shows him interacting with Cleveland

Browns fans who seem to genuinely like him as he signs autographs and takes pictures with them. In the video, Johnson takes the opportunity to show that he is much more gracious and friendly than the media portrays him. In addition, he tries to appeal to fans, suggesting that, even though he is one of the most well-known athletes in the United States, he is a regular guy who just wants to be liked by his friends.

Johnson's willingness to interact with fans extends not just within the world of football, but to fans of many other sports, as well as nonsports fans. During the course of his playing career, he appeared in numerous venues outside of sports, for example, VH1's 2010 reality television program *Ochocinco: Ultimate Catch*, a talk show on the Versus Network with then-teammate Terrell Owens entitled *The T.Ocho Show*, and as a contestant on the popular ABC prime-time program *Dancing with the Stars* in 2010. In addition, he made forays into other sports, including trying out for Major League Soccer's Sporting Kansas City team during the 2011 NFL lockout, and he performed at a Professional Bull Riders competition, where he lasted 1.5 seconds riding a 1,500-pound bull.[18] As might be expected, Johnson skillfully promoted himself using Twitter while participating in these events, which helped increase his celebrity status outside the sporting world. Through his continued use of social media and Twitter, it seemed likely that his popularity would remain intact long after his NFL playing career was finished.

As with all things in life, with the good comes the bad. Put in more scientific terms, Newton's Third Law of Physics states that for every action, there is an equal but opposite reaction. Newton intended for this to apply to objects in motion; however, metaphorically, this law of physics applies equally to human activities and the repercussions for those actions as they interact with other people in society. For the majority of his time on Twitter, Chad Johnson boosted his celebrity status and became one of the most high-profile Internet figures in the world of sports, and he did so in a relatively positive manner. Even though he had the reputation of being truculent with authority and acting as a selfish teammate, his exploits usually bordered on lighthearted tomfoolery, which made him a likable figure both on the field and with the various social media sites he frequently utilized. In his autobiography entitled *Ocho Cinco: What Football and Life Have Thrown My Way* (2009), he even calls attention to the fact that since he was in the NFL, he has never been arrested, accused of illicit drug or alcohol abuse, suspended for using performance-enhancing drugs, or beaten up any of his girlfriends.[19] Claims of this nature, along with the level of recognition Johnson attained throughout his career, can leave any public figure vulnerable for committing even the slightest transgression. As a result, anything a celebrity in Johnson's position does, good or bad, will attract a great deal of attention from the general public.

Newton's Third Law of Physics provides a good analogy for what happened to Johnson as his fortunes took a turn for the worse prior to the 2012 NFL season. Once he left the Cincinnati Bengals for the New England Patriots, and then later for the Miami Dolphins, his on-the-field production declined considerably. This happens to most athletes as they age in any sports simply because they are incapable of performing as well as they did at their physical prime. As a result, most aging athletes slip away from the spotlight unless some off-the-field incident draws the public's attention, usually through a controversy initiated by legal or financial problems or troubles in their personal lives (think O. J. Simpson). In the summer of 2012, while Johnson was vying for a roster spot on the Miami Dolphins, his personal life began to overshadow his athletic career due to several problems that arose soon after his marriage to *Basketball Wives* star Evelyn Lozada in July 2012. In true Chad Johnson fashion, he used Twitter to communicate with his fans during the wedding ceremony. Through the following Tweets, he portrayed himself as a typical groom, while infusing his own trademark humor in reaching out to his nearly 3.6 million followers (please note that I retain the language and grammar in the original Tweets):

- Live tweeting from my wedding . . . should be a first I'm assuming, music is playing, can't see my guest right now but they're here . . . #nervous.
- I'm breathing like a pregnant lady in lamaze class right now . . . I was hoping continuing to tweet with y'all support would calm me down.
- Here we go . . . Proverbs 18:22 . . . I love you guys . . . If I do it right the 1st time I won't have to do it again . . . Turn up . . .

- Small issue, I'm the only person that didn't/doesn't drink alcohol n every 1 is wasted including my WIFE, can't relate 2 this shit, now what?

The third Tweet is crucial regarding what would happen in the weeks following the wedding. By indicating that he was looking forward to being married and only once specifically, along with infusing the Tweet with a religious tone through the Proverbs 18:22 reference, which states, "He who finds a wife finds what is good and receives favor from the Lord,"[20] he opened himself up to even greater scrutiny than would be expected for any act of infidelity he might potentially commit against his new wife. This claim proved to be ironic once the truth came out regarding another way he was adeptly using social media to his advantage in reaching out to a more exclusive group of Twitter followers than his rank-and-file fans.

As it turned out, while Johnson used Twitter for so many years communicating with his football fans to increase his popularity, he was also using it in a more clandestine fashion in making connections with women for amorous encounters. According to an unnamed source from the website *Radar Online* (www.radaronline.com), "He [Johnson] is constantly scouring Twitter flirting with women, and if he sees someone he likes, he has them direct message their number to him so they can meet up in person."[21] The source further states that Johnson had been cheating on his wife as far back as during their engagement, indicating that he "has been carrying out a number of illicit affairs with several women for the past year, during which time he took them to his favorite bars, brazenly tweeted with them, and even let one girlfriend drive the Smart Car that *Basketball Wives* star Lozada [Johnson's former wife] bought him." Based on these claims, it appears that Johnson had a long history of using Twitter to facilitate his online salacious pursuits that ran concurrent with his employment of the social media site to promote himself as a "nice-guy" sports celebrity.

In spite of all this, it is quite possible that none of this information would have seen the light of day if a highly publicized domestic violence incident never occurred between Johnson and his new wife only one month into their marriage. The inciting incident occurred on August 11, 2012, when police were called to the couple's home after Johnson headbutted Lozada during an argument that broke out when she found a receipt for a box of condoms in the trunk of his car. As a result of this highly publicized incident, Johnson was charged with misdemeanor domestic battery and later released from jail on a $2,500 bond.[22]

Before the dust settled from his arrest, numerous accusations of womanizing and infidelity sprung up from various sources on the Internet. The day following Johnson's release from jail, a Boston woman by the name of Beverly Shiner claimed that she had an affair with Johnson while he was engaged to Lozada. Shiner claimed that, "she enjoyed a four-month-long relationship with Johnson, who [initially] asked her out for dinner after she contacted him through Twitter."[23] Johnson also had a romantic relationship with a stripper from Atlanta, Georgia, Amber Priddy, where Johnson allegedly paid her $2,000 a month to cover her rent until he was cut from the Miami Dolphins in August 2012.[24] As if this was not enough, it was later revealed that Johnson was having another affair with a woman by the name of Bianca Zuluga, who lived in Miami, Florida. The following Tweets by Zuluga suggest that the two had a long-standing romantic relationship that involved numerous sexually charged trysts (please note that I retain the language and grammar in the original Tweets). (As a point of reference, David's Cafe in Miami was their secret meeting place, and every time Zuluga uses the term *chocolate* she is directly referencing Johnson.):

- @Zulubibi I can't take this anymore I need chocolate!!! My body is going into shock! Sent 5/23/12 6:20 AM.
- @Zulubibi After driving a unique smart car today I'm in [three yellow emoticons with a smiley face and two red hearts for eyes] Sent 6/10/12 6:32 PM [in reference the Smart Car Lozada purchased for Johnson when they were engaged].
- @Zulubibi Ok my company really needs to stop tweeting! And David's cafe hits the spot so right!!! Sent 6/16/12 1:44 PM.
- @Zulubibi Omggggggg I want chocolate soooooooo bad!!!! Sent 6/27/12 9:01 PM.
- @Zulubibi Some people on my Twitter need to stop hating my preference for chocolate!!!, Sent 7/4/12 12:44 PM [the day of the wedding].[25]

In addition, another one of his mistresses, Amber Priddy, posted the following Tweet one week after Johnson's wedding as insults directed at Evelyn Lozada: "@amberpriddy U can marry him today, he's still mine!!! #thatsmyhoe2." This was followed by, "@amberpriddy Lmafo all of Evelyn's little fans are tweeting me talkin shit!!! Lol get a [expletive] life.[26]

These Tweets suggest that, despite Johnson's sentimental Twitter comments about the sanctity of marriage during his wedding, he had no plans to terminate any of his illicit affairs after he was married to Lozada. Most remarkable about these illicit affairs is that Johnson and his mistresses were openly brazen about their sexual exploits on Twitter, doing little to cover their tracks on one of the most popular gossip websites on the Internet. Johnson's carelessness is astonishing given what should have been a keen awareness on his part regarding the potential dangers of a high-profile figure, like himself, being exposed for facilitating unseemly sexual encounters through Twitter during his engagement with Lozada. He of all Twitter users should have understood how any type of information, no matter how coded or cleverly masked, can spread so quickly and ubiquitously on the Twitterverse.

The old adage "you live by the sword, you die by the sword" is an apt summation of Johnson's long journey to Internet stardom and eventual fall from grace through his prolific use of Twitter in drawing attention to himself. His experience is a seminal case study indicating the positive and negative aspects of both the proficient and reckless uses of Twitter by prominent athletes. As of now, almost all high-profile athletes use Twitter and other social media websites to communicate with fans and promote themselves both on and off the field. Johnson's example shows that Twitter and social media use can have a tremendous impact on an athlete's popularity and infamy. In the past, athletes have always been open to great scrutiny with mass media outlets for their positive activities, as well as their transgressions. Now, with the Internet and Twitter specifically, the margin for error with athletes, or any public figure, for that matter, is razor thin, and the slightest misdeed can result in disastrous pervasive negative publicity. Consequently, all celebrity athletes should navigate the Internet and social media cautiously, knowing that their actions are being viewed under the microscope of public scrutiny and have the potential to either elevate them to the heights of veneration or plummet them into the depths of ignominy.

THE 2012 LONDON SUMMER GAMES OF THE XXX OLYMPIAD, A.K.A. THE TWITTER OLYMPICS

Twitter and sports are ideally suited for one another. Given its simplicity and the fact that events occur so quickly during sporting events, Twitter is the perfect communication mechanism that allows sports fans attending a live event or watching it on television to make timely remarks with the potential to reach worldwide audiences. Twitter usage usually spikes during such high-profile occurrences as award ceremonies, political elections, celebrity weddings, and so on. One of the most commonly Tweeted-about incidents usually surrounds sporting events, where records for the number of Tweets per second (TPS) during the past few years have been set and then broken days later. For instance, during the 2010 Fédération Internationale de Football Association (FIFA) World Cup, 30 seconds after Japan scored against Cameron on June 14, 2010, 2,940 TPS broke the existing record.[27] Just three days later, on June 17, 2010, the record was broken after the Los Angeles Lakers won the NBA Championship when users posted 3,085 TPS.[28] Then, on June 25, 2010, the record was broken again soon after Japan's FIFA victory over Denmark, at 3,283 Tweets per second. This indicates not only how quickly Tweets per second records can change, but also that these records are often established during sporting events around the world as sports fans clamor to broadcast their opinions and comments to a worldwide audience.

The current record stands at 25,088 Tweets in one second, which occurred during the Japanese television broadcast of the Anime film *Castle in the Sky* (1986) on December 9, 2011, where fans sent Tweets at the same time to symbolically help the movie's character cast a spell; however, more than half of the current top 15 TPS records occurred during sporting events, including 15,358 TPS during the 2012 European Championship game, when Spain scored the winning goal against Italy, at number 2 on the list, along with the conclusion of Super Bowl XLVI at 12,233 TPS and Madonna's 2012 Super Bowl halftime performance at 10,245 TPS at the third and fourth spots, respectively.[29] [30] With the exception of some nontrivial events, including the death of Osama bin Laden at 6,939 TPS,[31] Steve Jobs's death at 6,049 TPS, and at one point after the 2011 Japanese earthquake at 5,530 TPS, this data clearly shows that, along with events that are of interest to the Japanese, sporting events elicit the most buzz and short-term interest in popular culture that result in the largest punctuated aggregations of instantaneous comments and opinions posted on Twitter.

The Olympic Games have always been one of the most high-profile and most watched sporting events. In the past, for those not in attendance at the official Olympic venue, Olympic fans had to rely on television broadcasts or mass media news reports to get any information about the events. Now, with the widespread use of social media for those fans willing to alter their sleeping patterns, Olympic spectators in remote parts of the world can witness live events as they occur on their portable viewing devices, all without having to rely on television network broadcast schedules. Along with having more control over when and how they view the Olympics, social media offers contemporary Olympic Games fans the ability to communicate their reactions and opinions with other fans around the world and the Olympic athletes themselves, where Twitter is at the forefront of Olympic fan-to-fan and fan-to-athlete interactions.

The connection between the Olympic Games and Twitter started in earnest during the 2008 Summer Games in Beijing; however, the exponential increase in Twitter activity from the 2008 Olympic Games to the 2012 London Summer Olympics is staggering, showing that fans are utilizing Twitter as their main form of communication about the event. According to the Neilson Company, "research revealed that there were more Tweets about the Olympics on the day of the 2012 London Games Opening Ceremony than during the entire duration of the 2008 Beijing Olympics."[32] Anticipating the eventual popularity of Twitter during the 2012 Olympic Games, NBC, the official broadcaster of the event for the United States, announced that, "Twitter [would] be the official narrator of the London Olympics," where Twitter staffers were enlisted to work in conjunction with NBC's social media team to ensure that news and other content appears in a timely fashion.[33] In addition, "NBC set up a Twitter hub during the games with televised messages showing the #Olympics hashtag" so that fans could make comments that would appear on the screen as events were taking place.[34] To facilitate the potential for even greater interaction between fans and athletes, the International Olympic Committee developed a "social media destination called 'the Olympic Athletes' Hub' that aggregates social media feeds from more than 1,000 athletes, including real-time updates on their Facebook and Twitter accounts, and actively encouraged athletes to post, blog, and Tweet their experiences during the games."[35] Clearly, all parties involved in providing coverage of the 2012 Olympics foresaw the potential to reach a vast number of viewers through Twitter and other social media outlets and sought to exploit these newfound technical means in allowing fans and athletes to more directly engage with one another in an unprecedented manner.

One of the main problems with the Olympic Games in terms of broadcasting the events worldwide in a timely manner lies in the different times zones that span the globe, where 12-hour differences in time are common between where the Olympics are being held and where they are being broadcast on television. For example, since Beijing is 13 hours ahead of New York, if fans in the United States wanted to watch Michael Phelps compete in the finals of the 200 meters freestyle medley relay live during the 2008 Olympics, they would have to watch the event in the middle of the night on a television network broadcast. Because of this time disparity, viewers often had to rely on tape-delayed broadcasts of their favorite events. More importantly, fans had to avoid mass media outlets if they wanted the results of the event to remain unknown until they had the chance to witness it for themselves, which was the common practice even as recently as the 2008 Beijing Olympic Games.

During the 2012 London Olympic Games, Twitter forever changed this dynamic. Real-time updates from both fans during the event and athletes soon after competitions ended became the way most fans around the world received information about the games. In this way, Twitter became a direct threat to the same mass media outlets that worked so hard to incorporate the microblogging site into their coverage of the games to enhance the viewer's experience. In addition, this meant that Twitter users who wanted to avoid spoiler alerts were blindsided by the onslaught of posts regarding numerous details about almost every Olympic event, where the outcome of each contest was often revealed long before fans had a chance to watch the time-delayed event. This was the most immediate impact Twitter had on the 2012 London Olympics; however, this minor inconvenience paled in comparison to some of the unforeseen controversies that would arise from its prolific and nearly inexhaustible use by fans and athletes throughout the events.

One of the first controversies surrounding Twitter took place after Hope Solo, high-profile goalie for the U.S. Women's Soccer Team, posted a series of polemic Tweets in response to former U.S. women's soccer star and now color commentator for NBC coverage of Olympic soccer Brandi Chastain's harsh criticism of Solo's defensive teammates. During the broadcast of the U.S. women's soccer match against Columbia on July 28, 2012, Chastain made the following disparaging comment regarding the U.S. women's performance: "As a defender, your responsibilities are to defend . . . win the ball, and then keep possession. And that's something that Rachel Buehler actually needs to improve on in this tournament" (20 minutes into the match). This was followed with, "I give the U.S. team's performance an A-minus, mostly because of defensive issues" (at the conclusion of the match).[36]

Solo, who took great exception to Chastain's comments, generated the following series of Tweets, all on July 28, 2012, soon after the match against Columbia (I retain the language and grammar in the original Tweets):

- Its 2 bad we cant have commentators who better represents the team&knows more about the game @brandichastain! #fb.
- Lay off commentating about defending and gking until you get more educated @brandichastain the game has changed from a decade ago. #fb.
- Its important 2 our fans 2 enjoy the spirit of the olympics.Its not possible when sum1 on air is saying that a player is the worst defender!
- I feel bad 4 our fans that have 2 push mute, especially bc @arlowhite is fantastic.@brandichastain should be helping 2 grow the sport #fb.

Chastain avoided a potential heated battle with Solo in exchanging snarky Tweets, but she did respond to Solo's Twitter comments through the following diplomatic statement to the press: "My only comment is I am in London to cover the women's soccer for NBC in an honest and objective fashion, and that is what I have done, and what I will continue to do for the rest of the tournament."[37] While the Twitter incident between Solo and Chastain gained a great deal of coverage in the press, it soon abated in light of another Olympic Twitter controversy, which involved athletes posting racist comments to their Twitter accounts.

The Olympic Games was originally envisioned as a symbol of international goodwill; however, it has also been used as a high-profile event for countries to symbolically assert their national dominance through athletic competition on the world stage that borders on jingoism. During the Cold War, Olympic competitions between the United States and the Soviet Union, most notably the controversial finish to the gold medal basketball game during the 1972 Munich Olympic Games, served as metaphorical battlegrounds between the two nations' contrasting ideologies of capitalism and communism. Since the fall of the Soviet Union and the end of the Cold War, this ideological element no longer predominates the tone of the Olympics; however, racism remains intact as a controversial issue.

For instance, during the 2008 Beijing Olympics, a pre-Olympics advertising photo for the Spanish basketball team created quite a stir with what many believed was an overtly racist gesture toward their Chinese host. In the photo, all members from both the men's and women's squads, dressed in their official Olympic gear and standing around a dragon symbol in the center of the basketball court, are shown pulling back the skin over their eyes, calling reference to the negative "slant-eyed" Chinese stereotype. Even though some of the Spanish players defended the photo, including the team's center, Pau Gasol, of the National Basketball Association's (NBA) Los Angeles Lakers, who stated that, "it was something supposed to be funny or something but never offensive in any way," and point guard Jose Manuel Calderon, also an NBA player, who said, "We felt it was something appropriate, and that it would be interpreted as an affectionate gesture," this was not how the mainstream press viewed it.[38] Regardless, the incident was most likely the result of carelessness and insensitivity rather than malice. During the 2012 London Olympics, racism reappeared, which Twitter use by certain Olympic athletes has only exacerbated.

The first incident involving racist Tweets occurred before the start of the 2012 Olympics, when Greek triple jumper Paraskevi Papahristou posted the following Tweet in reference to a small outbreak of the West Nile Virus in Greece in 2012: "With so many Africans in Greece, at least the mosquitoes of West Nile will eat homemade food!!!" While she intended this as a joke, she was harshly criticized for her comments, and many people on the Twitterverse responded negatively to her Tweet, indicating that it was an insensitive, mocking gesture toward Greece's African immigrant population.[39] Papahristou's first response was to defend her comments, and she went back to Twitter and posted the following message: "I'm not a stuck CD! And if I make mistakes, I do not hit replay! I continue playing!" This Twitter comment appeared to be coded language indicating that she intended to defiantly stick by her statements. Being an outspoken supporter of the Conservative Party in Greece, she drew harsh criticisms from Greece's coruling Democratic Left Party, who demanded her expulsion from the team.[40] A few days later, sensing that her spot on the Greek Olympic team was in jeopardy, she posted the following comment on Twitter: "I would like to express my heartfelt apologies for the unfortunate and tasteless joke I published on my personal Twitter account. I am very sorry and ashamed for the negative responses I triggered, since I never wanted to offend anyone, or to encroach human rights."

Once she Tweeted this message, it seemed that all might be forgiven when she received 800 likes for her apology, along with support on other social media websites, including several Facebook pages requesting that she remain on the Greek Olympic team. Unfortunately for her, the damage had already been done. Wanting to avoid a potential backlash for her racially insensitive comment, the Hellenic Delegations' Administration Board removed her from the team, citing that, "her comments go against the values and ideals of Olympism."[41] Despite public support in Greece for Papahristou to be reinstated to the team, much of which came through Twitter and Facebook, the board was unwilling to relent, fearful that her presence on the team might help fuel a growing anti-immigrant sentiment among the Greeks during their 2012 fiscal crisis.[42] This may have been Papahristou's last chance to make the Greek Olympic team, given the fact that the games occur every four years and an athlete's window of opportunity to compete in the Olympics sometimes fails to coincide with when they are at their physical peak. Sadly, her exclusion from the team was not due to a lack of athletic ability, but rather the result of what she deemed a seemingly harmless Twitter comment that reached a hypercritical worldwide audience, where the margin for error in public opinion is incredibly slim.

In contrast to Paraskevi Papahristou's more nuanced racial comment, during the 2012 Olympics, a member of the Swiss soccer team posted an openly racist Tweet that was unquestionably hostile toward the intended target. After Switzerland lost a match to South Korea on July 29, 2012, Swiss defender Michel Morganella, suggesting that he was "provoked" by comments sent to his Twitter account after the match,[43] posted the following Tweet to his account (translated from French): "I want to beat up all South Koreans! Bunch of mentally handicapped retards!" As might be expected, there was a swift backlash against his comment, resulting in an immediate suspension of his Twitter account, which was later deleted to avoid further controversy. Soon after this, Swiss Olympic officials announced that Morganella would be summarily removed from the team. Realizing the severity of his statement and as an act of contrition, Morganella then issued the following apology through the press (not Twitter): "I am sincerely sorry for the people of South Korea, for the players, but equally for the Swiss delegation and Swiss football in general. It's clear that I'm accepting the consequences."

Most South Korean fans were unimpressed by Morganella's apology, which is understandable given the malicious nature of his racist Tweet, and they indicated that they felt as though "[their] entire country was looked down upon by the Swiss player."[44] To pacify the situation, Swiss Olympic team official Gian Gilli issued the following official apology to the South Korean National Olympic Committee: "[Morganella] discriminated against, insulted, and violated the dignity of the South Korea football team as well as the South Korean people."[45] Without anticipating the repercussions for his inflammatory statement, the 23-year-old Morganella may have caused permanent and irreparable damage to his budding professional soccer career. It seems that no matter how many apologies he may issue, or even how well he performs on the soccer pitch, it is likely he will be best known for his racist Tweet during the 2012 London Olympics.

Both this incident and the one involving Paraskevi Papahristou from Greece are a clear indication that national tensions are alive and well, and that the Olympics remains a symbolic battleground between countries. More importantly, they are prime examples of how the irresponsible use of Twitter can have an adverse effect on an athlete's career regardless of whatever reparations they might offer in retrospect. All athletes worldwide need to keep in mind the power that resides in these seemingly trivial 140-character-or-less statements and use caution when expressing themselves on Twitter with the understanding that they are being held to a higher standard of conduct, even though they are just as emotional, flawed, and prone to making stupid comments as the fans who follow them.

THE TWEET HEARD 'ROUND THE SPORTS WORLD: KEVIN DURANT AND GEORGE OVERBEY PLAY INTRAMURAL FLAG FOOTBALL

The 1979 Coca-Cola commercial featuring then Pittsburgh Steelers All-Pro defensive lineman Mean Joe Greene is an idyllic depiction of how adoring fans and athletes interact. The narrative of the famous commercial depicts an injured Mean Joe Greene limping toward the locker room when a small boy offers him an ice-cold Coca-Cola. After Greene takes the soda and downs it in a few gulps, he calls out to the boy, saying, "Hey, kid. Catch." The boy catches the NFL star's sweaty jersey, wide-eyed in delight at having just received a matchless sports souvenir, and says, "Gee, thanks!" In reality, when sports fans and athletes meet in person, it is not quite so cinematic or sentimental. Most often, these types of interactions involve a starstruck fan mumbling a few banal words of admiration at a usually accommodating but often annoyed athlete who just wants a bit of privacy.

I remember the first time I met one of my favorite athletes in person as a child, Frank White, All-Star second basemen from the Kansas City Royals, at an autograph signing at a shopping mall in Omaha, Nebraska, during the off season. Even though the interaction was much more impersonal than the cloying scenario in the Mean Joe Greene Coca-Cola commercial, being in the presence of this larger-than-life figure from the 1985 World Series championship team was one of the most exciting moments I can recall as a young sports fan.

The second time I met a professional athlete in person it was as a young adult, and the meeting occurred by chance when I (literally) ran into Charles Barkley, famous NBA star, at a restaurant in Phoenix, Arizona. One of things I remember most about this meeting was the disparity in size from the towering, bulky figure he appeared to be on television when I watched him play for the Philadelphia 76ers and Phoenix Suns compared to his actual size, which was still considerable, at 6′6", but much more slender than I expected. What I found even more surprising was that he was much more humble, soft-spoken, and low-key than he conducted himself in interviews. At least when I saw him that night signing autographs and shaking hands with gawking fans as he patiently negotiated his way to his table, he proved to be very gracious with his fans, even with the ones who invaded his personal space.

These types of interactions can be thrilling for sports fans; however, in reality, moments like this are hard to come by without having an inside contact with a sports team. Even with the aid of the Internet and social media, making direct contact with famous athletes usually occurs through chance and simply being at the right place at the right time. This is exactly what happened in the fall of 2011, when a college student answered a Tweet from a NBA player that resulted in a unique and unprecedented interaction between sports fans and a professional athlete and attracted attention in mass media and the Internet.

The 2011–2012 NBA season was delayed due to a labor dispute where the owners locked out the players. While representatives from the National Basketball Player's Association negotiated with the ownership, NBA players could do little more than wait until a settlement was reached. On October 31, 2011, Halloween night, frustrated with the NBA lockout, Oklahoma City Thunder star Kevin Durant sent the following message on Twitter (please note that the following Tweets remain unedited for grammar and spelling): "This lockout is really boring . . . anybody playing flag football in Okc..I need to run around or something!" Within a few minutes, Oklahoma State University student George Overbey responded, Tweeting, "Got a game tonight in Stillwater!! I need a deep threat!!RT." Not expecting a reply from the NBA All-Star, Overbey was surprised and delighted at what transpired through additional exchanges of Twitter messages between him and Durant. Durant responded, "Can I play." Overbey came back, "Can you catch?? Weve won the 'ship for three years! Tonight @ 10 RT." Durant continued, "Forreal?" "Only if you bring your A game. Yes for real! Come up early and hangout, go over some plays RT," Overbey answered.

Figure 6.1. Kevin Durant towering over the other players on the field. ***Image courtesy of KT King***

Overbey then gave Durant his cell phone number over Twitter so they could meet before the game to work on some plays. Still incredulous that this was not a prank, he was amazed when Durant first called him for directions and even more so when Durant showed up at Overbey's house with his entourage and security guards. Overbey stated that, "When his car pulled up at the house, I was like, this is really happening. My friends didn't believe me."[46] Once Durant and Overbey met and practiced a bit with Overbey's team, they went to the Oklahoma State intramural fields to play the game. Once word quickly spread through Twitter and other social media sites that Kevin Durant was about to play in a flag football game with a bunch of Oklahoma State students, more than 500 spectators came to watch this historic interaction.[47]

Along with having the largest crowd in attendance for an intramural sport at Oklahoma State University, Kyle Porter, lead blogger for the school's sports blog, *Pistols Firing*, put together a sequence of updates from Twitter interspersed with photos from the game entitled "Kevin Durant—First Millionaire Flag Football Player . . . Ever." Twitter user

Figure 6.2. Oklahoma State University students on the sidelines taking pictures of Durant with their smart phones. ***Image courtesy of KT King***

@A_McGee (Andrew McGee) Tweeted, "So KD at the Intramural fields?" Tweeter @james ocolly (James Polling) then texted, "OU Sucks," which the crowd cheered loudly for. Then @ YoungRan1 (Joseph Randle) Tweeted, "Why is Kevin Durant really out here playing flag football at the flag football field?" Twitter user @ryancameron24 (Ryan Cameron) followed, texting, "Seeing pics of the crowd watching @KDTrey5 play flag football in Stillwater tonight, he may turn the intramural fields into Rucker Park West." And last, @KDTrey5 (Kevin Durant at the end of the game) Tweeted, "I had soooo much fun at Oklahoma st playing flag football! Shoutout to my new buddy @groverby [George Overbey] for inviting me! I threw 4 tds and had 3 ints!!"

After the game, several fans went to the "Kevin Durant—First Millionaire Flag Football Player . . . Ever" blog to post some of the following comments, praising Durant for playing in the game, complimenting Kyle Porter's skillful blogging of the event, and expressing wonder at how such an event could have occurred:

Figure 6.3. Kevin Durant making his move on the flag football field. ***Image courtesy of KT King***

"DJ Beck": I couldn't put my phone down. Thanks Kyle for bleeding orange and staying on top of things!

Brooke: Way to be timely—that was awesome! Love reading your blog, Kyle.

David Einstein: We need more people like Kevin Durant in the world. Simple as that.

"Vtrammell": Weirdest moment ever walking up to my 11 p.m. game and seeing 500 people there.

"Pogi2Woods": PFB [Pistols Firing Blog] just picked up by deadspin! /dong shot.

Ashley Acklin-Duren: Thank you Kevin for gracing us with your presence in Stillwater, Oklahoma last night!! You made a lot of people feel really special to get to meet you!!! You Rock!!!!

"K^2": This is UNREAL! Incredibly jealous of the other 13 guys on the field. That's a story they will be telling forever. This needs to hit the ESPN wire.

Figure 6.4. More students on the sidelines. ***Image courtesy of KT King***

The last comment proved to be prophetic when, the following day, ESPN took notice of the event. *SportsCenter* producers often allow fans to send in their homemade videos of high school sporting events or other interesting videos from the world of sports that ESPN camera crews are too busy to capture. These amateur videos mostly consist of a last-second full-court basket or a spectacular diving catch in baseball or football, and they usually get brief airplay, along with some commentary in *SportsCenter's* "Top 10 Plays of the Day" segment at the end of the program. Kevin Durant's flag football game with George Overbey and the students at Oklahoma State University not only caught the attention of the network, it also prompted *SportsCenter* to produce a featured segment devoted exclusively to the remarkable event. During the November 1, 2011, broadcast of *SportsCenter*, sportscasters started the segment by recounting the events leading up to the flag football game, citing the Twitter exchange between Durant and Overbey as the inciting incident. Once they set up the game, the image cut to amateur video footage of the game, where ESPN sports anchors provided voice-over commentary much like they would when recapping the highlights of a NFL game. The scene then cut back to the studio, where anchors

Figure 6.5. Kevin Durant getting into his car in front of a dense crowd of students taking pictures of him on their smart phones. ***Image courtesy of KT King***

interviewed Overbey via telephone, asking him to comment on how the event took place and his reactions to having the unique opportunity to play flag football with such a famous athlete, while a montage of images taken by Flickr user ShuttrKingKT illustrated some of the action that took place during the game.

Soon after the game ended the night before, LeBron James, superstar small forward of the Miami Heat, not wanting to miss out on the action and attention, learned about Durant's flag football game and Tweeted the following to Durant about the game: "I need that invite next time! That's really my sport!" Durant Tweeted back, "I got u, bro! But I'll lock u up, I had 3 picks..Coulda been 6." Not being one to shy away from the spotlight, James then challenged Durant to a flag football game, which was set to take place at the University of Akron a few days later, on November 30, 2011. Called the "LeBron Flag Football Challenge," this highly publicized event featured Team KD (Durant's team) versus Team Bron (James's team), and it was broadcast live on the Internet at UStream. The high-scoring game ended in Team Bron's favor, with a final score of 70–63, and it featured various highlights, including 108-yard interception return for a touchdown by Durant and a 51-yard touchdown catch by LeBron that sealed the victory for this team.[48] ESPN camera crews were there to capture some of the highlights, and the network featured video from the game in a segment devoted to the game on *SportsCenter* the following day. Along with no one getting injured as a result of the flag football game, much to the delight of the owners of the Miami Heat and Oklahoma City Thunder, the event was a resounding success with the public, and it helped alleviate some of the tensions between fans and NBA players while the 2011 labor dispute was being settled.

These remarkable events took place as a result of an ingenious use of social media, which was initiated by a prominent athlete reaching out to his fans though Twitter. Before social media and the Internet, for an event like this to have even the slightest chance of becoming a reality, it would have taken months to plan and involved a slew of media professionals to execute. Social media, especially Twitter, now make it possible to remove the middle players, that is, mass media, in bringing sports celebrities and sports fans together. Using Twitter as a direct means of communication between athletes and fans, more events like the Kevin Durant flag football game are sure to take place and provide a few lucky sports fans with a chance to add to their 15 minutes of fame.

NOTES

1. Bianca Bosker, "Twitter Finally Shares Key Stats: 40 Percent of Active Users Are Lurkers," *Huffington Post*, 29 November 2012, www.huffingtonpost.com/2011/09/08/twitter-stats_n_954121.html#s353852&title=Twitter_Comms (29 November 2012).
2. Dan Farber, "Twitter Sets Its Sights to 2 Billion Users," *Cnet.com*, 27 April 2012, http://news.cnet.com/8301-1023_3-57423213-93/twitter-sets-its-sights-on-2-billion-users/ (29 November 2012).
3. David Sarong, "Twitter Founder Jack Dorsey Illuminates the Site's Founding Document. Part I," *Los Angeles Times*, 18 February 2009, http://latimesblogs.latimes.com/technology/2009/02/twitter-creator.html (28 November 2012).

4. Ryan Kelly, "Twitter Study Reveals Interesting Results About Usage: 40% Is Pointless Babble," *Pear Analytics*, 12 August 2009, www.pearanalytics.com/blog/2009/twitter-study-reveals-interesting-results-40-percent-pointless-babble/ (6 August 2012).

5. Danah Boyd, "Twitter: 'Pointless Babble' or Peripheral Awareness and Social Grooming?" *Apophenia*, 16 August 2009, www.zephoria.org/thoughts/archives/2009/08/16/twitter_pointle.html (28 November 2012).

6. "Bengals' Ochocinco Plans to Tweet During Games," *Dayton Daily News*, 8 July 2009, www.daytondailynews.com/news/sports/football/bengals-ochocinco-plans-to-tweet-during-games-1/nM2Yg/ (25 November 2012).

7. Nate Davis, "Bengals WR Chad Ochocinco Fined $25,000 for Using Twitter During Game," *USA Today*, 24 August 2010, http://content.usatoday.com/communities/thehuddle/post/2010/08/bengals-wr-chad-ochocinco-fined-25000-for-using-twitter-during-game/1#.ULPpKoUmatc (26 November 2012).

8. Adam Ostrow, "How Chad Ochocinco Plans to Tweet During NFL Games," *Mashable Social Media*, 26 August 2009, http://mashable.com/2009/08/26/ocho-cinco-tweets/ (26 November 2012).

9. Jason La Canfora, "In-Game Tweet Costs Bengal's Ochocinco $25,000," *NFL.com*, 24 August 2010, www.nfl.com/news/story/09000d5d819fb95a/article/ingame-tweeting-costs-bengals-ochocinco-25000?module=HP_headlines (26 November 2012).

10. Davis, "Bengals WR Chad Ochocinco Fined $25,000 for Using Twitter During Game," http://content.usatoday.com/communities/thehuddle/post/2010/08/bengals-wr-chad-ochocinco-fined-25000-for-using-twitter-during-game/1#.ULPpKoUmatc.

11. Darren Rovell, "Chad Ochocinco Tops Most Influential Athletes in Social Media List," *CNBC*, 25 April 2011, www.cnbc.com/id/42749405 (26 November 2012).

12. Amy K. Nelson, "Fan, Friends Connected with Ochocinco," *ESPN.com*, 31 January 2011, http://sports.espn.go.com/nfl/news/story?id=4868696 (26 November 2012).

13. Nelson, "Fan, Friends Connected with Ochocinco," http://sports.espn.go.com/nfl/news/story?id=4868696.

14. Nelson, "Fan, Friends Connected with Ochocinco," http://sports.espn.go.com/nfl/news/story?id=4868696.

15. Nelson, "Fan, Friends Connected with Ochocinco," http://sports.espn.go.com/nfl/news/story?id=4868696.

16. Nelson, "Fan, Friends Connected with Ochocinco," http://sports.espn.go.com/nfl/news/story?id=4868696.

17. "Real Dude: Chad Ochocinco Connects With His Fans! (Paid for Everyone's Meal and Drinks)," *World Star Hip Hop*, 15 January 2011, www.worldstarhiphop.com/videos/video.php?v=wshhNut9Ids5k96YPHFo (26 November 2012).

18. Gary Mihoces, "Chad Ochocinco Continues Flirtation with Professional Bull Riders," *USA Today*, 11 May 2011, http://content.usatoday.com/communities/thehuddle/post/2011/05/chad-ochocinco-continues-flirtation-with-professional-bull-riders/1#.ULQrIIUmatc (26 November 2012).

19. Chad Johnson and Jason Cole, *Ocho Cinco: What Football and Life Have Thrown My Way* (New York: Crown Publishers, 2009), 6–7.

20. "Proverbs 18:22 (New International Version)," *Bible Gateway.com*, www.biblegateway.com/passage/?search=Proverbs+18%3A22&version=NIV (27 November 2012).

21. Debbie Emery, "Chad 'Ochocinco' Johnson Scores Dates on Twitter, Third Mistress He Picked Up Is Revealed!" *Radar Online.com*, 24 August 2012, www.radaronline.com/exclusives/2012/08/chad-ochocinco-johnson-twitter-third-mistress (27 November 2012).

22. James Walker, "Dolphins Cut WR Chad Johnson," *ESPN NFL*, 13 August 2012, http://espn.go.com/nfl/trainingcamp12/story/_/id/8263326/chad-johnson-cut-miami-dolphins-karlos-dansby-hates-move (27 November 2012).

23. "Chad 'Ochocinco' Johnson Cheated With Mistress for Four Months Before his Wedding as Wife Speaks Out for the First Time Since Attack and Files for Divorce," *Daily Mail Online*, 14 August 2012, www.dailymail.co.uk/news/article-2188278/Chad-Johnson-NFL-star-mistress-engagement.html (27 November 2012).

24. Emery, "Chad 'Ochocinco' Johnson Scores Dates on Twitter," www.radaronline.com/exclusives/2012/08/chad-ochocinco-johnson-twitter-third-mistress.

25. "Chad Johnson and Alleged Mistress Tweet," *Radar Online*, 23 August 2012, www.radaronline.com/photos/image/187633/2012/08/chad-johnson-and-alleged-mistress-tweet#image-load (27 November 2012).

26. "Two More Alleged Mistresses of Chad 'Ocho Cinco' Johnson Revealed (photos)," *Rucuss.com*, 24 August 2012 www.rucuss.com/gossip/two-more-alleged-mistresses-of-chad-ochocinco-johnson-revealed-photos/ (27 November 2012).

27. Tianyin Xu, Yang Chen, Lei Jiao, Ben Y, Zhao, Pan Hui, and Xiaoming Fu, "Scaling Microblogging Services With Divergent Traffic Demands" *Middleware 2011* (2011): 1.

28. Claire Cain Miller, "Sports Fans Break Record on Twitter," *New York Times*, 18 June 2010, http://bits.blogs.nytimes.com/2010/06/18/sports-fans-break-records-on-twitter/ (28 November 2012).

29. Brian Anthony Hernandez, "The Top 15 Tweets per Second Records," *Mashable.com*, 6 February 2012, http://mashable.com/2012/02/06/tweets-per-second-records-twitter/ (29 November 2012).

30. Nathan Olivarez-Giles, "Super Bowl XLVI Sets New Tweets per Second Record," *Los Angeles Times*, 6 February 2012, www.latimes.com/business/technology/la-twitter-super-bowl-46-new-york-giants-new-england-patriots-eli-manning-tom-brady-madonna-20120206,0,1184572.story (30 November 2012).

31. "Tweets per Second Mark Set During Finals," *ESPN*, 18 July 2011, http://espn.go.com/sports/soccer/news/_/id/6779582/women-world-cup-final-breaks-twitter-record (28 November 2012).

32. "The 'Socialympics' Ignites London," *Neilson.com*, 15 August 2012, http://sites.nielsen.com/london2012/the-socialympics-ignites-london/ (29 November 2012).

33. Erik Sass, "NBC Taps Twitter as 'Official Narrator' for Olympics," *Media Post Blogs*, 23 July 2012, www.mediapost.com/publications/article/179366/nbc-taps-twitter-as-official-narrator-for-olympi.html?edition=49332#axzz2DdfH5F58 (29 November 2012).

34. Sass, "NBC Taps Twitter as 'Official Narrator' for Olympics," www.mediapost.com/publications/article/179366/nbc-taps-twitter-as-official-narrator-for-olympi.html?edition=49332#axzz2DdfH5F58.

35. Sass, "NYT Hosts Google+ Hangouts with Olympic Athletes," www.mediapost.com/publications/article/178586/nyt-hosts-google-hangouts-with-olympic-athletes.html?edition=48908#axzz2DdfH5F58.

36. Matt Kryger, "Hope Solo Bashes Brandi Chastain on Twitter," *USA Today*, 29 July 2012, http://usatoday30.usatoday.com/sports/olympics/story/2012-07-28/hope-solo-twitter-brandi-chastain-olympics-soccer-tweets/56561338/1 (30 November 2012).

37. Allison Corneau, "Exclusive: Brandi Chastain Responds to Hope Solo's Twitter Rant," *US Weekly*, 31 July 2012, www.usmagazine.com/celebrity-news/news/brandi-chastain-responds-to-hope-solos-twitter-rant-2012317#ixzz22Dl4fHUw (30 November 2012).

38. "Spanish Players Defend Racially Controversial Photo," *USA Today*, 13 August 2008, http://usatoday30.usatoday.com/sports/olympics/beijing/2008-08-13-spain-basketball_N.htm (1 December 2012).

39. Alon Harish, "Greek Jumper Expelled for Racist Tweet," *ABC News*, 25 July 2012, http://abcnews.go.com/International/greek-olympic-jumper-expelled-racist-tweet-defenders-flock/story?id=16856393#.ULpg5oUmate (1 December 2012).

40. "Greek Triple Jumper Paraskevi Papahristou Withdrawn from Olympics Following Racist Tweet about African Immigrants," *Independent*, 25 July 2012, www.independent.co.uk/sport/olympics/news/greek-triple-jumper-paraskevi-papachristou-withdrawn-from-olympics-following-racist-tweet-about-african-immigrants-7976442.html (1 December 2012).

41. Harish, "Greek Jumper Expelled for Racist Tweet," http://abcnews.go.com/International/greek-olympic-jumper-expelled-racist-tweet-defenders-flock/story?id=16856393#.ULpg5oUmate.

42. Harish, "Greek Jumper Expelled for Racist Tweet," http://abcnews.go.com/International/greek-olympic-jumper-expelled-racist-tweet-defenders-flock/story?id=16856393#.ULpg5oUmate.

43. Graham Dunbar, "Swiss Olympic Team Expels Player for Racist Tweet," *CBS News*, 31 July 2012, www.cbsnews.com/8301-505245_162-57483445/swiss-olympic-team-expels-player-for-racist-tweet/ (1 December 2012).

44. Dunbar, "Swiss Olympic Team Expels Player for Racist Tweet," www.cbsnews.com/8301-505245_162-57483445/swiss-olympic-team-expels-player-for-racist-tweet/.

45. Dan Evon, "Racist Tweet Gets Michel Morganella Kicked off the Swiss Olympic Soccer Team," *Inquisitor*, 30 July 2012, www.inquisitr.com/288467/racist-tweet-gets-michel-morganella-kicked-off-swiss-olympic-soccer-team/ (1 December 2012).

46. "NBA Star Durant Plays in Intramural Flag Football Game on Oklahoma State Campus," *Houston Chronicle*, 1 November 2011, http://blog.chron.com/hottopics/2011/11/nba-star-durant-plays-in-intramural-flag-football-game-on-oklahoma-state-campus/ (2 December 2012).

47. Kyle Porter, "Kevin Durant—First Millionaire Flag Football Player . . . Ever," *Pistols Firing: OK State Sports Blog*, 31 October 2011, www.pistolsfiringblog.com/kevin-durant-first-millionaire-flag-football-player-ever#more-2861 (2 December 2012).

48. Tom Weir, "The LeBrons Beat the Kevin Durants in Flag Football," *USA Today*, 1 December 2011, http://content.usatoday.com/communities/gameon/post/2011/12/the-lebrons-beat-the-kevin-durants-in-flag-football/1#.ULvNcYUmatc (2 December 2012).

7

CONCLUSION

SOCIAL MEDIA'S IMPACT ON MODERN SOCIETY

A few years ago, the aphorism "if you are not on Facebook, it is quite possible that you don't exist" was intended as a clever joke.[1] Today, this statement serves more as a fitting description about one's status in contemporary society rather than an ironic quip. Social media has become so prolific in modern society that those who fail to use it on a regular basis are considered by some to be abnormal. Psychologist Christopher Moeller supports this claim by suggesting that using Facebook and other social media applications has become a sign of a person being well adjusted and having a healthy social network.[2] Going a step further, according to *Forbes*:

> Human resources departments across the [United States] are becoming more wary of young job candidates who don't use the site [Facebook]," which they say the "common concern among bosses is that a lack of Facebook could mean the applicant's account could be so full of red flags that it had to be deleted.[3]

Soon after the July 20, 2012, fatal theater shooting in Aurora, Colorado, on the opening night of *The Dark Knight Rises* (2012), the *Daily Mirror* published an article suggesting that,

> Not having a Facebook account could be the first sign that you are a mass murder, and that theater shooter James Holmes, who is accused of killing 12 people and an unborn child and wounding 58 others at a movie theater in Aurora, Colorado, and Norwegian mass murder Anders Behring Breivik, who murdered 77 people with a car bomb and mass shooting, did not use Facebook and had small online footprints.[4]

Advice columnist Emily Yoffee, writing for *Slate.com*, adds the following assessment when referring to social media and romantic relationships: "If you're of a certain age and you meet someone who you are about to go to bed with, and that person doesn't have a Facebook page, you may be getting a false name. It could be some kind of red flag."[5]

Although claims like this are debatable and much research would need to be conducted to substantiate these statements, social media is nevertheless a vital component of the way people interact with one another in almost every aspect of today's hypermediated, fast-paced society. In all likelihood, the vast majority of people who avoid using Facebook are not as maladjusted as the aforementioned statements suggest; however, those who do not use social media are likely to remain outliers in modern popular culture, as a growing number of people are choosing to shun mass media while simultaneously increasing their engagement with the world through the Internet and social media.

On the other hand, there are some who take the opposite stance, claiming that social media is detrimental and inhibits healthy interpersonal interactions. In direct response to the various previously mentioned claims, Erik Sass from Media Post Blogs wrote an article as a counterpoint entitled "9 Reasons to Quit Social Media Now." In the article, he states that, "people who fail to use social media on a regular basis are not psychopaths, we may be highly employable, and we have good reasons for not using social media."[6] The following are Sass's nine reasons to either reduce or completely avoid using social media, along with studies and other justifications supporting each one of the reasons people should avoid using it:

- It is a waste of time. A survey conducted in November 2011 by Ryan Linton of Zynga, the company that specializes in online social games, says that the average user spends 6.5 hours per week playing games—games [that] are precisely engineered to suck you in by being just the right level of hard but not too hard.
- It is addictive and unhealthy. Researchers in Norway have indicated that people use Facebook to forget about personal problems, and they use it so much that it has a negative impact on their job, studies, or personal lives.
- It encourages envy and narcissism. A study by the University of Salford, in Britain, found several negative outcomes from social media use, including feelings of insecurity or lack of confidence when users compared their online achievements to that of their friends.
- It takes you away from the real world. Sass himself points out that by inviting you to pore over other people's (carefully crafted representations of their own) lives, or obsess over how you choose to represent your own life to them, social media ironically distracts you from actually living it.
- It encourages superficial relationships. Sass poses the questions, is it really safe to assume your friends are telling you everything that's going on with them through social media? Is it possible that they would share something more private over a bottle of wine or a game of racquetball?
- It brings up privacy concerns and unethical business practices. Sass asserts that this alone should be enough to convince most people not to use social media.
- It can be personally and professionally dangerous. Sass points out that once something is on the Internet, it will live there forever, and one inappropriate comment can permanently damage someone's reputation [look no further than the racist Tweets posted by Olympic athletes during the 2012 London Olympic Games and the ensuing controversies discussed in Chapter 6, "Twitter's Impact on Sports"].
- It is expected. Sass indicates that using social media is a secondary layer of social norms [that] should be completely optional, much like other personal life choices, and that people should not be looked down upon if they chose to avoid using social media.

- It is only going to get worse. Since many social media companies are constantly looking for new ways to continually increase everyone's engagement with social media through every means available, more businesses are likely to exploit and manipulate people as their personal information becomes more public through social media analysis and tracking.[7]

Whether or not either of these diametrically opposed viewpoints regarding the use of social media proves accurate, social media is a powerful driving force in society that will affect almost every aspect of civilized life and continue to do so for many generations to come. As such, spectators and athletes alike will need to learn and properly navigate the rules of engagement with social media in staying informed in the world of sports and being recognized for their activities as sports fans and players, respectively.

THE FUTURE OF SOCIAL MEDIA AND SPORTS

An AT&T commercial that aired during the 2012 college football season features a running back for an unnamed high school performing a spectacular front flip over a defender on the way to a touchdown. The commercial then shows a person in the crowd watching the game and filming the remarkable play on their smart phone video camera. Immediately after the play, the person who captured the video shares it on YouTube and spreads word about it on Twitter. A quick montage follows, indicating that the video spreads to a wide range of people across the United States through social media. Near the climax of the commercial, Oklahoma Sooners head coach Bob Stoops visits the high school running back to recruit him for his football team, suggesting that he did so because of the viral video of the running back's performance that spread to him through Twitter and social media.

While this commercial specifically features a high-profile college football coach being able to make contact with a potential recruit who would otherwise be separated by great physical distance through social media as its main narrative, the advertisement also illustrates the power of Twitter and other social media applications in facilitating communication between sports fans and athletes at a grassroots level. The fact that a large mass media corporation like AT&T produced a commercial featuring this scenario testifies to the power social media sites the likes of Twitter have in bridging the gap between sports fans and sports celebrities. Numerous real-life examples have recently emerged that mirror the situation in the AT&T advertisement, and they are clear indications about the ways in which sports fans and athletes are currently interacting and will continue to interact in the future. As more and more social media options rise to prominence with users, and with what are certain to be vast improvements in smart phones, tablets, and whatever the next generation of personal computing devices will be, the virtual gap between sports fans and celebrity athletes will continue to shrink. Moreover, social media will be used as a platform for businesses in reaching out to existing sports fans and attracting new ones as potential media consumers.

SPORTS SPECTATORSHIP AUDIENCE ANALYSIS THROUGH SOCIAL MEDIA

Social media serves as an effective way to track a wide range sports fans' online activities. This type of information is highly sought after, and marketing firms draw upon it when targeting potential customers with micro-ads on Facebook and other social media websites. In the past, businesses needed to conduct long-term studies through phone surveys and other forms of time-consuming methods of data collection to chart consumer viewing trends in all types of media entertainment. Now, potential advertisers have the ability to collect massive amounts of data in a relatively short period of time by utilizing algorithms in software programs to monitor trends and patterns regarding user activity on popular social media websites. Armed with this highly focused information regarding the online viewing habits of sports fans, businesses can better tailor advertisements for specific audiences and maximize their efforts in reaching the largest number of consumers in the most efficient manner.

The State of the Media: U.S. Digital Consumer Report Q4-Q4 2011 is a study conducted by the Nielson Company. It provides a wide range of information regarding the online habits of several demographics in the United States. The study also provides a breakdown of what devices certain groups are likely to use when accessing the Internet. The report provides a surplus of information that could help advertisers target specific demographics by examining their classifications of specific device and application usages based on age and gender.

The report begins by charting significant milestones in the development of the Internet from 2000 to 2011. It lists the following milestones and statistics regarding changes in Internet usage patterns during the past decade:

- As of 2011, 275 million Americans have Internet access, which is more than double the amount in 2000 (132.2 million).
- In 2009, social networks/blogs became the top online destination, accounting for 9.2% of Internet time, surpassing e-mail as the top category.
- In 2011, 81 billion minutes were spent on social media networks/ blogs.
- Also in 2011, 64% of mobile phone time was spent on applications, and 42% of tablet users used their devices daily while watching television.
- The number of laptops surpassed the number of desktop computers within homes with televisions.[8]

This information indicates that since so many people in the United States have Internet access in homes with televisions, and that many of the same people engage with their personal computers or tablets while watching television, companies can no longer exclusively rely on television as a way to reach their customers. In addition, this data clearly shows that users spend the majority of their time on the Internet visiting social networks and blogs; therefore, the Internet exists as fertile ground in reaching a huge number of potential media consumers through a wide range of social media platforms.

Another bit of significant information from this report indicates that most people use some type of personal computing device to access the Internet while watching television. The study provides the following breakdown of what types of online activities users are performing while watching television during television programs:

57% checked e-mail.

44% surfed for information unrelated to the program they were watching.
44% visited social networking sites.

The following is a similar breakdown of the online activities these same users perform during television commercial breaks:

59% checked e-mail.
44% surfed for information unrelated to the program they were watching.
44% visited social networking sites.

The report also provides the following ranking of the top websites users visit while watching television:

1. Facebook
2. YouTube
3. Zynga
4. Google Search
5. Yahoo! Mail
6. Craigslist
7. eBay
8. Electronic Arts (EA) Online
9. MSN/Windows Live/Bing
10. Yahoo! Homepage

This data shows where television multiscreen multitaskers are spending the majority of their time on the Internet and on which specific sites they are likely to visit while watching television. Although it is extremely difficult to know where these users might be surfing for unrelated information while watching television, the data points to e-mail and social networking sites as popular destinations for these multitaskers. This provides advertisers with clear online targets in sending timely ads and messages to potential customers during television broadcasts.

The report then delivers the following breakdown of the specific activities these multiscreen television viewers are performing online:

45% used a downloadable application.
34% checked sports scores.
29% looked up information related to the television program they were watching.

19% looked up product information for an ad they saw on television.
16% looked up information about coupons or deals related to an advertisement they saw on television.

This information provides advertisers with an even greater level of differentiation regarding online activities during television broadcasts, giving them knowledge of what behaviors they should follow and appeal to when placing online advertisements. More importantly, the fact that 19% of these viewers looked up information regarding an advertisement they saw during a broadcast and 16% did the same about coupons or deals related to a commercial they saw creates a rippling effect in the spread of their advertisements. Much like an echo, if people who witness a television advertisement are likely to research that product online after viewing the ad, the message of an advertisement can be self-propagating on the Internet and, through this "echo-advertising," allow for even greater exposure about a product beyond the original broadcast of the commercial. In addition, because many of these same viewers (44%) spend time on social networking sites both during television broadcasts and commercial breaks, even greater reach is possible as these users spread the word about an advertisement that caught their attention with their Facebook and Twitter friends. With this information, businesses are taking the initiative in providing direct links on the screen regarding a product during commercial advertisements where consumers can learn more about a product and spend more time engaging with information about the benefits of a product than the original 30- or 60-second commercial spot allows. For example, Sun Drop soda produced a series of popular commercials featuring a young woman and young man performing comical dances. These advertisements became the most buzzworthy on the Internet, generating 255,000 social media comments.[9]

Information from this report can help businesses reach more multitasking sports fans online as they watch television. As indicated by the fact that 34% of these same viewers are checking sports scores, there is a great interest among many of these television viewers in gaining sports information online during their viewing experience, even if they are not watching a sports-related program. As such, information gleaned from this report and other forms of analyses of social media sites could assist businesses in determining which demographics are more likely to use a specific social media application during a particular television broadcast. For instance, advertisers might see that 63.7% of married men who use Facebook and list football as their main interest can microtarget Facebook pages of this demographic with ads that will likely appeal to this group in maximizing their advertising costs.[10] In addition, targeting specific social media sites like Twitter and Facebook with online advertisements during commercial breaks on television broadcasts allows for deeper penetration of product advertisement to audiences. Moreover, these ads have the potential for even greater reach to online users who might not have actually seen a buzzworthy advertisement but gained information about the ad's content on social media from other users who saw the ad.

Having an awareness of the location and activities of potential consumers on the Internet is important information that all businesses work hard to generate and obtain. In this way, social media analysis provides a constantly updated data stream of user activity on almost all aspects of consumption in modern society. This type of analysis has led to corporate mass media outlets, including sports networks, incorporating social media as much as possible in their long-term programming and advertising strategies.

THE 2012 NFL PRO-BOWL IN-GAME TWITTER EXPERIMENT: WILL THIS BE THE NORM?

National Football League (NFL) football is one of the most popular forms of sports entertainment. The Super Bowl alone is the most watched live sports television program in the United States. In 2012, the game attracted 111.3 million viewers, supplanting the previous year's Super Bowl at the top spot in American television history.[11] According to Glen Levy from Time NewsFeed.com, "until the 2010 Super Bowl broadcast when the New Orleans Saints beat the Indianapolis Colts, the series finale of *M*A*S*H* had famously held the record for 27 years with an impressive tally of just [fewer than] 106 million, but [at that time] the Super Bowl [took] over the top two spots, as well as numbers four and five."[12] Pat McDonough, senior vice president for insight and analysis at the Nielsen Company, states that the "number of people watching NFL games has never been higher, with 24% more people watching the average NFL game this year than just five years ago. The Super Bowl continues to be in a category of its own."[13] This trend is expected to repeat with successive Super Bowls, making it not just a popular sporting event, but also a cultural and social phenomenon in the United States that attracts a wide continuum of viewers, ranging from avid football fans to people who might not watch any other sporting event the entire year.

In addition, even regular-season NFL football games top the television ratings charts on a weekly basis. NBC's *Sunday Night Football* often ranks as one of the most-viewed television programs during its time slot. A stark example of the drawing power of NFL football with television viewers occurred on October 28, 2012. On this night, the *Sunday Night Football* regular-season game between the New Orleans Saints and Denver Broncos earned 16.17 million viewers, while the final game of the 2012 Major League Baseball (MLB) World Series between the San Francisco Giants and Detroit Tigers drew only 15.5 million viewers on Fox.[14] According to the Nielson Company, *Sunday Night Football* is often number one on the charts of prime time broadcast total viewership each week. On December 2, 2012, " *Sunday Night Football* was again the highest-rated program among adults 18–49, and it was also number 1 with total viewers," beating out CBS's *Big Bang Theory*, ABC's *Modern Family*, and NBC's *The Voice*.[15] Clearly, NFL games, whether regular-season or postseason, are some of the hottest television properties, and they consistently attract large numbers of viewers across many demographics.

There is one NFL game that has never been as popular with television audiences as regular-season and postseason games: the NFL Pro Bowl. This is the NFL's all-star game, which usually occurs the week after the Super Bowl, and even though it is the most-watched all-star event in American professional sports, it seems to lack luster with many NFL enthusiasts.[16] In an attempt to draw more fans and improve the quality of the Pro Bowl, the NFL temporarily suspended one of their rules regarding social media during the games and allowed Pro Bowl athletes to communicate with fans on the sidelines using Twitter, Facebook, and other social media applications during the 2012 Pro Bowl. They even went so far as to provide players with computers on the sidelines to allow them to constantly update content on their social media sites. The following are some of the Tweets the players posted during the game (please note that I retain the language and grammar in the original Tweets):

- Jimmy Graham, New Orleans Saints: Almost Kick off time at Aloha stadium . . . excited to play in my first Pro Bowl . . . go NFC. YOLO.
- Eric Weddle, San Diego Chargers: Now that's what I call a pregame performance that was beautiful #godblessamerica.
- Mike Wallace, Pittsburgh Steelers: Having a great time out here with some awesome players!! Plus we get to tweet on top of that!!!!
- Brandon Marshall, Miami Dolphins: The ball just fell in my hands!! All glory to god. I promise it wasn't me. Fins up![17]

Unfortunately, not all the Tweets were so well-received by the NFL. The following Tweet posted by Washington Redskins linebacker London Fletcher caught the ire of league officials and caused a minor controversy during the game: "$500 to whoever predicts the final score. Must be my follower. $1000 if you predict the score and MVP. deadline halftime." Fletcher admits that he made this offer simply as a goodwill gesture to his fans; however, the NFL viewed it as an endorsement of gambling. Gambling is obviously a huge part of all professional sports, and NFL games inspire a rather sizable amount of wagering, both legal and otherwise; however, the league does not publicly endorse gambling, going so far as to "prevent its broadcast partners [from discussing] point spreads on games."[18] Therefore, since the league encouraged Pro Bowl players to communicate with their fans through social media and then facilitated it by providing them with computers on the sidelines, the NFL had to distance themselves from Fletcher's friendly wager.

NFL officials immediately informed Fletcher that he would have to rescind his offer or face a fine. Soon after this request by the league, Fletcher posted the following Tweet: "Just found from the NFL i can't make that offer . . . sorry. i'll think of something for you all later that won't get me in trouble." After consulting with NFL officials, Fletcher came up with a compromise, as illustrated in the following Twitter comment: "Autographed pro bowl jersey to the 1st person that predicts final score! 3rd Quarter deadline must 1 of my followers!" This offer of giving away an autographed jersey was acceptable with NFL officials. All parties were satisfied, allowing the league to distance itself from the perception that they were endorsing gambling and helping Fletcher save face with his Twitter followers. Aside from the London Fletcher Twitter incident, the rest of the Tweets from the Pro Bowl game came from players sharing details about particular plays or relaying some other bit of innocuous information to fans.

Whether or not the NFL ultimately decides to allow players to communicate through social media during games as a regular practice during the regular season and playoffs remains to be seen. With the number of entertainment options available to media consumers that involve direct engagement through social media, in all likelihood, the NFL might have to concede on their in-game social media ban at some point in the near future. Even though all professional sports leagues in the United States have strict rules against their athletes communicating with fans through social media during competitions, league officials might want to rethink their positions, because lifting these bans would allow for an exponential increase in their respective fan bases. As evidenced by the response Brad Keselowski received from his fans by Tweeting during the 2012 Daytona 500, where he added 130,000 followers in the three and half hours it took to compete in the race,[19] incorporating social media as part of the live game experience with athletes appears to be a surefire way to attract previously unreachable demographics, especially those that engage with popular culture primarily through social media.

SOCIAL MEDIA AT THE STADIUM AND LIVE SPORTING EVENTS

Another area that is becoming a more important consideration in the world of sports is how to better incorporate social media as part of the live sporting event entertainment experience at sports stadiums and arenas. Professional and college sports teams have found that attracting fans to live games is more challenging than ever, especially with the widespread availability of high-definition televisions. In addition, new devices and applications are being developed at a rapid pace to help increase sports fan interactivity with almost every aspect of sports from anywhere in the world. With this in mind, the only way to get more people "off the couch" and into the stadium is to make the viewing experience at the ball park as entertaining and comfortable as it is watching the game at home.

At the most basic level, to encourage more spectators to attend games in person, professional and college teams are working to provide spectators with free Wi-Fi Internet access in existing stadiums and arenas. In a NPR interview conducted by Ben Bergman with David Holland, who runs the sports and entertainment division of tech giant Cisco, the two discussed the importance of integrating social media into the live sports viewing experience and how this has become a primary concern for many parties involved in the sports entertainment world. In the interview, Holland states that, "The next generation of sports fans really expect to have more of an integrated experience, watching a live event [with the ability] to surf the Internet or access social networking aspects [much in the same way] that they engage in [these practices] throughout their day."[20] He further indicates that his company is experimenting with some upgrades in the digital experience at live sporting events through social media, including setting up applications that allow fans to order food and drinks from their portable devices and have the ability to watch "customizable instant replays on [their] smart phones at anytime from anywhere in the stadium."[21]

In addition, many sports stadiums in the United States, as well as worldwide, now offer fans several new social media applications that help simulate the home-viewing experience. Along with providing fans with elaborate, high-definition jumbotrons, for example, the world's largest video board at Cowboy's Stadium in Dallas, Texas, Gillette Stadium in Foxboro, Massachusetts, provides fans with a specialized application known as "Patriots Game Live." This new application "gives fans with smart viewing devices four live camera feeds of the game they are watching, as well as the NFL RedZone channel, providing highlights and live action from every game in the NFL," which, in many ways, is a direct accommodation to the millions of fantasy sports owners.[22] These new social media features are the first of many innovative designs that both sports teams and Internet providers will offer to sports fans in an attempt to lure them away from the comfort of their own homes to experience the event at the live sporting venue.

This might be a distant reality given the many difficulties contemporary teams have in trying to incorporate Digital Age technology in stadiums and arenas that were built long before Internet connectivity was a part of the planning and construction process. For example, historic stadiums like Fenway Park, home field for the Boston Red Sox, might be one of the most popular MLB parks, but the design of the stadium is troublesome when it comes to getting a good digital communications signal inside the park. According to Red Sox IT director Steve Conley, in the past, "if you were an AT&T user at Fenway you essentially walked into a black hole by the time the first pitch happened, and service would return at the end of the game."[23] Stanford University's home stadium in Northern California is another older stadium where it is difficult to get a strong Wi-Fi or cellular signal. Stanford's athletic director, Kevin Blue, once said the following regarding the problem: "They view connectivity as a business problem, in that our constituency is particularly comfortable with technology and has high expectations. Stanford Stadium is sometimes the only place in Silicon Valley where people can't use their mobile devices, and that's troubling to us."[24]

Even though upgrades to digital technology infrastructures in older stadiums is an ongoing process, integrating Wi-Fi and cellular signals into the everyday experience of live sports viewing at stadiums designed prior to the Digital Era is likely to be a problem for the foreseeable future, thereby making it more difficult to attract more fans to the venues.

FANATIX: THE SPORTS FANS' IDEAL SOCIAL MEDIA APPLICATION

Even though sports fans have been utilizing social media outlets like Twitter and Facebook, among many others, to engage in the world of mediated sports, as of 2012, there is no social media application in the United States devoted solely to information sharing among sports fans. That is, until now. In October 2011, a United Kingdom–based company created a social media application called fanatix, which *Forbes* magazine says is a

> free iOs 'social TV app' exclusively for sports fans, providing them a personalized stream of sports content—news updates, tweets, video clips, live scores, and stats—and enabling easy sharing of that content to personalized groups, known within the app as "huddles," which consist of group chats for sports fans.[25]

According to fanatix's chief executive officer and founder, Will Muirhead, when questioned as to what inspired the creation of the social television app, also speaking for his cocreators, he claims, "Our original thinking was that you find yourself watching sports alone, and that's ridiculous." He continues, saying that as sports fans themselves, they grew tired of having to "dig through a Twitter stream to find relevant Tweets or worry that the message will be lost among a plethora of others unrelated to the live game being watched."[26] The following is the description of the fanatix application that appears on the iTunes store website:

- Official video highlights from English football club channels, Serie A, Ligue 1, MLS, and Brasileiro.
- Real-time feed of all the latest sports news from the leading sports blogs and websites around the world.
- One-touch personalization for a feed of only articles from the teams you follow.
- Official Instagram feeds from the clubs you follow.
- Official Twitter feeds from the clubs you follow.

Soccer fans currently dominate the main user base of fanatix, but the company is confident that it is only a matter of time before the application catches on with all other types of sports. After launching their site in October 2011, in Europe, the website has "received more than 250,000 downloads and has a daily active user base of [more than] 35,000, [and] the average *fanatix* user, who [is] mostly [13 to 24 years of age and male], accesses the app five-and-a-half times a day, with the average registered user accessing the service [more than] 10 times per day."[27] While still working out some of the bugs in the earliest versions of the application, judging by the following customer reviews on the iTunes store page, fanatix seems to be an effective and popular sports information-sharing application:

- “Cntrlvsoption,” October 23, 2011 (regarding version 1.0): “Really like this app! Don’t really have anything that will let me talk to my friends at a game except SMS. I guess I can also chat with my friends, not at the game too. Really cool. I can also see which events my mates are going to. I can’t wait to use it at the next game. Go Rangers!”
- “greekst,” November 1, 2011 (about version 1.0): “Works as described. Great concept!”
- “Unclee81” (about version 1.2): “Awesome app. Very useful and fun.”
- “Carlos chaplin, October 8, 2012 (regarding version 2.4): “Chile premier division por favor,” requesting that fanatix include coverage of the Chilean First Division of Professional Football on the application.

In an effort to reach out to markets around the world, fanatix created partnerships with several high-profile sports outlets, including Manchester City, ESPN, and Eurosport, and, according to Muirhead, they plan to make many more U.S.-based partnership announcements in the near future. On October 30, 2012, fanatix launched the first version of its U.S. application, which is currently available on iOS—Apple’s mobile operating system—but an Android app should be available some time in 2013. Muirhead further indicates that, “Coming to the United States presents a big opportunity for us, because we feel like we’re bringing something new to U.S. sports fans—and there are a lot of ’em!”[28] As for the timing of introducing the application in the United States in October, Muirhead explains that, “October through December is the ‘most jam-packed time in American sports,’ with the World Series (which the app actually just missed), the NFL season at the midway point, the NBA season starting Tuesday night, and the college football season [underway].[29]

Since fanatix was released in the United States and extended to include such U.S. sports as the NFL, NBA, and MLB, users of the application seem pleased with it and offer the following five-star reviews on the iTunes Preview webpage (please note that these reviews have been left in their original form):

- "Gonzo90210": "Big NFL fan—news on here probably better than NFL app itself."
- "Mozart Face": "Loving this app. Live scores and the huddle feature are great. Getting push notifications when goals happen is awesome, then add all the highlights and the personalized news feed . . . brilliant."
- "ShakyandGeorge": "Latest update made this app even more 'unputdownable.'"

Judging by its positive reception in the United States and worldwide, fanatix appears to be on the verge of becoming an important social media application among devoted sports fans. Moreover, the fact that this application provides sports fans with the ability to monitor a wide range of sports simultaneously will make it a vital tool for the millions of Fantasy sports fans that crave a steady stream of sports-related information updated on a continual basis.

While there are other sports information-sharing social media applications, including Thuuz, Bleacher Report, and PlayUp, among others, Muirhead asserts that the "Huddle feature, where groups of likeminded sports fans can come together, separates fanatix from the competition."[30] Muirhead also indicates that "trying to stay on top of news relevant to your team is a tricky process, and we make it easy and . . . social. It is all about easy discovery of content and easy sharing of content." The last part of Muirhead's statement is an apt description of the way social media has drastically changed the way both sports fans and athletes connect with one another in the world of sports. Moreover, because an ever-increasing number of sports fans choose to engage the mediated world through social media, applications like fanatix that are specifically intended for sports information sharing are likely to increase in number and sophistication to meet this demand.

SPORTS VIDEO GAMES AND SOCIAL MEDIA: *OVERDOG* LEADING THE WAY

From the simple, two-dimensional, 8-bit visual reality of the Atari 2600 Football game first introduced in 1978, to the three-dimensional, high-definition quality of modern sports video games like the *Madden NFL* series, sports video games have undergone significant changes in graphics and levels of game action verisimilitude. In many of the new sports video games, popular athletes the likes of LeBron James of the Miami Heat (NBA), All-Star pitcher Tim Lincecum of the San Francisco Giants (MLB), and Calvin Johnson of the Detroit Lions (NFL) actually serve as templates for their video game counterparts through motion-capture technology, which provides gamers with a close approximation of playing as one of the high-profile athletes in some of the more popular video games. In this way, sports video game technology helps close the virtual gap between fans and athletes and gives sports fans an even greater sense of participation in the playing action of professional and college sports.

Because of social media, sports video gamers are no longer relegated to obscurity for their efforts and accomplishments, which, in the past, received little recognition beyond their small circle of friends. Now, sports video gamers can compete online with other sports fans and share the results and details of their games on social media sites like Facebook, Twitter, and YouTube. In addition, since such mass media outlets as ESPN and the Major League Gaming Network (devoted solely to broadcasting people playing video games) are starting to cover sports video game competitions, successful sports video gamers can display their talents to nationally televised audiences. For instance, in the past few years, ESPN2 has broadcast championship competitions of *Madden NFL* in a reality TV format, where gamers compete against one another on the sprawling video boards on Fremont Street in downtown Las Vegas and talk to the camera about how they made it into the competition. Moreover, EA Sports and Virgin Mobile sponsor a yearly sports video gaming competition, where video gamers battle against one another on *Madden NFL*, *FIFA*, and *NHL* video games in the EA Sports Challenge Series. On February 9, 2013, the event took place in Las Vegas, Nevada, where the finalists of each of the three video games played in front of a live audience.

Sports video games are starting to branch out through social media to integrate the gaming experience in bringing fans and athletes closer together through the online video gaming experience. A new application called OverDog is currently in development as of the writing of this book. This app will allow sports fans to play video games against high-profile athletes online. Former Chicago Bears linebacker Hunter Hillenmeyer, OverDog's chief executive officer and founder, envisioned the application as a way for sports fans to have the "opportunity to beat the real pros on the virtual field with his new company."[31] One of the cofounders of OverDog, retired NFL kicker Chris Kluwe, formerly of the Minnesota Vikings, had the following to say to ESPN regarding the application: "I think it can fill a niche that people would really enjoy. I know I personally get requests to play games from fans all the time, and I imagine it's the same for many other athletes. All of the guys I've talked to think it's a great idea, and those that game are excited to be a part of it."[32]

In developing OverDog, Hillenmeyer and his team have negotiated with the NFL Players Association to enlist some of the sport's top athletes. The union has been lending their support, indicating that, "Anything we can do to put our athletes in contact with fans with an experience that both sides are already active in, it's a good thing for the players, good thing for the fans, good thing for that team, and a good thing for that league's brand as a whole."[33] The main website provides the following information about the application:

> A game-changing experience! You love playing video games with your buddies. So do we. Our buddies just happen to be professional athletes. Care to join us?
> OverDog connects fans with their favorite athletes via any video game title (*Madden*, *FIFA*, *NBA2K*, and *Call of Duty*, to name a few). You're a Patriots fan who wants to exorcise your demons by beating a NY Giant in *Madden 2013*? OverDog can make that happen. You want to play *FIFA* against MLS guys while they're in their locker room pregame? They're already playing—OverDog just provides you with the connection. Whatever your game, whatever your sport—with [more than] 3,000 professional athletes already enrolled in the platform, OverDog is your access point for athlete gamers.
> We're in the last stages of development, but we'd love your feedback. Use this site to shoot us an e-mail or a suggestion. And check back frequently—we're going to be releasing exciting new videos and athlete testimonials in the coming weeks. We can't wait for you to see the fun we have in store.[34]

Along with being able to play sports video games against athletes, visitors of the site can also watch the pros play from the virtual sidelines. Hillenmeyer says that OverDog will allow fans not directly competing against sports celebrities in video game competitions to "ask [athletes] questions and be in the metagame or the same ecosystem or arena even if you're not the one sitting on the other side playing him."[35] Set to launch in the first quarter of 2013, OverDog appears to have great potential in allowing sports fans to more directly interact with their favorite athletes through online sports video gaming.

Given my inability to play many of these sports video games, I am unlikely to try my luck against an athlete online through this application; however, I would love to be a virtual spectator of another sports fan battling it out with a professional athlete in an online sports video game. This feature, the ability to operate as a virtual sports spectator, is one of the most ingenious aspects of OverDog. The spectatorial component of the application gives it the potential to attract not just avid sports video gamers, but people who are fascinated by the spectacle of watching people playing video games against a high-profile celebrity. Moreover, knowing that there is an audience for these online sports video game competitions, advertisers could post ads during these gaming events to further approximate the overall game-day experience of athletic competition in virtual reality, which could also serve as a potential revenue stream for the application.

FINAL THOUGHTS

Sports fans have always wanted to be more directly involved in the world of sport. Even before the Internet, sports fans fought hard to have their voices and opinions heard on a public platform. Having to rely on the limited number of ways they could actively engage with sporting events in the past, fans like Morganna the Kissing Bandit and Rollen Stewart had to exert considerable and consistent effort at live sporting events to get the level of fame and recognition they earned as sports celebrities. With the increased level of access social media gives anyone with a smart device to almost any aspect of popular sports culture, sports fans are no longer content to remain on the sidelines and operate as passive viewers. Social media has made it possible for fans to cross the virtual barriers that separate them from the sports they love and allows them to express themselves to a worldwide audience.

As more and more applications the likes of fanatix and OverDog make their way into the market, social media will become an even more important component of sports spectatorship and mediated sports fan participation in the near future. From my perspective as a sports fan and media scholar, or "acafan," I will need to maintain and even expand my presence on social media if I want to stay properly informed regarding the most current trends in sports. If nothing else, armed with the proper smart device and application, I will be able to get instant updates on my Fantasy Football team and, more importantly, engage in timely smack talk with my opponents while LMAO ROTF (laughing my ass off rolling on the floor).

NOTES

1. Kashmir Hill, "Business Card: I'm On Facebook," *Forbes*, 4 March 2010, www.forbes.com/sites/kashmirhill/2010/03/04/business-card-im-on-facebook/ (2 December 2012).

2. Katrin Schulze, "*Nach dem Attentat von Denver* Machen sich Facebook-Verweigerer verdächtig?" [After the Denver Murders: Facebook Holdouts Become Suspicious?], *Der Tagesspiegel*, 24 July 2012, www.tagesspiegel.de/weltspiegel/nach-dem-attentat-von-denver-kein-facebook-profil-kein-job-angebot/6911648-2.html (2 December 2012).

3. Kashmir Hill, "Beware Tech Abandoners: People without Facebook Accounts Are 'Suspicious,'" *Forbes*, 6 August 2012, http://www.forbes.com/sites/kashmirhill/2012/08/06/beware-tech-abandoners-people-without-facebook-accounts-are-suspicious/ (2 December 2012).

4. "Is Not Joining Facebook a Sign You're a Psychopath? Some Employers and Psychologists Say Staying Away from Social Media Is 'Suspicious,'" *Daily Mail*, 6 August 2012, www.dailymail.co.uk/news/article-2184658/Is-joining-Facebook-sign-youre-psychopath-Some-employers-psychologists-say-suspicious.html (2 December 2012).

5. Farhad Manjoo and Emily Yoffe, "Revenge of the Facebook Stalker (Transcript): I Hooked Up with a Jerk with a Girlfriend—Should I Rat Him Out Online?" *Slate*, 6 March 2012, www.slate.com/articles/podcasts/manners_for_the_digital_age/2012/03/transcript_facebook_stalker_should_i_tell_a_cheating_guy_s_girlfriend_that_we_hooked_up_.single.html (2 December 2012).

6. Erik Sass, "9 Reasons to Quit Social Media Now," *Media Post Blogs*, 8 August 2012, www.mediapost.com/publications/article/180465/9-reasons-to-quit-social-media-now.html?edition=49844#axzz2DwfeXapB (2 Dec. 2012).

7. Sass, "9 Reasons to Quit Social Media Now," www.mediapost.com/publications/article/180465/9-reasons-to-quit-social-media-now.html?edition=49844#axzz2DwfeXapB.

8. Nielson Company, *The State of the Media: U.S. Digital Consumer Report Q4-Q4 2011*, www.nielsen.com/us/en/insights/reports-downloads/2012/us-digital-consumer-report.html (9 December 2012).

9. Nathan Edelsburg, "Exclusive: The Most Social Commercials and Brands on TV," *Lost Remote*, 5 September 2012, http://lostremote.com/exclusive-the-top-brands-on-social-tv-from-bluefin-labs-infographic_b33639 (9 December 2102).

10. Matt Carmichael, "The Demographics of Social Media: Ad Age Looks at the Users of Major Social Media Sites," *AdAge.com*, 16 May 2011, http://adage.com/article/adagestat/demographics-facebook-linkedin-myspace-twitter/227569/ (5 December 2012).

11. Scott Collins, "The Superbowl Is on a New Ratings High," *Los Angeles Times*, 7 February 2012, http://articles.latimes.com/2012/feb/07/entertainment/la-et-super-bowl-ratings-20120207 (7 December 2012).

12. Glenn Levy, "Super Bowl Sets Record Viewing Figures of 111M," *Time NewsFeed.com*, http://newsfeed.time.com/2011/02/08/super-bowl-sets-record-viewing-figures-of-111m/ (7 December 2012).

13. Levy, "Super Bowl Sets Record Viewing Figures of 111M," http://newsfeed.time.com/2011/02/08/super-bowl-sets-record-viewing-figures-of-111m/.

14. Adam Chitwood, "Sunday TV Ratings: *Sunday Night Football* Beats San Francisco's World Series Win, *Once Upon a Time*, and *The Mentalist* Up," *Collider*, 29 October 2012, http://collider.com/ratings-world-series-football-once-upon-a-time/207226/ (7 December 2012).

15. Amanda Kondolojy, "TV Ratings Broadcast Top 25: *Sunday Night Football* Tops Week 10 Viewing Among Adults 18–49 and Is Number 1 with Total Viewers," *TV by the Numbers*, http://tvbythenumbers.zap2it.com/2012/12/04/tv-ratings-broadcast-top-25-sunday-night-football-tops-week-10-viewing-among-adults-18-49-and-is-number-1-with-total-viewers/160209/ (7 December 2012).

16. Sara Bibel, "2012 NFL Pro Bowl to Air on NBC Sunday, January 27, 2013," *TV by the Numbers*, 30 May 2012, http://tvbythenumbers.zap2it.com/2012/05/30/2012-nfl-pro-bowl-to-air-on-nbc-sunday-january-27-2013/136241/ (7 December 2012).

17. Rebecca Ford, "Pro Bowl 2012: Did the Experiment Work?" *Hollywood Reporter*, 30 January 2012, www.hollywoodreporter.com/news/pro-bowl-2012-twitter-nfl-285816 (7 December 2012).

18. Norman Chad, "The NFL's Stance on Gambling Is Absurd," *SI.com*, 20 September 2009, http://sportsillustrated.cnn.com/2009/writers/norman_chad/09/20/delware.gambling/index.html (7 December 2012).

19. Amanda Kooser, "NASCAR Driver Tweets During Race, Add 130,000 Followers," *Cnet*, 28 February 2012, http://news.cnet.com/8301-17938_105-57386971-1/nascar-driver-tweets-during-race-adds-130000-followers/ (7 December 2012).

20. Ben Bergman, "Sports Stadium Vie to Win Technology Race," *NPR*, 22 November 2011, www.npr.org/2011/11/22/142670767/stadiums-vie-to-win-technology-race (2 December 2012).

21. Bergman, "Sports Stadium Vie to Win Technology Race," www.npr.org/2011/11/22/142670767/stadiums-vie-to-win-technology-race.

22. Jon Brodkin, "Why Your Smart Device Can't Get Wi-Fi in the Home Team's Stadium: AT&T Explains Why Some Stadiums Get Strong Networks and Others Don't," *Ars Technica*, 26 August 2012, http://arstechnica.com/features/2012/08/why-your-smart-device-cant-get-wifi-in-the-home-teams-stadium/ (2 December 2012).

23. Brodkin, "Why Your Smart Device Can't Get Wi-Fi in the Home Team's Stadium," http://arstechnica.com/features/2012/08/why-your-smart-device-cant-get-wifi-in-the-home-teams-stadium/.

24. Brodkin, "Why Your Smart Device Can't Get Wi-Fi in the Home Team's Stadium," http://arstechnica.com/features/2012/08/why-your-smart-device-cant-get-wifi-in-the-home-teams-stadium/.

25. Darren Heitner, "Social TV App Exclusively for Sports Fans Raises $2 Million, Seeks to Cure Watching Sports Alone," *Forbes*, 1 November 2012, www.forbes.com/sites/darrenheitner/2012/11/01/social-tv-app-exclusively-for-sports-fans-raises-2-million-seeks-to-cure-watching-sports-alone/ (2 December 2012).

26. Heitner, "Social TV App Exclusively for Sports Fans Raises $2 Million," www.forbes.com/sites/darrenheitner/2012/11/01/social-tv-app-exclusively-for-sports-fans-raises-2-million-seeks-to-cure-watching-sports-alone/.

27. Heitner, "Social TV App Exclusively for Sports Fans Raises $2 Million," www.forbes.com/sites/darrenheitner/2012/11/01/social-tv-app-exclusively-for-sports-fans-raises-2-million-seeks-to-cure-watching-sports-alone/.

28. Steven Loeb, "Fanatix Comes to the U.S., Raises $1M in Angel Funding," *Vator News*, 30 October 2012, http://vator.tv/news/2012-10-30-fanatix-comes-to-the-us-raises-1m-in-angel-funding (8 December 2012).

29. Loeb, "Fanatix Comes to the U.S.," http://vator.tv/news/2012-10-30-fanatix-comes-to-the-us-raises-1m-in-angel-funding.

30. Loeb, "Fanatix Comes to the U.S.," http://vator.tv/news/2012-10-30-fanatix-comes-to-the-us-raises-1m-in-angel-funding.

31. Charles Curtis, "OverDog Pits Athletes Against Online Gamers," *ESPN*, 6 December 2012, http://espn.go.com/blog/playbook/tech/post/_/id/3224/overdog-pits-athletes-against-gamers-online#more (10 December 2012).

32. Curtis, "OverDog Pits Athletes Against Online Gamers," http://espn.go.com/blog/playbook/tech/post/_/id/3224/overdog-pits-athletes-against-gamers-online#more.

33. Curtis, "OverDog Pits Athletes Against Online Gamers," http://espn.go.com/blog/playbook/tech/post/_/id/3224/overdog-pits-athletes-against-gamers-online#more.

34. "OverDog: Where Athletes Come to Play," www.theoverdog.com/about.aspx (10 December 2012).

35. Curtis, "OverDog Pits Athletes Against Online Gamers," http://espn.go.com/blog/playbook/tech/post/_/id/3224/overdog-pits-athletes-against-gamers-online#more.

BIBLIOGRAPHY

"15 Impressive Free Throw Distractions," *Total Pro Sports.com*, 12 March 2012, www.totalprosports.com/2012/03/02/15-impressive-free-throw-distractions/ (22 August 2012).

"15 Most Famous (or Infamous) Cases of Streaking in Sports," *Total Pro Sports.com*, www.totalprosports.com/2012/07/06/15-most-famous-or-infamous-cases-of-streaking-in-sports/ (6 August 2012).

"The 100 Most Iconic Internet Videos," *urlesque.com*, 7 April 2009, www.urlesque.com/2009/04/07/the-100-most-iconic-internet-videos/ (5 October 2012).

Adams, Cecil. "A Straight Dope Classic from Cecil's Storehouse of Human Knowledge, January 23, 1987 Archive: What's with Those 'John 3:16' Signs That People Hold Up at Football Games?" *Straight Dope.com*, www.straightdope.com/columns/read/457/whats-with-those-john-3 (8 October 2012).

Adelson, Suzanne. "Rockin' Rollen, Fan of God, Takes a Message to Every Game," *People Magazine*, vol. 29, no. 4 (February 1, 1988), www.people.com/people/archive/article/0,,20098186,00.html (8 October 2012).

"The Alabama Face Guy: Los Angeles," *FunnyorDie.com*, www.funnyordie.com/videos/a5cf524f12/the-alabama-face-guy-los-angeles (24 November 2012).

"Alabama Face Guy Jack Blankenship Stops by *Late Night with Jimmy Fallon* to Talk Basketball(video)," *Huffington Post*, 22 February 2012, www.huffingtonpost.com/2012/02/22/alabama-face-guy-jack-blankenship-jimmy-fallon-video_n_1293456.html (25 August 2012).

"Bengals' Ochocinco Plans to Tweet During Games," *Dayton Daily News*, 8 July 2009, www.daytondailynews.com/news/sports/football/bengals-ochocinco-plans-to-tweet-during-games-1/nM2Yg/ (25 November 2012).

Bergman, Ben. "Sports Stadium Vie to Win Technology Race," *NPR*, 22 November 2011, www.npr.org/2011/11/22/142670767/stadiums-vie-to-win-technology-race (2 December 2012).

Bibel, Sara. "2012 NFL Pro Bowl to Air on NBC Sunday, January 27, 2013," *TV by the Numbers*, 30 May 2012, http://tvbythenumbers.zap2it.com/2012/05/30/2012-nfl-pro-bowl-to-air-on-nbc-sunday-january-27-2013/136241/ (7 December 2012).

Bosker, Bianca. "Twitter Finally Shares Key Stats: 40 Percent of Active Users Are Lurkers," *Huffington Post*, 29 November 2012, www.huffingtonpost.com/2011/09/08/twitter-stats_n_954121.html#s353852&title=Twitter_Comms (29 November 2012).

Boyd, Danah. "Twitter: 'Pointless Babble' or Peripheral Awareness and Social Grooming?" *Apophenia*, 16 August 2009, www.zephoria.org/thoughts/archives/2009/08/16/twitter_pointle.html (28 November 2012).

Bradford, Harry. "Papa John's Anti-Obamacare Meme Goes Viral (photos)," *Huffington Post*, 14 November 2012, www.huffingtonpost.com/2012/11/14/papa-johns-obamacare-boycott-meme_n_2129800.html?1352910915&ncid=edlinkusaolp00000009 (15 November 2012).

"Brett Evens Score with Kissing Bandit," *Tri City Herald*, 13 September 1977, http://news.google.co.uk/newspapers?id=zok1AAAAIBAJ&sjid=rokFAAAAIBAJ&pg=3190,3272324&hl=en (6 October 2012).

"Britain's First Streaker Meets His Match: It Was Cold. He Didn't Have Anything to Be Proud Of," *Guardian*, 21 April 2006, www.guardian.co.uk/sport/2006/apr/22/gdnsport3.sport (5 August 2012).

Brodkin, Jon. "Why Your Smart Device Can't Get Wi-Fi in the Home Team's Stadium: AT&T Explains Why Some Stadiums Get Strong Networks and Others Don't," *Ars Technica*, 26 August 2012, http://arstechnica.com/features/2012/08/why-your-smart-device-cant-get-wifi-in-the-home-teams-stadium/ (2 December 2012).

Burke, Kevin. "Letterman Perceptive, Friendly, Reports Ball State Senior," Ball State University, 5 September 2007, www.bsu.edu/news/article/0,1370,--54420,00.html (5 October 2012).

Burke, Monte. "John 3:16: Where Is He Now? The Original Sports-Event Prosthelytizer Strayed Severely from His Holy Ways," *Forbes*, 12 November 2009, www.forbes.com/2009/11/12/john-316-sign-lifestyle-sports-rainbow-man-today.html (8 October 2012).

Carmichael, Matt. "The Demographics of Social Media: Ad Age Looks at the Users of Major Social Media Sites," *AdAge.com*, 16 May 2011, http://adage.com/article/adagestat/demographics-facebook-linkedin-myspace-twitter/227569/ (5 December 2012).

"Central Florida Packer Backers," *Central Florida Packer Backers Blog Spot*, October 2011, http://centralfloridapackerbackers.blogspot.com/2011/10/win-lambeau-leap-tickets-eat-free-brats.html (6 August 2012).

Chad, Norman. "The NFL's Stance on Gambling Is Absurd," *SI.com*, 20 September 2009, http://sportsillustrated.cnn.com/2009/writers/norman_chad/09/20/delware.gambling/index.html (7 December 2012).

"Chad Johnson and Alleged Mistress Tweet," *Radar Online*, www.radaronline.com/photos/image/187633/2012/08/chad-johnson-and-alleged-mistress-tweet#image-load (27 November 2012).

"Chad 'Ochocinco' Johnson Cheated with Mistress for Four Months Before His Wedding as Wife Speaks Out for the First Time Since Attack and Files for Divorce," *Daily Mail Online*, 14 August 2012, www.dailymail.co.uk/news/article-2188278/Chad-Johnson-NFL-star-mistress-engagement.html (27 November 2012).

Chase, Chris. "A Brief History of the Green Bay Packers' Lambeau Leap," *Yahoo! Sports*, 3 February 2009, http://sports.yahoo.com/nfl/blog/shutdown_corner/post/A-brief-history-of-the-Green-Bay-Packers-Lambea?urn=nfl-316361 (6 August 2012).

Chitwood, Adam. "Sunday TV Ratings: *Sunday Night Football* Beats San Francisco's World Series Win, *Once Upon a Time*, and *The Mentalist* Up," *Collider*, 29 October 2012, http://collider.com/ratings-world-series-football-once-upon-a-time/207226/ (7 December 2012).

Coakley, Jay, and Richard Lapchick. "Psychology and the Road to Professional Baseball." *North American Journal of Psychology*, vol. 9, no. 2 (2007): 1–20.

"Coca-Cola Classic Ad: Mean Joe Green (full version) (1979)," *YouTube*, www.youtube.com/watch?v=xffOCZYX6F8 (9 August 2012).

Cohen, Ben. "The Godfather of Tebowing Tells All," *Wall Street Journal Blogs*, 27 October 2011, http://blogs.wsj.com/dailyfix/2011/10/27/the-godfather-of-tebowing-tells-all/ (17 November 2012).

Collins, Scott. "The Superbowl Is on a New Ratings High," *Los Angeles Times*, 7 February 2012, http://articles.latimes.com/2012/feb/07/entertainment/la-et-super-bowl-ratings-20120207, (7 December 2012).

Corneau, Allison. "Exclusive: Brandi Chastain Responds to Hope Solo's Twitter Rant," *US Weekly*, 31 July 2012, www.usmagazine.com/celebrity-news/news/brandi-chastain-responds-to-hope-solos-twitter-rant-2012317#ixzz22Dl4fHUw (30 November 2012).

Cornish, Audie. "Don't Count on a U.S. Medal in Badminton, Canoeing: Audie Cornish Talks to David Wallechinsky About the United States' Olympic Weak Spots. What Are the Sports and Events Americans Rarely—If Ever—Win Medals For? And What Countries Excel in Those Areas?" *All Things Considered*, NPR, 23 July 2012, www.npr.org/2012/07/23/157248905/dont-count-on-a-u-s-medal-in-badminton-canoeing (24 July 2012).

"Could You Cover Jerry Rice?" *Pros vs. Joes*, Season 1, Episode 1, Spike TV, original air date 6 March 2006.

Crowe, J. D. "Budget Face," *Alabama.com*, 23 February 2012, http://blog.al.com/jdcrowe/2012/02/budget_face.html (24 November 2012).

Crowe, Jerry. "Rainbow Man's Dark Side Keeps Him from Getting Out," *Los Angeles Times*, 19 May 2008, http://articles.latimes.com/2008/may/19/sports/sp-crowe19 (8 October 2012).

Curtis, Charles. "OverDog Pits Athletes Against Online Gamers," *ESPN*, 6 December 2012, http://espn.go.com/blog/playbook/tech/post/_/id/3224/overdog-pits-athletes-against-gamers-online#more (10 December 2012).

"CWS Memories: Dave Winfield's Final Pitch," *The Quad: The New York Times College Sports Blog*, 28 June 2010, http://thequad.blogs.nytimes.com/2010/06/28/c-w-s-memories-dave-winfields-final-pitch/ (18 July 2012).

Davis, Nate. "Bengals WR Chad Ochocinco Fined $25,000 for Using Twitter During Game," *USA Today*, 24 August 2010, http://content.usatoday.com/communities/thehuddle/post/2010/08/bengals-wr-chad-ochocinco-fined-25000-for-using-twitter-during-game/1#.ULPp-KoUmatc (26 November 2012).

Dawkins, Richard. *The Selfish Gene*, 2nd ed. (New York: Oxford University Press, 1989).

Dessart, George. "Standards and Practices," *Museum of Broadcast Communications*, www.museum.tv/eotvsection.php?entrycode=standardsand (5 September 2012).

Drehs, Wayne. "The Streaker Does Hollywood," *ESPN.com*, 26 January 2005, http://sports.espn.go.com/espn/page2/story?page=drehs/050126, (5 August 2012).

Dunbar, Graham. "Swiss Olympic Team Expels Player for Racist Tweet," *CBS News*, 31 July 2012, www.cbsnews.com/8301-505245_162-57483445/swiss-olympic-team-expels-player-for-racist-tweet/ (1 December 2012).

Dunham, Curtis, and John Innes. *Wurra-Wurra: A Legend of Saint Patrick at Tara* (New York: Desmond Fitzgerald, 1911).

Edelsburg, Nathan. "Exclusive: The Most Social Commercials and Brands on TV," *Lost Remote*, 5 September 2012, http://lostremote.com/exclusive-the-top-brands-on-social-tv-from-bluefin-labs-infographic_b33639 (9 December 2102).

Eisenband, Jeffery. "Robert Griffin III Could've Been an Olympic Hurdler," *ThePostGame, Yahoo! Sports*, 9 August 2012, www.thepostgame.com/blog/london-calling-2012/201208/robert-griffin-iii-olympics-hurdles-baylor-track-heisman (16 August 2012).

Emery, Debbie. "Chad 'Ochocinco' Johnson Scores Dates on Twitter, Third Mistress He Picked Up Is Revealed!" *Radar Online.com*, 24 August 2012, www.radaronline.com/exclusives/2012/08/chad-ochocinco-johnson-twitter-third-mistress (27 November 2012).

Eng, Joyce. "Top Oscar Moments: Tears for a Joker, Million-Dollar Babies, and More," *TV Guide*, 23 February 2009, www.tvguide.com/News/2009-Oscar-Moments-1003234.aspx (5 October 2012).

"ESPN, NFL Agree to Eight-Year Deal," *ESPN.com*, 8 September 2011, http://espn.go.com/nfl/story/_/id/6942957/espn-nfl-television-deal-keeps-monday-night-football-network-2021 (26 August 2012).

Evon, Dan. "Racist Tweet Gets Michel Morganella Kicked off the Swiss Olympic Soccer Team," *Inquisitor*, 30 July 2012, www.inquisitr.com/288467/racist-tweet-gets-michel-morganella-kicked-off-swiss-olympic-soccer-team/ (1 December 2012).

"Extremely Exciting Entertainment in NFL, Week 3," *Hartford Informer*, 28 September 2003, http://hartfordinformer.com/2011/09/sports/extremely-exciting-entertainment-in-nfl-season-week-3/ (9 August 2012).

Farber, Dan. "Twitter Sets Its Sights to 2 Billion Users," *Cnet.com*, 27 April 2012, http://news.cnet.com/8301-1023_3-57423213-93/twitter-sets-its-sights-on-2-billion-users/ (29 November 2012).

Farrar, Doug. "Jim McMahon: 'My Memory's Pretty Much Gone,'" *Shutdown Corner, Yahoo! Sports Blog*, 10 November 2011, http://sports.yahoo.com/nfl/blog/shutdown_corner/post/Jim-McMahon-My-memory-s-pretty-much-gone-?urn=nfl-284214 (21 July 2012).

Ford, Rebecca. "Pro Bowl 2012: Did the Experiment Work?" *Hollywood Reporter*, 30 January 2012, www.hollywoodreporter.com/news/pro-bowl-2012-twitter-nfl-285816 (7 December 2012).

Fowler, Bob. "The Bandit: Morganna Kisses and the Victims Tell of Stolen Busses," *Spokane Chronicle*, 26 May 1986, http://news.google.com/newspapers?nid=1345&dat=19860528&id=HutWAAAAIBAJ&sjid=xfkDAAAAIBAJ&pg=5399,2637165 (7 October 2012).

Gorightly, Adam. "'Somewhere Over the Rainbow,' Man," *Kooks Museum.com*, 1999, http://home.pacifier.com/~dkossy/rainbow.html (8 October 2012).

"Greek Triple Jumper Paraskevi Papahristou Withdrawn From Olympics Following Racist Tweet About African Immigrants," *Independent*, 25 July 2012, www.independent.co.uk/sport/olympics/news/greek-triple-jumper-paraskevi-papachristou-withdrawn-from-olympics-following-racist-tweet-about-african-immigrants-7976442.html (1 December 2012).

Grossinger, Paul. "The Worst Announcers in Sports," *Bleacher Report.com*, 12 August 2012, http://bleacherreport.com/articles/1294448-the-worst-announcers-in-sports (27 September 2012).

Gutierrez, Paul. " Catching Up With Bengals Running Back Ickey Woods, " CNNSI.com , 9 December 1997, http://sportsillustrated.cnn.com/features/1997/weekly/catchingup/1215/ (7 August 2012).

Harish, Alon. "Greek Jumper Expelled for Racist Tweet," *ABC News*, 25 July 2012, http://abcnews.go.com/International/greek-olympic-jumper-expelled-racist-tweet-defenders-flock/story?id=16856393#.ULpg5oUmate (1 December 2012).

Heitner, Darren. "Social TV App Exclusively for Sports Fans Raises $2 Million, Seeks to Cure Watching Sports Alone," *Forbes*, 1 November 2012, www.forbes.com/sites/darrenheitner/2012/11/01/social-tv-app-exclusively-for-sports-fans-raises-2-million-seeks-to-cure-watching-sports-alone/ (2 December 2012).

Helene, David. "Watch: ESPN Announcer Accidentally Calls Citi Field 'Shitty Field,'" *SportsGrid.com*, 29 July 2010, www.sportsgrid.com/mlb/watch-espn-announcer-accidentally-calls-citi-field-shitty-field/ (3 October 2012).

Hernandez, Brian Anthony. "The Top 15 Tweets per Second Records," *Mashable.com*, 6 February 2012, http://mashable.com/2012/02/06/tweets-per-second-records-twitter/ (29 November 2012).

Hersch, Hank. "Miami or Bust," in *Sports Illustrated Presents: That Championship Season, Nebraska 1994*, ed. David Bauer (Tampa, FL: Time, 1995), 74–77.

Hill, Kashmir. "Beware Tech Abandoners: People Without Facebook Accounts Are 'Suspicious,'" *Forbes*, 6 August 2012, www.forbes.com/sites/kashmirhill/2012/08/06/beware-tech-abandoners-people-without-facebook-accounts-are-suspicious/ (2 December 2012).

Hill, Kashmir. "Business Card: I'm On Facebook," *Forbes*, 4 March 2010, www.forbes.com/sites/kashmirhill/2010/03/04/business-card-im-on-facebook/ (2 December 2012).

Huff, Richard. "Fans Rule on ESPN2's *SportsNation*," *New York Daily News*, 4 July 2009, www.nydailynews.com/entertainment/tv-movies/fans-rule-espn2-sportsnation-article-1.425807 (26 August 2012).

"'Ichiro' Interferes with Play," *MLB.com*, 3 August 2011, http://mlb.mlb.com/video/play.jsp?content_id=17595817 (8 August 2012).

"Ickey Woods," *Pro-Football-Reference.com*, 2012, www.pro-football-reference.com/players/W/WoodIc00.htm (7 August 2012).

"Introduction to the Sports Industry," Plunkett Research, Inc., 2012, www.plunkettresearch.com/sports-recreation-leisure-market-research/industry-and-business-data (27 July 2012).

"Is Not Joining Facebook a Sign You're a Psychopath? Some Employers and Psychologists Say Staying Away From Social Media Is 'Suspicious,'" *Daily Mail*, 6 August 2012, www.dailymail.co.uk/news/article-2184658/Is-joining-Facebook-sign-youre-psychopath-Some-employers-psychologists-say-suspicious.html (2 December 2012).

"Jack Blankenship for UA [University of Alabama] President," *YouTube*, 29 March 2012, www.youtube.com/watch?v=-XOfoxg4Glo&feature=player_embedded (25 August 2012).

Jean, Al. Commentary for "Stark Raving Dad," in *The Simpsons: The Complete Third Season* [DVD], 2003, 20th Century Fox.

Jenkins, Henry. "Acafandom and Beyond: Concluding Thoughts (weblog post)," *Confessions of an Acafan: The Official Weblog of Henry Jenkins*, 22 October 2011, http://henryjenkins.org/2011/10/acafandom_and_beyond_concludin.html (28 June 2012).

Jenkins, Henry. *Textual Poachers: Television Fans and Participatory Culture* (New York and London: Routledge, Chapman, and Hall, 1992).

Johnson, Chad, and Jason Cole. *Ocho Cinco: What Football and Life Have Thrown My Way* (New York: Crown Publishers, 2009).

Johnson, K. C. "The Invisible Fan: The Scapegoat Bartman Has Managed to Stay Undetected for 8 Years," *Chicago Tribune*, 26 September 2011, http://articles.chicagotribune.com/2011-09-26/sports/ct-spt-0927-bartman-chicago--20110927_1_cubs-five-outs-scapegoat-bartman-alex-gibney (6 August 2012).

Kelly, Ryan. "Twitter Study Reveals Interesting Results about Usage: 40% Is Pointless Babble," *Pear Analytics*, 12 August 2009, www.pearanalytics.com/blog/2009/twitter-study-reveals-interesting-results-40-percent-pointless-babble/ (6 August 2012).

Kondolojy, Amanda. "TV Ratings Broadcast Top 25: *Sunday Night Football* Tops Week 10 Viewing Among Adults 18–49 and Is Number 1 With Total Viewers," *TV by the Numbers*, http://tvbythenumbers.zap2it.com/2012/12/04/tv-ratings-broadcast-top-25-sunday-night-football-tops-week-10-viewing-among-adults-18-49-and-is-number-1-with-total-viewers/160209/ (7 December 2012).

Kooser, Amanda. "NASCAR Driver Tweets During Race, Adds 130,000 Followers," *Cnet.com*, 28 February 2012, http://news.cnet.com/8301-17938_105-57386971-1/nascar-driver-tweets-during-race-adds-130000-followers/ (7 December 2012).

Kryger, Matt. "Hope Solo Bashes Brandi Chastain on Twitter," *USA Today*, 29 July 2012, http://usatoday30.usatoday.com/sports/olympics/story/2012-07-28/hope-solo-twitter-brandi-chastain-olympics-soccer-tweets/56561338/1 (30 November 2012).

La Canfora, Jason. "In-Game Tweet Costs Bengal's Ochocinco $25,000," *NFL.com*, 24 August 2010, www.nfl.com/news/story/09000d5d819fb95a/article/ingame-tweeting-costs-bengals-ochocinco-25000?module=HP_headlines (26 November 2012).

Lane, Tahree. "Mad for Alfred: A New Exhibit Shows *Mad* Magazine's Poster Boy Has a Checkered Past," *Toledo Blade*, 20 January 2008, www.toledoblade.com/Art/2008/01/20/Mad-for-Alfred-A-new-exhibit-shows-Mad-magazine-s-poster-boy-has-a-shadowy-past.html (13 November 2012).

Levy, Glen. "Super Bowl Sets Record Viewing Figures of 111M," *Time NewsFeed.com*, http://newsfeed.time.com/2011/02/08/super-bowl-sets-record-viewing-figures-of-111m/ (7 December 2012).

Loeb, Steven. "Fanatix Comes to the U.S., Raises $1M in Angel Funding," *Vator News*, 30 October 2012, http://vator.tv/news/2012-10-30-fanatix-comes-to-the-us-raises-1m-in-angel-funding (8 December 2012).

Manjoo, Farhad, and Emily Yoffe. "Revenge of the Facebook Stalker (Transcript): I Hooked Up with a Jerk with a Girlfriend—Should I Rat Him Out Online?" *Slate*, 6 March2012, www.slate.com/articles/podcasts/manners_for_the_digital_age/2012/03/transcript_facebook_stalker_should_i_tell_a_cheating_guy_s_girlfriend_that_we_hooked_up_.single.html (2 December 2012).

Marger, Eli. "Which Athletes Are Most Like These Superheroes?" *Los Angeles Times*, 13 October 2011, http://bleacherreport.com/articles/891052-which-athletes-are-most-like-these-superheroes (3 December 2012).

McCarthy, Michael. "ESPN: Beadle Gone, Is Erin Andrews Next?" *USA Today*, 15 May 2012, http://content.usatoday.com/communities/gameon/post/2012/05/espn-announces-that-michelle-beadle-will-leave-network/1#.UDrTNEQls7A (26 August 2012).

McCarthy, Michael. "ESPN's Ron Jaworski Curses Live on *Monday Night Football*," *USA Today*, 12 September 2011, http://content.usatoday.com/communities/gameon/post/2011/09/live-tv-sports-blog-new-england-patriots-vs-miami-dolphins/1#.UGyjyxgls7A (3 October 2012).

McFedries, Paul. "Snowclone Is the New Cliché," *ieeeSpectrum.com*, February 2008, http://spectrum.ieee.org/at-work/education/snowclone-is-the-new-clich (15 November 2012).

Mellisy, Dave. "20 Top Memes of 2010: The Internet Has a Mind of Its Own, and That Mind Has Some Odd Interests," *About.com Web Humor*, December 2010, http://humor.about.com/od/bestofthebest/tp/top_memes_2010.htm (15 November 2012).

Mendelson, Brandon. "Every Team Makes Theirs Marvel in *ESPN Magazine*," *Comics Alliance*, 25 October 2010, www.comicsalliance.com/2010/10/25/espn-magazine-nba-marvel-covers-gallery/ (24 July 2012).

"Men's 100m Butterfly: Day 8 Review, Phelps Ends Career in Golden Fashion," *London2012.com*, 2 August 2012, www.london2012.com/swimming/event=swimming-men-100m-butterfly/ (7 August 2012).

Men's Senior Baseball League, www.msblnational.com/About-Us.html (7 July 2012).

Mihoces, Gary. "Chad Ochocinco Continues Flirtation with Professional Bull Riders, " *USA Today*, 11 May 2011, http://content.usatoday.com/communities/thehuddle/post/2011/05/chad-ochocinco-continues-flirtation-with-professional-bull-riders/1#.ULQrIIUmatc (26 November 2012).

Miller, Claire Cain, "Sports Fans Break Record on Twitter," *New York Times*, 18 June 2010, http://bits.blogs.nytimes.com/2010/06/18/sports-fans-break-records-on-twitter/ (28 November 2012).

Moffitt, Chase. "CWS Dasher Speaks Out," *Wowtv.com*, 27 June 2012, www.wowt.com/home/headlines/CWS_Field_Dasher_Speaks_Out_160632545.html (20 October 2012).

Moore, Jack. "A 17-Year-Old's Quest to Touch Two Baseball Players' Butts," *BuzzFeed.com*, June 2012, www.buzzfeed.com/jpmoore/a-17-year-olds-quest-to-touch-two-baseball-player (24 October 2012).

"Morganna the Kissing Bandit," *Springfield Historical Society @ mcgarnagle.com*, 24 June 2011, http://mcgarnagle.com/2011/06/24/morganna-the-kissing-bandit/ (7 October 2012).

Murphy, B. O., and T. Zorn. "Gendered Interaction in Professional Relationships," in *Gendered Relationships: A Reader*, ed. T. J. Wood (Mountain View, CA: Mayfield, 1996), 218.

"NBA Star Durant Plays in Intramural Flag Football Game on Oklahoma State Campus," *Houston Chronicle*, 1 November 2011, http://blog.chron.com/hottopics/2011/11/nba-star-durant-plays-in-intramural-flag-football-game-on-oklahoma-state-campus/ (2 December 2012).

Nelson, Amy K. "Fan, Friends Connected with Ochocinco," *ESPN.com*, 31 January 2011, http://sports.espn.go.com/nfl/news/story?id=4868696 (26 November 2012).

Nielson Company. *The State of the Media: U.S. Digital Consumer Report Q4-Q4 2011*, www.nielsen.com/us/en/insights/reports-downloads/2012/us-digital-consumer-report.html (9 December 2012).

Nudd, Tim. "Ad of the Day: Errol Morris Brilliantly Profiles the Craziest Sports Fans Around: Those Who Cheer for Their Teams Even in Death," *Adweek*, 1 August 2012, www.adweek.com/news/advertising-branding/ad-day-espn-142390 (1 August 2012).

Olivarez-Giles, Nathan. "Super Bowl XLVI Sets New Tweet per Second Record," *Los Angeles Times*, 6 February 2012, www.latimes.com/business/technology/la-twitter-super-bowl-46-new-york-giants-new-england-patriots-eli-manning-tom-brady-madonna-20120206,0,1184572.story (30 November 2012).

Ostrow, Adam. "How Chad Ochocinco Plans to Tweet During NFL Games," *Mashable Social Media*, 26 August 2009, http://mashable.com/2009/08/26/ocho-cinco-tweets/ (26 November 2012).

"Patriots Fan Runs onto the Field and Wins the Game," *ebaumsworld.com*, 21 November 2011, www.ebaumsworld.com/video/watch/82033228/ (5 December 2012).

"Philadelphia Eagles vs. San Francisco 49ers Snowball Fight," *YouTube*, www.youtube.com/watch?v=2isksLw0jW8 (22 August 2012).

Porter, Kyle. "Kevin Durant—First Millionaire Flag Football Player . . . Ever," *Pistols Firing: OK State Sports Blog*, 31 October 2011, www.pistolsfiringblog.com/kevin-durant-first-millionaire-flag-football-player-ever#more-2861 (2 December 2012).

Posnanski, Joe. "His 21,038,400 Minutes of Fame: Give It Up for Steve Sabol, Who Over 40 Years Has Transformed the NFL with Pop Art," *SI.com*, 8 February 2012, http://sportsillustrated.cnn.com/vault/article/magazine/MAG1165530/index.htm (3 October 2012).

"Proverbs 18:22 (New International Version)," *Bible Gateway.com*, www.biblegateway.com/passage/?search=Proverbs+18%3A22&version=NIV (27 November 2012).

Quercia, Jacopo della. "7 Memes That Went Viral Before the Internet Existed," *Cracked.com*, 11 April 2011, www.cracked.com/article_19119_7-memes-that-went-viral-before-internet-existed.html (14 November 2012).

"Raiders Legend Otto Undergoes Right Leg Amputation," *ESPN.com*, 1 August 2007, http://sports.espn.go.com/nfl/news/story?id=2957868 (21 July 2012).

Raley, Dan. "An All-Star Memory Sealed with a Kiss," *Seattle Post-Intelligencer*, 5 July 2001, www.seattlepi.com/news/article/An-All-Star-memory-sealed-with-a-kiss-1058973.php (6 October 2012).

"Real Dude: Chad Ochocinco Connects with His Fans! (Paid for Everyone's Meal and Drinks)," *World Star Hip Hop*, 15 January 2011, www.worldstarhiphop.com/videos/video.php?v=wshhNut9Ids5k96YPHFo (26 November 2012).

Reilley, Mike, and T. J. Simers. "Irritated by Insults, Everett Goes After Cable Talk Show Host: Media: Former Rams Quarterback Attacks Jim Rome After Being Called 'Chris Everet' During an ESPN2 Interview," *Los Angeles Times*, 4 April 1994, http://articles.latimes.com/1994-04-07/sports/sp-43089_1_talk-show-host-jim-rome (25 August 2012).

"Ron Jaworski Gaffe: ESPN Announcer Says 'Shit' on *Monday Night Football* (video)," *Huff Post Sports*, 13 September 2011, www.huffingtonpost.com/2011/09/13/ron-jaworski-verbal-gaffe-shit_n_959710.html (3 October 2012).

Rothstein, Michael. "How *SportsNation* Became an ESPN Staple and Developed an Emerging Star in Michelle Beadle," *Ann Arbor.com*, 23 September 2010, www.annarbor.com/sports/um-football/how-sportsnation-became-a-espn-reality-and-developed-an-emerging-star-in-michelle-beadle/ (26 August 2012).

Rovell, Darren. "Chad Ochocinco Tops Most Influential Athletes in Social Media List," *CNBC*, 25 April 2011, www.cnbc.com/id/42749405 (26 November 2012).

"Rush *Moving Pictures* Sighting on *Mike and Mike in the Morning*," *Rush Is a Band*, 7 July 2009, www.rushisaband.com/display.php?id=1895&p=3&n=10&o=DESC#comments (3 December 2012).

Sarong, David. "Twitter Founder Jack Dorsey Illuminates the Site's Founding Document. Part I," *Los Angeles Times*, 18 February 2009, http://latimesblogs.latimes.com/technology/2009/02/twitter-creator.html (28 November 2012).

Sass, Erik. "9 Reasons to Quit Social Media Now," *MediaPost Blogs*, 8 August 2012, www.mediapost.com/publications/article/180465/9-reasons-to-quit-social-media-now.html?edition=49844#axzz2DwfeXapB (2 December 2012).

Sass, Erik. "NBC Taps Twitter as 'Official Narrator' for Olympics," *Media Post Blogs*, 23 July 2012, www.mediapost.com/publications/article/179366/nbc-taps-twitter-as-official-narrator-for-olympi.html?edition=49332#axzz2DdfH5F58 (29 November 2012).

Sass, Erik. "NYT Hosts Google+ Hangouts with Olympic Athletes," *Media Post Blogs*, 11 July 2012, www.mediapost.com/publications/article/178586/nyt-hosts-google-hangouts-with-olympic-athletes.html?edition=48908#axzz2DdfH5F58 (30 November 2012).

Scalici, Matt. "Jack 'the Face' Blankenship Appears on the *Today Show*," *Alabama Live.com*, 21 February 2012, www.al.com/sports/index.ssf/2012/02/jack_the_face_blankenship_appe.html (25 August 2012).

Schulze, Katrin. "*Nach dem Attentat von Denver* Machen sich Facebook-Verweigerer verdächtig?" [After the Denver Murders: Facebook Holdouts Become Suspicious?], *Der Tagesspiegel*, 24 July 2012, www.tagesspiegel.de/weltspiegel/nach-dem-attentat-von-denver-kein-facebook-profil-kein-job-angebot/6911648-2.html (2 December 2012).

"Sky Sports Fanzone Gets Feminine for a Day," *Awful Announcing.com*, 28 April 2009, http://awfulannouncing.blogspot.com/2009/04/sky-sports-fanzone-gets-feminine-for.html (3 October 2012).

Smith, Michael David. "Robert Griffin III: 'It Sucks' Watching Olympic Track Trials," *NBC Sports*, 29 June 2012, http://profootballtalk.nbcsports.com/2012/06/29/robert-griffin-iii-it-sucks-watching-olympic-track-trials/ (4 August 2012).

"The 'Socialympics' Ignites London," *Neilson.com*, 15 August 2012, http://sites.nielsen.com/london2012/the-socialympics-ignites-london/ (29 November 2012).

Soper, Taylor. "Fake Ichiro Unwittingly Gets into the Action," *Official Website of the Seattle Mariners*, 3 August 2011, http://seattle.mariners.mlb.com/news/article.jsp?ymd=20110803&content_id=22690656&vkey=news_sea&c_id=sea (6 August 2012).

"Spanish Players Defend Racially Controversial Photo," *USA Today*, 13 August 2008, http://usatoday30.usatoday.com/sports/olympics/beijing/2008-08-13-spain-basketball_N.htm (1 December 2012).

"Sport and Painkillers," *The Sporting Body Themes and Issues: Investigations into the Organisation of the Body in Sports*, http://sportingbody.edublogs.org/painkillers-and-sport/ (7 August 2012).

"Sporting Streakers (photos)," *TripleM.com*, www.triplem.com.au/melbourne/sport/photos/sporting-streakers (6 August 2012).

"Sports Fans Continue the Conversation Online: Brands Seek Opportunities Outside the Commercial Breaks," *eMarkerter.com*, 6 July 2012, www.emarketer.com/PressRelease.aspx?R=1009174 (7 August 2012).

"Star Wars Kid Is Top Viral Video: A Two-Minute Clip of a Teenage Boy Pretending to Wield a Lightsaber Has Become the Most Popular Viral Video on the Internet," *BBC News*, 27 November 2006, http://news.bbc.co.uk/2/hi/entertainment/6187554.stm (14 November 2012).

"Steelers Fan Goes to Recliner in the Sky," *Seattle Times*, 7 July 2005, http://community.seattletimes.nwsource.com/archive/?date=20050707&slug=steelerfan)07 (11 August 2012).

Steinberg, Dan, and Sarah Kogod. "DC Sports Bog: RGIII on Two Catalog Covers," *Washington Post*, 25 July 2012, www.washingtonpost.com/blogs/dc-sports-bog/post/rgiii-on-two-catalog-covers/2012/07/25/gJQADkpt8W_blog.html (5 August 2012).

"The Steve Bartman Incident—Any Excuse Will Do," *The Chicago Cubs Suck.com*, http://chicagocubssuck.com/the-steve-bartman-incident-%E2%80%93-any-excuse-will-do.php (6 August 2012).

"Streaking," *Streaking.org*, www.streaking.org/ (6 August 2012).

Symon, Evan V. "5 Fans Who Ruined Sports," *Cracked*, 27 November 2011, www.cracked.com/article_19529_5-sports-fans-who-ruined-sports_p2.html (8 October 2012).

"Tebowing," *Know Your Meme.com*, http://knowyourmeme.com/memes/tebowing#fn16 (17 November 2012).

"Tebowing Accepted Into the English Language: Six-Week Rise of the Global Phenomenon," *Global Language Monitor.com*, 11 December 2011, www.languagemonitor.com/new-words/tebowing-accepted-into-english-language/ (19 November 2012).

"They Were Throwing Batteries: Phillies Fans Hurl Insults, Projectiles at J. D. Drew," *CNNSI.com*, 11 August 1999, http://sportsillustrated.cnn.com/baseball/mlb/news/1999/08/10/cardinals_phillies_ap/#more (22 August 2012).

Total Football Forums, www.totalfootballforums.com/forums/topic/78172-fan-announcers-for-premier-league-games/#entry1146838 (1 October 2012).

"Tweets per Second Mark Set During Finals," *ESPN*, 18 July 2011, http://espn.go.com/sports/soccer/news/_/id/6779582/women-world-cup-final-breaks-twitter-record (28 November 2012).

"Two More Alleged Mistresses of Chad 'Ocho Cinco' Johnson Revealed (photos)," *Rucuss.com*, 24 August 2012, www.rucuss.com/gossip/two-more-alleged-mistresses-of-chad-ochocinco-johnson-revealed-photos/ (27 November 2012).

U.S. Bureau of Labor Statistics. *Occupational Outlook Handbook, 2010 – 11 Edition* (Lanham, MD: Bernan Associates, 2010).

U.S. Bureau of Labor Statistics. "Professional Athlete," 19 March 2010, www.bls.gov/k12/sports02.htm (6 November 2011).

U.S. Census Bureau. www.census.gov/ (6 November 2011).

Walker, Mark. "Oceanside: Football Great Junior Seau, 43, Dead in Apparent Suicide," *North County Times*, 2 May 2012, www.nctimes.com/article_bccb943a-ba7e-56f3-8756-13d9c81a8258.html (21 July 2012).

Walker, James. "Dolphins Cut WR Chad Johnson," *ESPN NFL*, 13 August 2012, http://espn.go.com/nfl/trainingcamp12/story/_/id/8263326/chad-johnson-cut-miami-dolphins-karlos-dansby-hates-move (27 November 2012).

Walker, James. "Patriots Pull Shocker with Jeff Demps," *ESPN NFL*, *AFC East Blog*, 17 August 2012, http://espn.go.com/blog/afceast/post/_/id/46315/patriots-pull-shocker-with-jeff-demps (17 August 2012).

"Was Jim Rome vs. Jim Everett Staged?" *DanOnTheStreet.com*, 30 July 2012, http://danonthestreet.com/news/2010/07/31/was-jim-rome-vs-jim-everett-staged/ (25 August 2012).

Wasserman, Todd. "Papa John's Gets Bludgeoned by Memes for Obamacare Stance," *Mashable.com*, 13 November 2012, http://mashable.com/2012/11/13/papa-johns-memes/#101181-2 (15 November 2012).

Wei, William. "Where Are They Now? The 'Boom Goes the Dynamite' Kid Is Now a Real Reporter," *Business Insider*, 19 May 2010, http://articles.businessinsider.com/2010-05-19/tech/29969850_1_newscast-shooting-video-sportscenter (4 October 2012).

Weir, Tom. "The LeBrons Beat the Kevin Durants in Flag Football," *USA Today*, 1 December 2011, http://content.usatoday.com/communities/gameon/post/2011/12/the-lebrons-beat-the-kevin-durants-in-flag-football/1#.ULvNcYUmatc (2 December 2012).

"What Happened to Sky Sports Fanzone?" *Digital Sky.com*, 3 March 2012, http://forums.digitalspy.co.uk/showthread.php?t=1636781 (2 October 2012).

"What Is the Average NFL Player's Career Length? Longer Than You Might Think, Commissioner Goodell Says," *NFL Communications*, 18 April 2011, http://nflcommunications.com/2011/04/18/what-is-average-nfl-player%E2%80%99s-career-length-longer-than-you-might-think-commissioner-goodell-says/ (21 July 2012).

"What Is an Internet Meme?" *TechTarget.com*, February 2009, http://whatis.techtarget.com/definition/Internet-meme (14 November 2012).

Williamson, Bill. "Time for Elway to Think Post-Tebow," *ESPN NFL*, *AFC East Blog*, 30 October 2011, http://espn.go.com/blog/afcwest/post/_/id/34680/time-for-elway-to-think-post-tebow#comments (19 November 2012).

Wilson, Dave. "Alabama Fan Uses 'the Face' to Distract Opponents," *ESPN.com*, February 2012, http://espn.go.com/espn/page2/index?id=7578845 (21 August 2012).

Winter, George. *The Rainbow Man Blog Spot*, http://therainbowman.blogspot.com/2004_11_01_archive.html (17 October 2012).

Wojciechowski, Gene. "Despite 'Worst' Sportscast, Collins Says He'd Try Again," *ESPN.com*, 6 March 2007, http://sports.espn.go.com/espn/columns/story?id=2785830 (5 October 2012).

Wolford, Josh. "Alabama Face Guy Starts Viral Campaign for Presidency of the University," *WebProNews.com*, 30 March 2012, www.webpronews.com/alabama-face-guy-viral-campaign-for-president-2012-03 (25 August 2012).

Wortman, Marc. "Over 30s Play Ball: Once a Game Only for the Boys of Summer, Amateur Baseball Leagues Are Now Filled With Thousands of Men Over 30," *Cigar Afficionado*, September/October 1998, www.cigaraficionado.com/webfeatures/show/id/Over-30s-Play-Bal_7391 (27 July 2012).

Xu, Tianyin, Yang Chen, Lei Jiao, Ben Y, Zhao, Pan Hui, and Xiaoming Fu."Scaling Microblogging Services with Divergent Traffic Demands," *Middleware 2011* (2011): 1.

Yoder, Matt. "The Pammie Awards," *Awful Announcing.com*, 26 September 2012, www.awfulannouncing.com/pammies/pammy-awards/ (28 September 2012).

Yoder, Matt. "Your Week 4 Pammies Winners and Updated Standings," *Awful Announcing.com*, 26 September 2012, www.awfulannouncing.com/pammies/pammy-awards/your-week-4-2012-pammies-winners-updated-standings.html (28 September 2012).

INDEX

ABOUT THE AUTHOR

After holding numerous jobs ranging from health inspector to stand-up comedian, high school chemistry teacher to dog track announcer, **David M. Sutera's** career has converged into a sports media scholar, writer, and aspiring university professor working on his Ph.D. in film and media studies at the University of Kansas. In addition, Sutera is an active filmmaker with an M.F.A. in film production from the University of Utah, and he has produced several award-winning short films, including *Amber Waves* (2012), *Glass Half Full* (2009), *Space Invaders* (2007), *Messages from the Burning Shrub* (2004), and *Fryday* (2003). He is currently working on his first feature-length documentary film/travelogue novel with Scarecrow Press, *Vaudeville on the Diamond*. When not writing about sports or making a sports film, Sutera is a proud, frustrated athlete who still plays fast-pitch baseball in the Men's Senior Baseball League.